TRAIN TO WIN
IN A COMPLEX WORLD

THE OFFICIAL U.S. ARMY GUIDE TO TRAINING DEVELOPMENT

CURRENT, FULL-SIZE EDITION

FM 7-0
(TC 25-10)

Headquarters, Department of the Army

Train to Win in a Complex World: The Official US Army Guide to Training Development
Current, Full-Size Edition - FM 7-0 (TC 25-10)

U.S. Army

This edition first published 2017 by Carlile Military Library. "Carlile Military Library" and its associated logos and devices are trademarks. Carlile Military Library is an imprint of Carlile Media. The appearance of U.S. Department of Defense (DoD) visual information does not imply or constitute DoD endorsement. New material copyright © 2017 Carlile Media. **All rights reserved.**

Published in the United States of America.

ISBN-13: 978-1-9794-5616-6
ISBN-10: 197945616X

*FM 7-0

Field Manual
No. 7-0

Headquarters
Department of the Army
Washington, DC, 5 October 2016

TRAIN TO WIN IN A COMPLEX WORLD

Contents

		Page
	PREFACE	v
	INTRODUCTION	vii
Chapter 1	**TRAINING OVERVIEW**	**1-1**
	Train to Win	1-1
	Principles of Training	1-1
	Training Proficiency	1-1
	The Role of Leaders	1-5
	Battle Focus	1-8
	Training Environment	1-10
	Training for Battle Rhythm	1-11
	Commanders' Dialogues	1-17
	Reserve Component Training Considerations	1-18
Chapter 2	**DEVELOPING THE UNIT TRAINING PLAN**	**2-1**
	Training Readiness	2-1
	The Army Operations Process	2-2
	Command Training Guidance	2-2
	The Unit Training Plan	2-3
	Training Briefing	2-21
Chapter 3	**CONDUCTING TRAINING EVENTS**	**3-1**
	Overview	3-1
	Plan	3-2
	Prepare	3-5
	Execute	3-6
	Assess	3-7
Appendix A	**REALISTIC TRAINING**	**A-1**
Appendix B	**TRAINING AND EVALUATION OUTLINES**	**B-1**

Distribution Restriction: Approved for public release; distribution is unlimited.

*This manual supersedes TC 25-10, dated 26 August 1996.

Contents

Appendix C	COMPANY TRAINING MEETINGS	C-1
Appendix D	AFTER ACTION REVIEWS	D-1
Appendix E	LANE TRAINING	E-1
Appendix F	UNIT TRAINING PLAN	F-1
Appendix G	ALL TRAINING BRIEFINGS	G-1
Appendix H	T-WEEK CONCEPT	H-1
Appendix I	ORGANIZATIONAL INSPECTION PROGRAM FOR TRAINING	I-1
	GLOSSARY	Glossary-1
	REFERENCES	References-1
	INDEX	Index-1

Figures

Figure 1-1. Sustaining proficiency within a band of excellence 1-3
Figure 1-2. Top-down training guidance and bottom-up feedback 1-4
Figure 1-3. Overlapping training responsibilities 1-8
Figure 1-4. Battle focus integration of collective and individual training 1-9
Figure 1-5. Planning horizons for training 1-10
Figure 1-6. UTP publication timelines within a notional Regular Army brigade 1-13
Figure 1-7. UTP publication timelines within a notional Reserve Component flag officer command 1-13
Figure 1-8. Multiechelon training task crosswalk 1-15
Figure 1-9. Notional training resource synchronization conference for a Regular Army brigade 1-17
Figure 1-10. Notional Reserve Component unit training long-range planning horizons 1-19
Figure 2-1. Receipt of training guidance begins the planning process 2-1
Figure 2-2. The Army operations process 2-2
Figure 2-3. Mission analysis helps determine battle focus 2-4
Figure 2-4. Notional mission analysis when prioritizing capabilities to train 2-5
Figure 2-5. Development of a METL for an assigned mission 2-6
Figure 2-6. Development of a METL for an assigned METL with other capabilities 2-6
Figure 2-7. Initial and projected start-of-training MET assessments 2-7
Figure 2-8. Mission analysis backbrief 2-8
Figure 2-9. Notional mission analysis vignette 2-8
Figure 2-10. Steps 3-6 of the MDMP as it relates to unit training 2-10
Figure 2-11. Multiechelon training events demonstrated in a notional UTP calendar 2-12
Figure 2-12. Sample brigade training objective 2-14
Figure 2-13. Example EXEVAL posted on a notional brigade UTP calendar 2-15
Figure 2-14. Sample of crawl-walk-run training events 2-15
Figure 2-15. Company crawl-walk-run training events on the UTP calendar 2-16

Figure 2-16. Sample LVC training mix from brigade to individual Soldier 2-18
Figure 2-17. COA approval 2-20
Figure 2-18. The approved COA becomes the unit training plan 2-21
Figure 2-19. Notional training briefing vignette 2-22
Figure 3-1. Plan phase of the operations process 3-2
Figure 3-2. The 8-step training model 3-3
Figure 3-3. Prepare phase of the operations process 3-6
Figure 3-4. Execute phase of the operations process 3-7
Figure 3-5. Assess phase of the operations process 3-8
Figure 3-6. Notional company training meeting vignette 3-9
Figure 3-7. Objective task evaluation criteria from a training and evaluation outline 3-11
Figure 3-8. Formal and informal evaluations 3-12
Figure A-1. Realistic training vignette A-2
Figure A-2. Graphic for realistic training vignette A-3
Figure B-1. Bottom-up feedback of task evaluations B-1
Figure B-2. Sample training and evaluation outline B-2
Figure B-3. Objective task evaluation criteria matrix B-5
Figure B-4. Sample extract from T&EO illustrating performance steps B-8
Figure B-5. Sample extract from T&EO illustrating performance measures B-9
Figure C-1. UTP processes from execution to MET proficiency C-2
Figure C-2. Sample preexecution checks questions C-8
Figure C-3. Notional hip-pocket training C-9
Figure D-1. After action review scenario D-10
Figure E-1. General sequence of activities during a lane training event E-5
Figure E-2. Detailed lane training process E-7
Figure E-3. Lane training execution process E-9
Figure E-4. Diagram of lane training E-10
Figure E-5. Example generic lane scenario E-11
Figure E-6. Example scenario for one collective task with three task steps E-12
Figure E-7. Example scenario with several supporting or related collective tasks E-13
Figure E-8. Scenario for a stationary unit E-14
Figure F-1. Production and dissemination of the UTP F-1
Figure F-2. Operation plan or operation order format F-2
Figure G-1. Sample slide for brigade training focus G-1
Figure G-2. Sample slide for training environment G-2
Figure G-3. Sample slide for battalion training focus G-2
Figure G-4. Sample slide for training guidance G-2
Figure G-5. First sample slide for concept of operations G-2
Figure G-6. Second sample slide for concept of operations G-3
Figure G-7. Third sample slide for concept of operations G-3
Figure G-8. Sample slide for assessment plans G-3
Figure G-9. Sample slide for key resources G-3

Figure G-10. Sample training risks G-4
Figure G-11. Sample training challenges G-4
Figure G-12. Sample slide for brigade training focus G-4
Figure G-13. Sample slide for training environment G-5
Figure G-14. Sample slide for battalion training focus G-5
Figure G-15. Sample slide for battalion assessments G-5
Figure G-16. Sample slide for last quarter training highlights G-5
Figure G-17. Sample slide for current quarter training highlights G-6
Figure G-18. Sample slide for future quarter training highlights G-6
Figure G-19. Sample slide for training resource synchronization conference G-6
Figure G-20. Sample slide for Soldier training assessment G-6
Figure G-21. Sample slide for school statuses G-7
Figure G-22. Sample slide for ammunition status and allocation G-7
Figure G-23. Sample slide for scheduled in gunnery G-7
Figure G-24. Sample for use of integrated training environment G-8
Figure G-25. Sample slide for commander's training issues G-8
Figure H-1. Sample training objectives H-5
Figure H-2. Example of individual training objectives H-7
Figure H-3. Sample leader development plan for an armor company H-12
Figure H-4. Sample logistic support plan for an armor company H-13
Figure H-5. Approval of company training schedules H-14
Figure H-6. Recommended approval process for changes H-14
Figure H-7. Example company training schedule H-15

Tables

Introductory table. New and modified terms vii
Table 1-1. Regular Army long-range planning by echelon 1-12
Table 1-2. Reserve Component long-range planning by echelon 1-12
Table 1-3. Commanders' dialogue at critical points in the training process 1-18
Table 2-1. Sample TDA collective tasks 2-9
Table B-1. School and proponent codes B-3
Table B-2. Echelon codes B-3
Table C-1. Times for training meeting agenda C-5
Table D-1. Comparison of formal and informal after action reviews D-2
Table E-1. Characteristics of lane training E-4
Table E-2. Key personnel in managing lane training E-6
Table E-3. Lane training activities E-6
Table E-4. Crawl-walk-run characteristics in lane training E-8
Table H-1. Illustrative T-Week concept H-2

Preface

FM 7-0, *Train to Win in a Complex World*, describes how the Army trains to win. With that focus, the Army develops training readiness and the capabilities that support Army and joint force commanders. FM 7-0 applies to all leaders at all organizational levels. All leaders are trainers. Leaders include officers, warrant officers, noncommissioned officers, and Department of the Army Civilians in leadership positions.

The principal audience for FM 7-0 is all members of the Profession of Arms, leaders, Soldiers, Army Civilians, and contractors who might be isolated from others during a mission. Trainers and educators throughout the Army will also use this publication.

Commanders, staffs, and subordinates ensure their decisions and actions comply with applicable United States, international, and in some cases, host-nation laws and regulations. Commanders at all levels ensure their Soldiers operate in accordance with the law of war and the rules of engagement (see FM 27-10).

FM 7-0 uses joint terms where applicable. Terms for which FM 7-0 is the proponent field manual (the authority) are indicated with an asterisk in the glossary. Definitions for which FM 7-0 is the proponent field manual are printed in boldface in the text. For other terms defined in the text, the term is italicized and the number of the proponent publication follows the definition.

FM 7-0 applies to the Active Army, the Army National Guard/Army National Guard of the United States, and the United States Army Reserve unless otherwise stated.

Headquarters, United States (U.S.) Army Combined Arms Center is the proponent for this publication. The preparing agencies are the Combined Arms Doctrine Directorate (CADD) and the Training Management Directorate (TMD) within the Combined Arms Center–Training (CAC-T). Both CADD and CAC-T are subordinate to the U.S. Army Combined Arms Center.

This page intentionally left blank.

Introduction

FM 7-0, *Train to Win in a Complex World*, expands on the fundamental concepts of the Army's training doctrine introduced in ADRP 7-0. The Army's operations process is the foundation for how leaders conduct unit training. It also places the commander firmly at the center of the process and as the lead of every facet of unit training. FM 7-0 supports the idea that training a unit does not fundamentally differ from preparing a unit for an operation. Reinforcing the concepts, ideas, and terminology of the operations process while training as a unit makes a more seamless transition from training to operations.

This publication focuses on training leaders, Soldiers, and Army Civilians as effectively and efficiently as possible given limitations in time and resources. It also aims to ensure that leaders incorporate ethical aspects (such as moral-ethical decision points and personal actions) into training scenarios or routinely discuss ethics during post-training after action reviews. FM 7-0 guides leaders to develop realistic training, which includes changing conditions and various operating environments.

FM 7-0 contains three chapters:

Chapter 1 introduces the Army's concepts of training and how units attain and maintain training readiness over time. It also reiterates the Army's principles of training outlined in ADRP 7-0.

Chapter 2 details the processes of how units determine the collective tasks to train and development of the unit training plan. This plan progressively trains the unit over time to collective task proficiency and sustainment of training readiness.

Chapter 3 discusses how units plan, prepare, execute, and assess each training event to maximize the outcome of each event to support training readiness.

FM 7-0 contains nine appendixes.

FM 7-0 introduces new and modifies existing terms for which it is proponent. See the introductory table.

Introductory table. New and modified terms

Term	Action	Reason
after action review	modified	Proponency moved from ADRP 7-0 to FM 7-0.
lane	modified	Proponency moved from TC 25-10. No longer formally defined term.
lane training	modified	Proponency moved from TC 25-10. No longer formally defined term.
lane training exercise	modified	Definition modified and proponency moved from TC 25-10 to FM 7-0.
mission-essential task	modified	Definition modified and proponency moved from ADRP 7-0 to FM 7-0.
mission-essential task list	modified	Definition modified and proponency moved from ADRP 7-0 to FM 7-0.
training and evaluation outline	modified	Definition modified and proponency moved from ADRP 7-0 to FM 7-0.
training environment	new	
training objective	modified	Proponency moved from ADRP 7-0 to FM 7-0.

This page intentionally left blank.

Chapter 1
Training Overview

TRAIN TO WIN

1-1. The Army trains to win in a complex world. To fight and win in a chaotic, ambiguous, and complex environment, the Army trains to provide forces ready to conduct unified land operations. The Army does this by conducting tough, realistic, and challenging training. Unit and individual training occurs all the time—at home station, at combat training centers, and while deployed.

1-2. Army forces face threats that will manifest themselves in combinations of conventional and irregular forces, including insurgents, terrorists, and criminals. Some threats will have access to sophisticated technologies such as night vision systems, unmanned systems (aerial and ground), and weapons of mass destruction. Some threats will merge cyberspace and electronic warfare capabilities to operate from disparate locations. Additionally, they may hide among the people or in complex terrain to thwart the Army's conventional combat overmatch. Adding to this complexity is continued urbanization and the threat's access to social media. This complex environment will therefore require future Soldiers to train to perform at the highest levels possible.

1-3. Training is the most important thing the Army does to prepare for operations. Training is the cornerstone of readiness. Readiness determines our Nation's ability to fight and win in a complex global environment. To achieve a high degree of readiness, the Army trains in the most efficient and effective manner possible. Realistic training with limited time and resources demands that commanders focus their unit training efforts to maximize training proficiency.

PRINCIPLES OF TRAINING

1-4. Units execute effective individual and collective training based on the Army's principles of training. See ADRP 7-0 for a discussion of each of these principles:
- Train as you fight.
- Training is commander driven.
- Training is led by trained officers and noncommissioned officers (NCOs).
- Train to standard.
- Train using appropriate doctrine.
- Training is protected.
- Training is resourced.
- Train to sustain.
- Train to maintain.
- Training is multiechelon and combined arms.

TRAINING PROFICIENCY

1-5. Proficiency in individual, leader, and collective tasks is measured against published standards. Proficiency is recognized as complete task proficiency, advanced task proficiency, basic task proficiency, limited task proficiency, and cannot perform the task.

Chapter 1

PROFICIENCY RATINGS

1-6. The proficiency ratings are as follows:
- T is fully trained (complete task proficiency).
- T- is trained (advanced task proficiency).
- P is practiced (basic task proficiency).
- P- is marginally practiced (limited task proficiency).
- U is untrained (cannot perform the task).

T (Fully Trained)

1-7. A T proficiency rating means a unit is fully trained. It has attained task proficiency to the Army standard, achieved a GO in 90% or more of both performance measures and leader performance measures, and has met 100% of all critical performance measures. The task is externally evaluated and meets the remaining requirements as outlined in the training and evaluation outline (T&EO) in accordance with the objective task evaluation criteria matrix. (See appendix B for a detailed explanation of the objective task evaluation criteria matrix.)

T- (Trained)

1-8. A T- proficiency rating means a unit is trained. It has attained advanced task proficiency free of significant shortcomings, achieved a GO in 80% or more of both performance measures and leader performance measures, and has met 100% of all critical performance measures. The unit's shortcomings require minimal training to meet the Army standard. The task is externally evaluated and meets the remaining requirements as outlined in the T&EO in accordance with the objective task evaluation criteria matrix.

P (Practiced)

1-9. A P proficiency rating means a unit is practiced. It has attained basic task proficiency with shortcomings, achieved a GO in 65% or more of all performance measures, achieved 80% or more of all leader performance measures, and has met 100% of all critical performance measures. The unit's shortcomings require significant training to meet the Army standard. The task is not externally evaluated and meets the remaining requirements as outlined in the T&EO in accordance with the objective task evaluation criteria matrix.

P- (Marginally Practiced)

1-10. A P- proficiency rating means a unit is marginally practiced. It has attained limited task proficiency with major shortcomings, achieved a GO in 51% or more of all performance measures, achieved less than 80% of all leader performance measures, and has met less than 100% of all critical performance measures. The unit's shortcomings require complete retraining of the task to achieve the Army standard. The task is not externally evaluated and does not meet the remaining requirements as outlined in the T&EO in accordance with the objective task evaluation criteria matrix.

U (Untrained)

1-11. A U proficiency rating means a unit is untrained. The unit cannot perform the task. It achieved a GO in less than 51% of all performance measures, less than 80% in all leader performance measures, and less than 100% in all critical performance measures. The unit requires complete training on the task to achieve the Army standard.

SUSTAINING PROFICIENCY—THE BAND OF EXCELLENCE

1-12. A unit's training readiness is directly tied to its training proficiency. That proficiency naturally fluctuates over time and in response to various factors. Each unit encounters and adjusts to these factors, including training frequency, key personnel turnover, new equipment fielding, and resource constraints. Well-trained units seek to minimize significant variances in achieved training proficiency over time. This is training in a band of excellence. This common sense approach precludes deep valleys in proficiency that occur when units lose their training proficiency. Failing to sustain proficiency requires more resources and time to retrain the unit. Training within a band of excellence is the key to sustaining long-range training readiness. See figure 1-1.

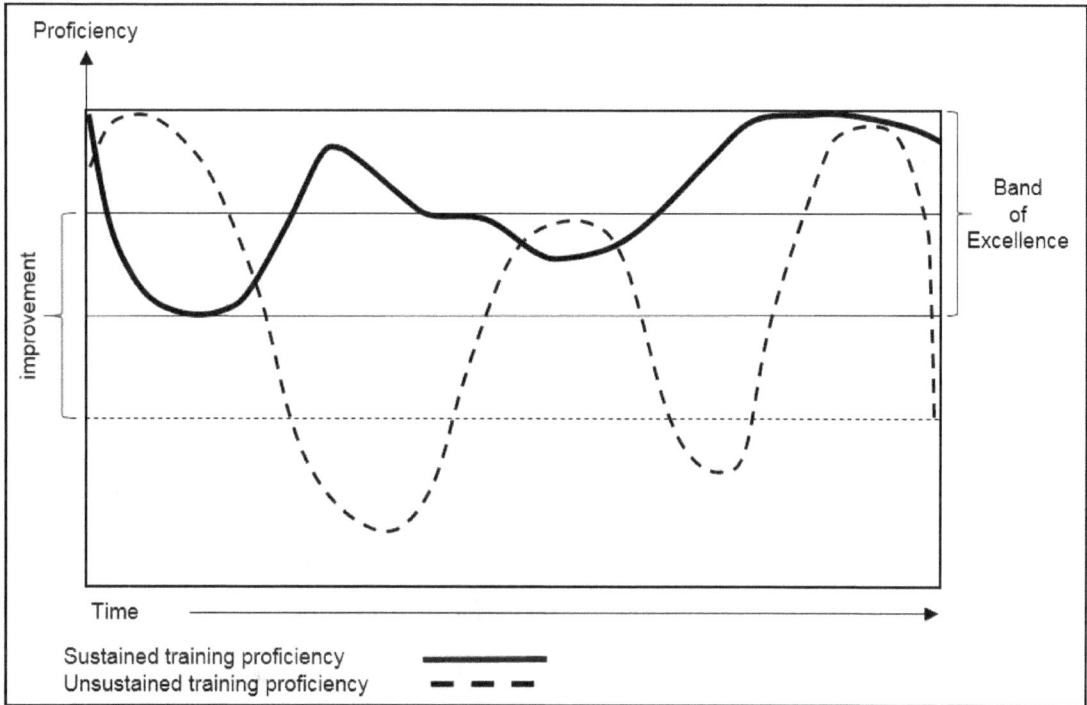

Figure 1-1. Sustaining proficiency within a band of excellence

1-13. Effective commanders take the unit from a training start point, attain the required training proficiency, and maintain that proficiency over time. Once training proficiency is attained, the unit strives to maintain that proficiency within a band of excellence. The commander who understands factors that negatively affect training proficiency can better plan so that unit training skills do not atrophy to a less than acceptable level.

1-14. To adjust to the anticipated highs and lows of training proficiency, commanders continually assess training plans and strategies to keep the unit mission-ready over long periods. This assessment may cover individual memory degradation, skill degradation, unit personnel turnover, changes in crew assignments, and changes in key leadership. Maintaining high levels of proficiency may prove more difficult than building proficiency from a training start point. By understanding and predicting the factors that affect training proficiency, commanders can mitigate those effects and maintain higher levels of training readiness longer.

TOP-DOWN/BOTTOM-UP APPROACH TO TRAINING

1-15. A top-down/bottom-up approach to training reflects a team effort with commanders and their subordinate leaders. Commanders provide top-down guidance in the training focus, direction, and resources while subordinate leaders provide feedback on unit task proficiency, identify needed training resources, and execute training to standard. This team effort helps maintain training focus, establishes training priorities, and enables effective communication between command echelons. See figure 1-2 on page 1-4.

Chapter 1

1-16. Training guidance flows from the top down and results in subordinate units' identification of specific collective and individual tasks that support the higher unit's mission. Subordinates provide bottom-up feedback. This input from the bottom up identifies the current state of training proficiency for collective and individual tasks at lower echelons. This input helps the commander objectively determine unit training readiness.

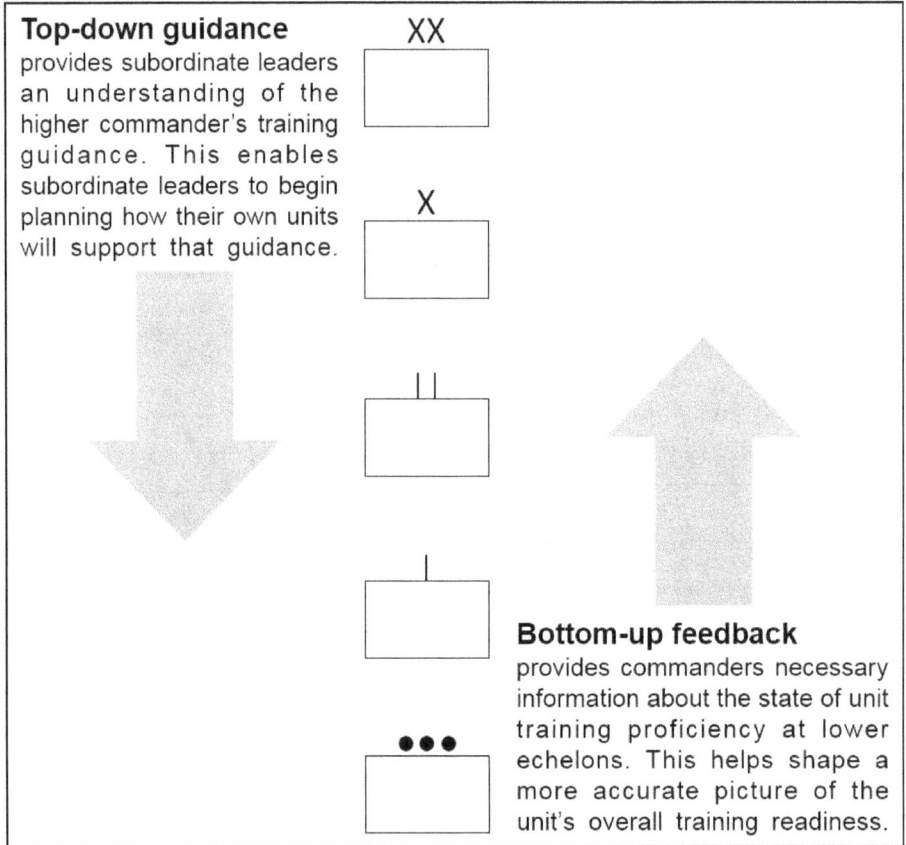

Figure 1-2. Top-down training guidance and bottom-up feedback

TRAINING SUBORDINATES IN MISSION COMMAND

1-17. *Mission command* is the exercise of authority and direction by the commander using mission orders to enable disciplined initiative within the commander's intent to empower agile and adaptive leaders in the conduct of unified land operations (ADP 6-0). As the Army's philosophy of command, mission command emphasizes that command is essentially a human endeavor. Successful commanders understand that their leadership directs the development of teams and helps establish mutual trust and shared understanding throughout the force. Commanders provide clear guidance that directs subordinates' actions while promoting freedom of action and initiative.

1-18. Subordinates, by understanding the commander's guidance and the overall common objective, can adapt to rapidly changing situations and exploit fleeting opportunities. They are given the latitude to accomplish assigned tasks in a manner that best fits the situation. Commanders influence the situation and provide direction and guidance while synchronizing operations. Likewise, subordinates understand they have an obligation to act and synchronize their actions with the rest of the force. Commanders encourage subordinates to take action, accept prudent risks to create opportunity, and seize the initiative.

1-19. To exercise mission command successfully during operations, leaders in units understand, foster, and frequently practice the principles of mission command during training. Using these principles during training enables subordinates to overcome obstacles. The principles of mission command apply to all levels of command.

1-20. Commanders aggressively train to overcome institutional obstacles that the Army's operational pace and personnel turbulence present. These obstacles can include frequent deployments of an organization comprised of units that have not trained together, personnel turbulence caused by operational commitments, and constrained financial resources. In particular, training creates common and shared experiences that increase trust and allow commands to acquire competence in mutual understanding. This training builds teams who can communicate explicitly and implicitly, conduct decentralized operations, and achieve unity of effort in uncertain situations. (For more information on mission command, see ADP 6-0 and ADRP 6-0.)

THE ROLE OF LEADERS

1-21. All unit leaders are responsible for quality training. Primary roles involve training subordinate leaders and developing teams. Leaders consist of commanders, NCOs, and unit leaders.

TRAIN AND DEVELOP SUBORDINATE LEADERS

1-22. Successful leaders build cohesive organizations with a strong chain of command, high ésprit de corps, and good discipline. As the unit trains, leaders mentor, guide, listen to, and think with subordinates to challenge their subordinates' depth of knowledge and understanding. These actions build trust among Soldiers and between Soldiers and their leaders. Commanders ensure that their subordinates know *how* to think instead of *what* to think. They develop their subordinates' confidence and empower them to make independent, situational-based decisions. Effective commanders develop subordinates with agile and adaptive approaches to problem solving that more easily translate to operations.

1-23. Effective Army leaders develop others and conduct team building. Holistic leader development plans contribute to unit cohesion, resilience, and agility by producing teams and leaders that are creative, life-long learners, adaptable, fully committed to the Army profession, and capable of exercising mission command.

DEVELOP COHESIVE AND EFFECTIVE TEAMS

1-24. Teamwork is the essence of how the Army operates. The Army trains confident and proficient individual Soldiers but employs them as teams that work together to meet every mission requirement and to overcome every obstacle. Whether training as a team of two Soldiers or as a large combined arms team, developing and encouraging teamwork in training sets the foundation for operating when deployed. Commanders instill and encourage teamwork as training is planned, prepared, executed, and assessed.

1-25. Teams and teamwork are as essential to unit training as they are to successful operations. Teams occur at every echelon and level of Army organizations. Teamwork begins with two Soldiers training together, progresses as they train on simple collective tasks, and evolves as they sustain their training on more complex collective tasks. A team is more effective than an individual is at achieving results. When Soldiers work together, they use their unique skills, experiences, and capabilities together to achieve task proficiency.

1-26. The mission command philosophy helps to set the conditions for training and developing cohesive and effective teams. Building a shared understanding among team members is the first step in developing a team. It gives the team a unifying and focused purpose. In a team-focused climate, members understand the reason for each action, the capabilities of each member of the team, and each members' contributions effects on the overall success of the organization.

THE ROLE OF COMMANDERS

1-27. In addition to the unit commander's activities—understand, visualize, describe, direct, lead, and assess—in training, commanders at all echelons fulfill their role in unit training with their continuous attention, physical presence, and energy to—

Chapter 1

- Develop and communicate a clear vision.
- Personally engage in training.
- Demand that training standards are achieved.
- Foster a positive training culture.
- Limit training distracters.
- Enforce a top-down/bottom-up approach to training.

See ADRP 7-0 for more on the commander's activities in training.

Develop and Communicate a Clear Vision

1-28. Published training guidance provides the vision, direction, purpose, and motivation necessary to prepare individuals and organizations to win. It is based on a comprehensive understanding of—

- Task proficiencies to attain—the *what* to train.
- Commander's guidance.
- Operational environments.
- Organizational and personnel strengths and weaknesses.
- The training environment.

Personally Engage in Training

1-29. Commanders are engaged in every aspect of training. Commanders are physically present to the maximum extent possible during the planning for and execution of training. As stewards of the Army Profession, they effectively resource training and protect subordinates' training time. They create a sense of stability throughout the organization by protecting approved training plans from training distracters. Commanders are responsible for executing the approved training to standard. Effective commanders provide timely, valuable feedback to all participants.

Demand Training Standards Be Achieved

1-30. Leaders anticipate that units may not perform some tasks to standard. When designing the training calendar, leaders allow time during training events for additional training for those tasks not performed to standard. It is better to train to standard on a limited number of tasks rather than attempt and fail to achieve the standard on too many tasks. Soldiers will remember the enforced standard, not the one that leaders discussed. Leaders cannot assume that time will be available to train to standard next time. Rationalizing that corrective action will occur during some later training period sets units up for failure rather than success. See appendix B for more information on task standards.

Foster a Positive Training Culture

1-31. Commanders create a training culture that listens to and rewards subordinates who are bold and innovative leaders and trainers. Commanders challenge the organization and each individual to train to their full potential. Such a challenge fosters a training culture so that organizations and individuals strive to not just attain task standards but to attain higher levels of task mastery.

Limit Training Distracters

1-32. Commanders plan and resource training events while limiting potential distractions. They ensure participation by the maximum number of Soldiers. Although commanders cannot ignore administrative support burdens, commanders can manage those burdens using an effective time management system. Additionally, commanders must support subordinates' efforts to train effectively by managing training distracters and reinforcing the requirement for all assigned personnel to be present during training.

Enforce a Top-Down/Bottom-Up Approach to Training

1-33. Senior commanders provide the lead in a top-down/bottom-up approach to training. Commanders provide the training focus, direction, and resources, while subordinate leaders provide feedback on unit training proficiency, identify specific training needs, and execute training to standard. This team effort maintains training focus, establishes training priorities, and enables effective communication between command echelons.

1-34. Training guidance flows from the top down and results in subordinate units' identification of the individual and collective tasks that support the higher unit's mission. Input from the bottom up is essential because it identifies training needs to achieve task proficiency. Leaders at all echelons communicate with each other about requirements as well as about planning, preparing, executing, and assessing training.

1-35. Commanders centralize planning to provide a consistent training focus from the top to the bottom of the organization. They decentralize execution to promote subordinate leaders' initiative to train their units. Commanders do not relinquish their responsibilities to supervise training, develop leaders, and provide feedback.

THE ROLE OF NONCOMMISSIONED OFFICERS

1-36. The NCO Corps has an enduring and foundational role in unit training. NCOs are responsible for the individual training of Soldiers, crews, and small teams. NCOs conduct standards-based, performance-oriented, battle-focused training. They—

- Identify specific individual, crew, and small-team tasks that support the unit's collective mission-essential tasks (METs).
- Plan, prepare, and execute training.
- Evaluate training and conduct after action reviews (AARs) to provide feedback to the commander on individual, crew, and small-team proficiency.
- Fulfill an important role by assisting in the professional development of the officer corps.

THE ROLE OF UNIT LEADERS

1-37. In addition to the commander and NCO roles and responsibilities, all leaders must require their subordinates to understand and perform their roles in training (see figure 1-3 on page 1-8). The commander assigns primary responsibility to officers for collective training and to NCOs for Soldier training. The commander is responsible to meld leader and Soldier training requirements into collective training events using multiechelon techniques. Additionally, all leaders must—

- Train the combined arms team to be proficient on its METs. This includes training Soldiers, leaders, subordinate units, and supporting elements. Proficiency requires training the leader with the unit. Additionally, leaders pay special attention to training newly assigned lieutenants and sergeants as they train with their platoons as well as to newly promoted sergeants as they train with their sections, squads, teams, and crews.
- Centralize training planning to maintain unit focus on the mission.
- Decentralize execution to allow subordinate leaders the flexibility to focus training on their units' strengths and weaknesses.
- Establish effective communications at all levels.
- Talk to and exchange information with other leaders. Guidance on missions and priorities flows down while Soldier, leader, and collective training requirements flow up. Training meetings, briefings, and AARs serve as the primary forums for exchanging training information among leaders.
- Demand units achieve training standards.

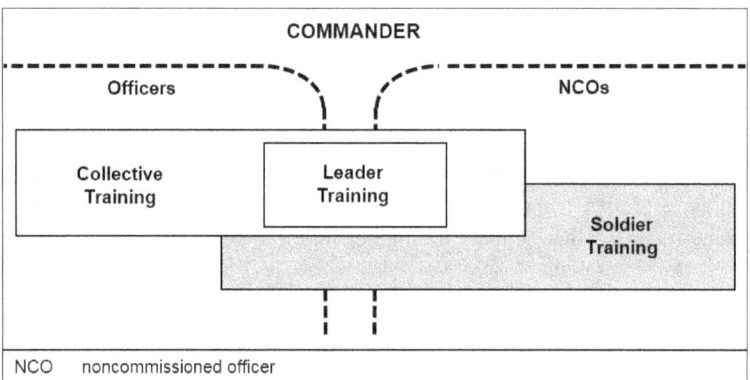

Figure 1-3. Overlapping training responsibilities

BATTLE FOCUS

1-38. A battle-focused unit trains selectively. It cannot train to standard on every task at once, whether due to time, or other resource constraints. A unit that attempts to train to proficiency all the tasks it could perform only serves to diffuse its training effort. A unit that simultaneously trains to all its capabilities at once will most likely never achieve a T or T- in all those tasks. Focusing on the tasks to train, based on the higher commander's guidance, and taking into account that time and resources are limited, is battle-focused training.

1-39. The battle focus concept involves understanding the responsibility for and the links between the collective METs and the individual tasks that support them. Figure 1-4 depicts the relationships and the proper sequence to derive optimum training benefits from each training opportunity.

1-40. The commander and command sergeant major—or first sergeant—coordinate the METs, collective tasks, and individual tasks on which the unit will focus during a given period. The command sergeant major or first sergeant identifies the supporting individual tasks for each collective task. The unit's Combined Arms Training Strategy (CATS) provides a resource for this coordination. The CATS contains a comprehensive listing of all collective tasks cross-referenced to supporting individual tasks by task number and title. Although NCOs have the primary role in training and sustaining individual Soldier skills, officers at every level are responsible for training to established standards during both individual and collective training. Commanders apply a battle focus to training for all capabilities or missions across the range of operations. The operations process guides the unit commander and all unit leaders through this coordination to achieve battle focus.

MISSION-ESSENTIAL TASK

1-41. Commanders rarely have enough time or resources to complete all necessary tasks. Each commander has to determine what is essential and then assign responsibility for accomplishment. The concept of METs provides the commander a process to provide the unit its battle focus. **A *mission-essential task* is a collective task on which an organization trains to be proficient in its designed capabilities or assigned mission. A *mission-essential task list* is a tailored group of mission-essential tasks.** Each MET aligns with the collective tasks that support it. All company and higher units have a mission-essential task list (METL). Units based on a table of organization and equipment (TOE) have an approved and standardized METL based on the type of unit by echelon. Standardized METLs can be found on the Army Training Network (ATN), Digital Training Management System (DTMS), and CATS. Units that do not have a standardized METL—like a unit based on a table of distribution and allowances (TDA)—develop its METs and METL.

Training Overview

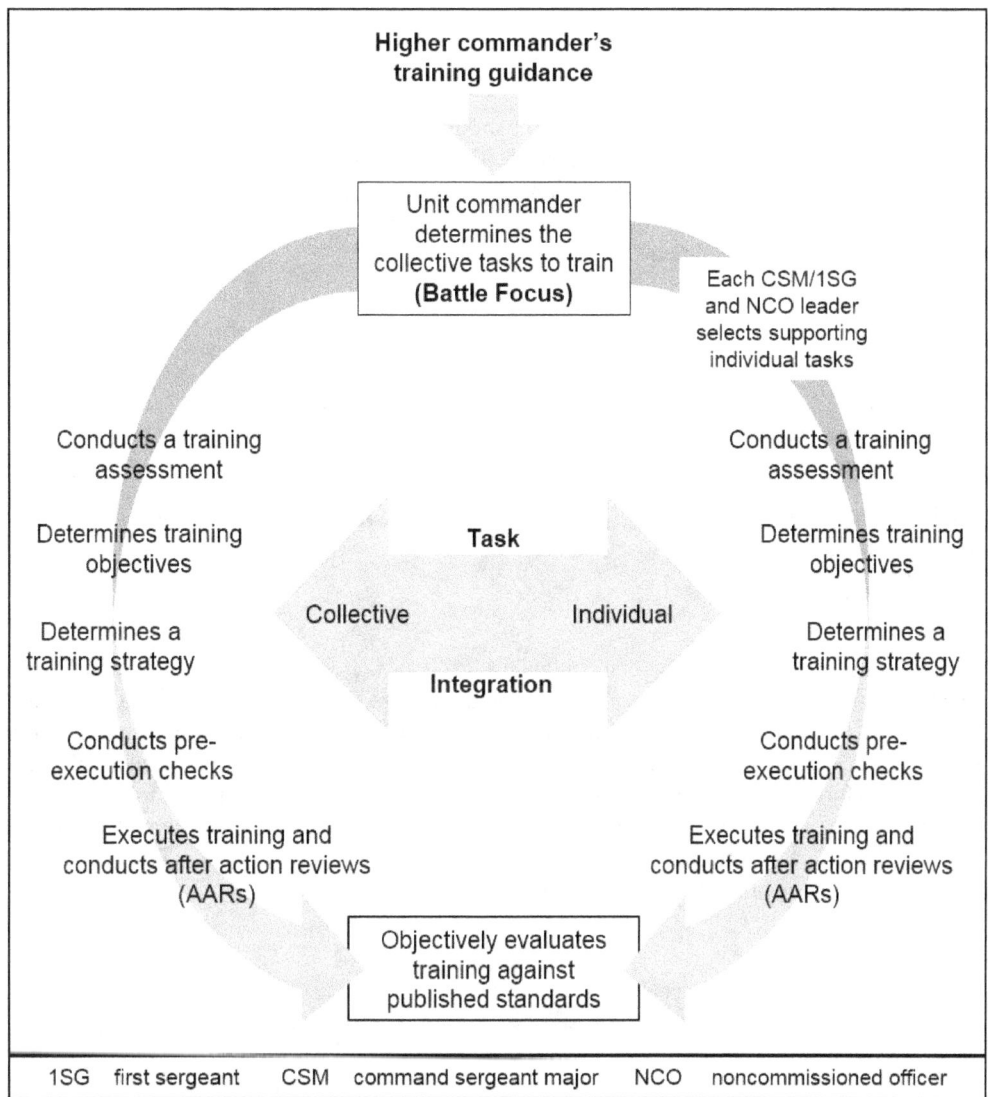

Figure 1-4. Battle focus integration of collective and individual training

Standardized Mission-Essential Task List

1-42. For company and larger units with a TOE, the applicable proponent develops the unit METL. This METL is referred to as the unit's standardized METL throughout this publication. It is developed and standardized by the responsible proponent; staffed with the Army commands and Army Service component commands; approved and published by the Headquarters, Department of the Army; and available on ATN. The unit's standardized METL is based on its echelon and design capabilities.

Mission-Essential Task List Development (Non-Standardized)

1-43. Not all Army units have a standardized METL. For company and larger units without a standardized METL (for example, a unit based on a TDA), the unit commander conducts a mission analysis, develops the unit METs, and has these approved by the next higher commander. The unit then publishes the METs and a METL in the DTMS. When no collective tasks exist for a TDA unit, the unit commander develops the METs and supporting collective tasks, develops the conditions and standards for the task, and has these approved by the next higher commander. The discussion beginning in paragraph 2-30 refers to METs for these type units.

BATTLE TASK

1-44. A battle task is a collective task on which a platoon or lower echelon trains that supports a company MET. A battle task can include any associated supporting collective tasks. Battle tasks are approved by the company commander. Platoon and lower echelons do not have METs or a METL. Based on the company METs and METL, the platoon leader—with the platoon sergeant—conducts a mission analysis to determine the platoon battle tasks that best support the company METs.

PLANNING FRAMEWORK

1-45. Senior commanders, as stewards of the Army Profession, provide the necessary resources to train, including time, and protect subordinate units from unprogrammed taskings or other training distractions. They publish training guidance (that includes a calendar) to give subordinate commanders adequate time to properly plan and resource training.

1-46. For training, senior commanders use a framework that involves three planning horizons:
- Long-range.
- Mid-range.
- Short-range.

A *planning horizon* is a point in time commanders use to focus the organization's planning efforts to shape future events (ADRP 5-0). A long-range planning horizon covers a unit's overarching training plan over an extended time (typically years). It synchronizes supporting units and agencies so that a unit can properly execute its training events. It is graphically depicted on a unit training plan (UTP) calendar. A mid-range planning horizon further refines the long-range planning horizon. It defines in more detail the broad guidance for training events, closer to the training start. A short-range planning horizon defines the specific actions (plan and prepare) prior to the start of training. (See appendix H for T-Week concept.) See figure 1-5 for the planning horizons. (See also ADRP 5-0 for a detailed discussion on planning horizons.)

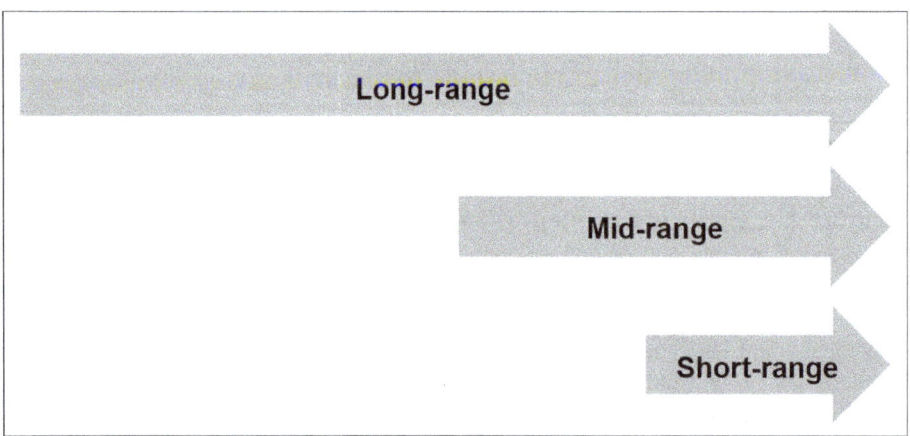

Figure 1-5. Planning horizons for training

TRAINING ENVIRONMENT

1-47. Units obtain effective training when they create a realistic and challenging training environment. A *training environment* is an environment comprised of conditions, supporting resources, and time that enables training tasks to proficiency. An effective training environment enables an individual or a unit to achieve proficiency in the individual and collective tasks trained. The commander sets the conditions of the tasks selected to train with as much realism as possible. Supporting resources provide the tools that enable modifying those conditions to be more challenging and complex for Soldiers and the entire unit. Commanders leverage available resources, to include the mix of live, virtual, and constructive (LVC) training enablers. When used properly, resources create a powerful training multiplier that more closely replicate an actual operational environment. The time available to train is often one aspect of the training environment of which there is never enough. Training within the limits of the planning horizon drives when the unit or individual is expected to be proficient in the tasks selected to train. Careful development of a training environment can produce exceptional results and ultimately increase training readiness. See appendix A for more information on creating realism in training.

TRAINING FOR BATTLE RHYTHM

1-48. Commanders integrate and synchronize training activities, meetings, briefings, conferences, and reports among their subordinates and with their higher commander. Commanders establish training for a unit's battle rhythm. *Battle rhythm* is a deliberate cycle of command, staff, and unit activities intended to synchronize current and future operations (FM 6-0). In the context of unit training, establishing a battle rhythm helps sequence the activities, events, and actions that regulate the flow and sharing of information that supports the training process. Effectively training for battle rhythm—

- Facilitates and establishes interactions related to training among the commander, staff, and subordinate units.
- Establishes a routine for staff interactions and coordination.
- Facilitates planning by the staff and decision making by the commander.

1-49. Training for a unit's battle rhythm consists of conducting periodic meetings and briefings, meeting report requirements, and experiencing other activities synchronized by time and purpose. These activities and products include, but are not limited to—

- Publishing command training guidance (CTG).
- Training meetings.
- T-Week concept.
- Training briefings.
- Installation training resource synchronization conferences.
- Commanders' dialogues.
- Time management cycles.
- UTP calendars.
- Company training schedules.
- Planning horizons (long, mid, and short).

1-50. The unit commander, in conjunction with the higher commander's guidance, establishes and enforces the training for the unit's battle rhythm. These activities are heavily influenced by policy, doctrine, unit standard operating procedures (SOPs), and training priorities established by the higher commander. All unit leaders understand and comply with the activities that comprise the training rhythm.

ESTABLISHING TRAINING FOR BATTLE RHYTHM IN UNITS

1-51. So that commanders and units have sufficient time to plan and coordinate long-range training, senior commanders publish CTG (further discussed in chapter 2). Published guidance communicates their training and readiness priorities throughout the command and provides subordinates sufficient time to develop and resource training that supports that guidance. Publication of the CTG establishes the unit's training for battle rhythm when it is not deployed on operations.

1-52. For the Regular Army and Reserve Component, each successive echelon publishes their nested CTG. For division and higher units, the format of the CTG is at the commander's discretion. For brigade and below units, the format is the UTP operation order (OPORD) (see appendix F). A published CTG always includes the corresponding training calendar.

Chapter 1

1-53. The timelines in table 1-1 provide guidance for when CTG or UTPs are published by echelon for the Regular Army. This separation by echelon ensures that long-range planning and guidance is timely and allows each command to conduct parallel and collaborative planning across the force. It also ensures that crucial training resources needed to train are identified well in advance and are available at the start of training. Table 1-2 shows the same information for the Reserve Component (known as RC). Note that Regular Army and Reserve Component units' CTG planning horizons significantly differ. For example, a Regular Army division commander's long-range planning horizon is two years, whereas a like echelon Reserve Component unit commander's long-range planning horizon is five years.

Table 1-1. Regular Army long-range planning by echelon

Echelon	Publishes CTG with calendar NLT[1]:	Planning horizon
Corps	12 months prior to training start	2 years
Division	10 months prior to training start	2 years
Installation	10 months prior to training start (calendar only)	1 year
Brigade	8 months prior to training start	1 year
Battalion[2]	6 months prior to training start	1 year

[1] Publication dates also apply to similar command-level TDA organizations or activities. For example, a TRADOC COE normally commanded by a major general follows the same planning cycle as a division commander.

[2] Companies develop and publish their own UTP. The battalion commander, in collaboration with subordinate company commanders and the battalion staff may develop a consolidated battalion UTP.

COE	center of excellence	TDA	table of distribution and allowances
CTG	command training guidance	TRADOC	Training and Doctrine Command
NLT	no later than	UTP	unit training plan

Table 1-2. Reserve Component long-range planning by echelon

Echelon	Publishes CTG with calendar NLT[1]:	Planning horizon
Flag officer CMD, separate brigade, regiment or group	18 months prior to training start	5 years
Brigade or separate battalion	10 months prior to training start	5 years
Battalion[2]	6 months prior to training start	2-3 years

[1] These actions also apply to similar command-level TDA organizations or activities. For example, a regional support command, commanded by a major general follows the same planning cycle as a division commander.

[2] Companies develop and publish their own UTP and calendar. The battalion commander, in collaboration with subordinate company or troop commanders, and the battalion staff may consolidated a battalion UTP.

CMD	command	TDA	table of distribution and allowances
CTG	command training guidance	UTP	unit training plan
NLT	no later than		

1-54. Within a brigade, on receipt of a division CTG, the brigade commander begins mission analysis to determine how best to meet the division commander's guidance. Adhering to the concept of collaborative and parallel planning, each subordinate unit also begins the same process to begin formulating how each echelon will support the higher commander's guidance. Effective collaborative planning ensures that each echelon publishes its plans well prior to the start of training. Because training relies on units having the right resources available at the right time, collaborative planning begins early enough in the planning cycle so units have the resources to train when they need them.

1-55. In figure 1-6, the timelines are by echelon within a Regular Army notional brigade. Figure 1-7 shows the publication timelines with a notional Reserve Component flag officer command. These timelines allow sufficient planning and publication time for each successive command to issue its UTP. They also allow sufficient time for collaborative planning, parallel planning, and coordination of resources prior to the start of training. Six weeks from the start of training, the company not only publishes its training schedule, but it also locks in company-level training (for the Reserve Component, this occurs three months or 90 days from the start of training [see figure 1-7]). Any changes to the approved company training are not authorized past this time unless approved by the next higher commander. See also appendix H for more information on training schedule publications.

Training Overview

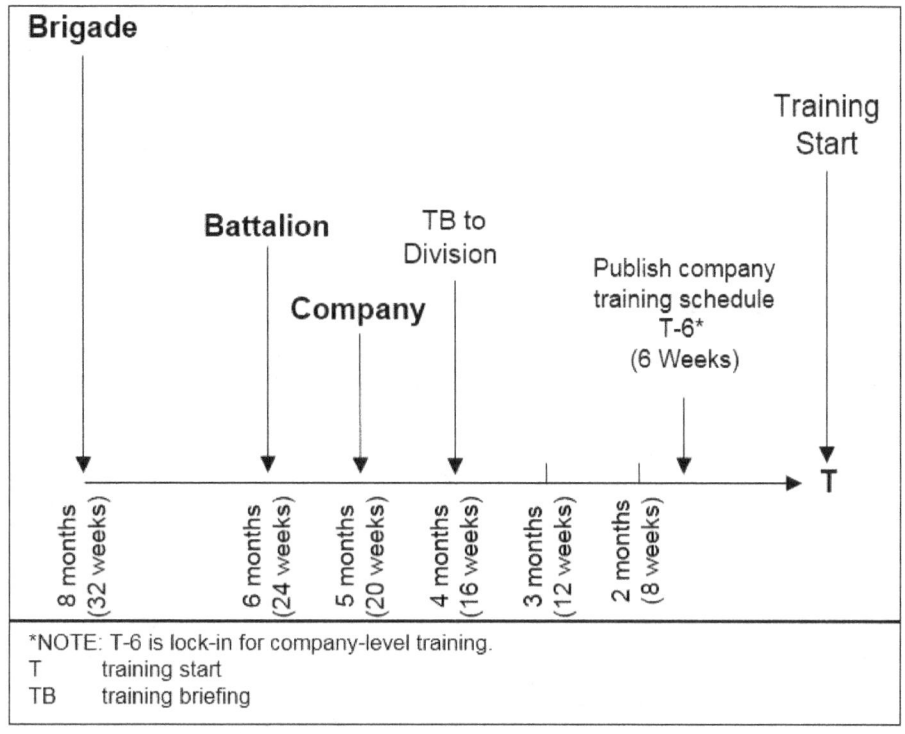

Figure 1-6. UTP publication timelines within a notional Regular Army brigade

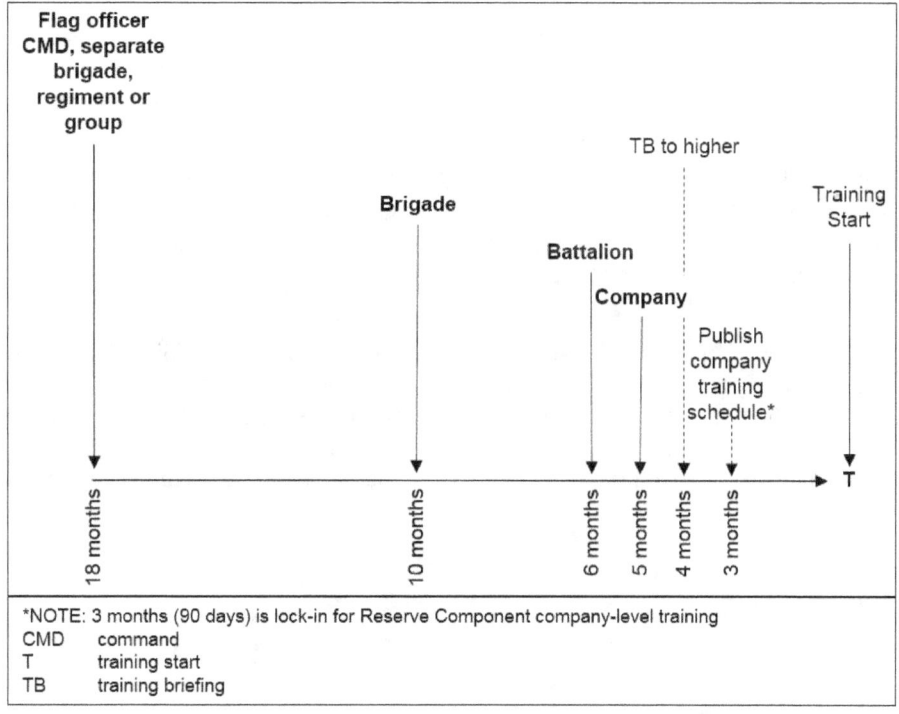

Figure 1-7. UTP publication timelines within a notional Reserve Component flag officer command

Chapter 1

TRAINING PLANS TIED TO RESOURCES NEEDED TO TRAIN

1-56. Without the right resources, effective training will not occur. Available resources directly affect unit training readiness. Each commander and staff understands the resource coordination and synchronization cycle on the installation on which units conduct training. Commanders and staffs coordinate and synchronize procedures for the normal classes of supply; training aids, devices, simulators, and simulations (TADSS); integrated training environment (ITE) considerations and resources; and available training facilities. At a home station, all training resources are limited and shared with other units on the installation. Commanders and staffs aware of an installation's resource cycle are more likely to secure the right training resources when they are needed to train.

MULTIECHELON TRAINING

1-57. *Multiechelon training* is a training technique that allows for the simultaneous training of more than one echelon on different or complementary tasks (ADRP 7-0). As each echelon conducts its mission analysis to determine the tasks to train, it provides a logic trail from individual Soldier tasks to brigade-level METs. An effective logic trail clearly nests from one echelon to the next and effectively crosswalks the tasks up the echelons and down the echelons. Although not an integral part of planning, this task crosswalk enables leaders to visualize how the top-down training guidance directly supports the bottom-up alignment of individual and collective tasks that support the higher unit.

1-58. To illustrate this concept, see figure 1-8. In this example, an infantry brigade combat team (known as IBCT) commander focuses training on offensive operations—specifically conduct a movement to contact—and states this in the training guidance. Through mission analysis, the subordinate artillery battalion commander determines that to support a brigade movement to contact, the battalion needs to focus training on the task, Conduct Battalion Fire Missions. Likewise, other subordinate commanders do their mission analyses to determine the collective tasks on which they must focus training to support the brigade commander's guidance.

Army Training Management System

1-59. The Army Training Management System (ATMS) is the Army enterprise program automating management of unit and individual training. ATMS consists of Web-based applications and centralized databases: ATN, CATS, and DTMS. The ATMS suite of applications automates routine command, unit, institution, and individual training and processes.

1-60. ATMS enablers directly support ADP 7-0, ADRP 7-0, this publication, and other relevant Army doctrine and policy guidance. The centrally managed enterprise databases—such as the individual training record—organize, store, and make available data for displays, reports, queries, and data sharing. Though centrally managed, the data collected from the ATMS belong to the commander. See the ATN for details on ATMS.

1-61. The ATN provides a single, Web-based portal with links to Army training doctrine, processes, and resources used by Army units. As a collaborative, online resource, the ATN relies on input from units and Soldiers. It is also the primary access point for CATS and DTMS. The ATN is also home to all published standardized METLs. The ATN is accessible at https://atn.army.mil. Users can access the ATN via an Army-issued common access card (known as CAC) and via the defense system log on with the appropriate credentials.

Training Overview

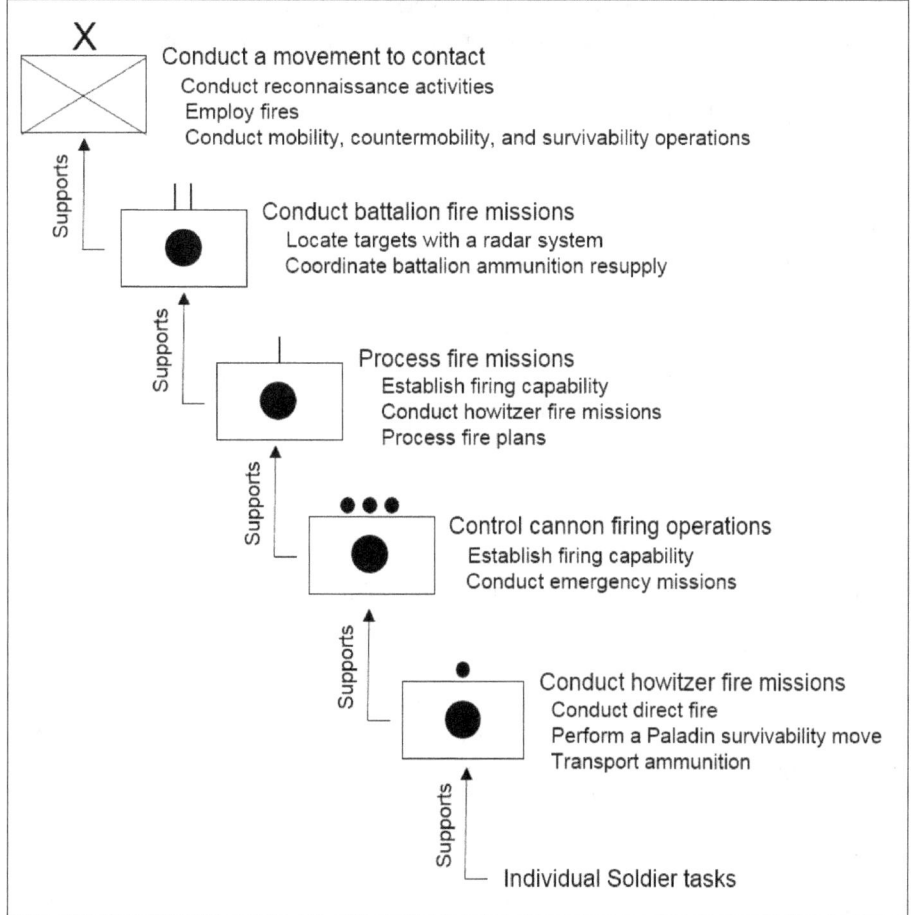

Figure 1-8. Multiechelon training task crosswalk

1-62. CATSs provide training strategies that are—
- Recommended by proponent.
- Based on tasks.
- Driven by events.
- Holistic.
- Focused on the METL (TOE units).

1-63. The strategies are based on analysis of the missions, functions, and capabilities as stated in the unit's TOE and the proponent-generated unit task list (known as UTL). CATSs utilize task sets as the primary building blocks of the UTP. Task sets are groups of collective tasks selected to be trained together that are necessary for a unit to achieve proficiency in a given capability or function. Task sets outline numerous training events using a crawl, walk, and run methodology to assist trainers to develop their UTPs. CATSs also provide the task, purpose, outcome, and execution guidance for each recommended training event. Each CATS identifies the types and frequencies of training events at the respective echelon that should be conducted to achieve proficiency. CATSs save planning time by providing descriptive, proponent-approved, and unit-vetted training strategies. Units can easily enter these strategies in DTMS as a training plan and then tailor them as needed. Users can access CATSs from the ATN homepage and DTMS at https://atn.army.mil.

1-64. DTMS automates specific training and management processes through its Web-based program. It provides the ability to digitally develop, record, and coordinate training plans within organizations as well

Chapter 1

as record training assessments, training completion, and training readiness. Users can access DTMS through ATN at https://atn.army.mil. DTMS enables leaders to perform some of the following functions:

- Review the higher commander's training guidance and disseminate other training documents.
- View and review unit METLs.
- Manage the UTP calendar.
- Manage mandatory, individual, collective, and deployment training tasks and requirements.
- Assess and record individual training records (known as ITRs) for Soldiers.
- View and update the digital job book.
- View and update the digital small-unit leader dashboard.
- Manage the Army's electronic individual training record.
- Use the common access card (known as CAC) to sign in to large-group training sessions.
- Enable bulk data uploads to allow units to record training completion.
- Use the Survey Tool to collect customer and user information.
- Use the Unit Individual Training Management (known as UITM) module to support central management of distributed individual training.

Other Supporting Training Resources

1-65. In addition to the Web-based resources available within ATMS, other additional resources provide information and access to data and knowledge to assist trainers. These include, but are not limited to the Central Army Registry (CAR) and Center for Army Lessons Learned (known as CALL).

1-66. The CAR is a Web-based digital catalog and repository that serves as the warfighters' one-stop source for training-related products such as doctrine, published tasks, training circulars, training support packages, and graphic training aids. Users can first search for training products in the CAR by identification, title, and keywords, and then browse the CAR catalog by product type and proponent. The CAR is available on ATN under the Unit Training Management or myTraining tabs. Users can directly access the CAR at https://atiam.train.army.mil/catalog/dashboard.

1-67. The Center for Army Lessons Learned is the Army's source for adaptive learning based on lessons and best practices from the Army. It provides timely and relevant knowledge by using integrated systems and interactive technology. Users can access the Center for Army Lessons Learned at http://usacac.army.mil/organizations/mccoe/call.

TRAINING RESOURCE SYNCHRONIZATION CONFERENCES

1-68. The senior commander on an installation hosts periodic installation-level resource synchronization conferences. Ideally, the senior commander schedules these training resource conferences every quarter (see figure 1-9). These conferences provide leaders two types of information. First, it identifies installation training resources. These resources may include training areas, ranges, ITE facilities and resources, and TADSS availability. Second, the conference shows the availability of any unscheduled resources.

1-69. As echelons develop UTP calendars, they coordinate and requisition training resources. The installation-level resource synchronization conferences verify that the senior commander acknowledges and validates that units require training resources to execute training. This validation is the senior commander's endorsement that the resources will be available when needed. Effective leaders—especially at the brigade and battalion levels—must attend these conferences to prepare their training plans. At these conferences, leaders learn of locally available installation training support resources and the method to schedule for their units' training cycle. Once training requirements are identified at the company level, brigade and battalion commanders and staff work diligently to properly resource company-level training.

1-70. The senior commander on the installation is responsible for prioritizing installation training resources (see AR 350-1). The higher commander determines the priority of units to training readiness and resources. Units with a higher priority often affect the availability of critical training resources for units with a lower priority. For example, a unit within six months of deploying has a higher priority for using ranges and

Training Overview

training areas than a unit that is not scheduled for deployment. Knowledgeable commanders know when these conferences and meetings occur, and they ensure their unit is represented by the right leader who can make decisions on behalf of the commander.

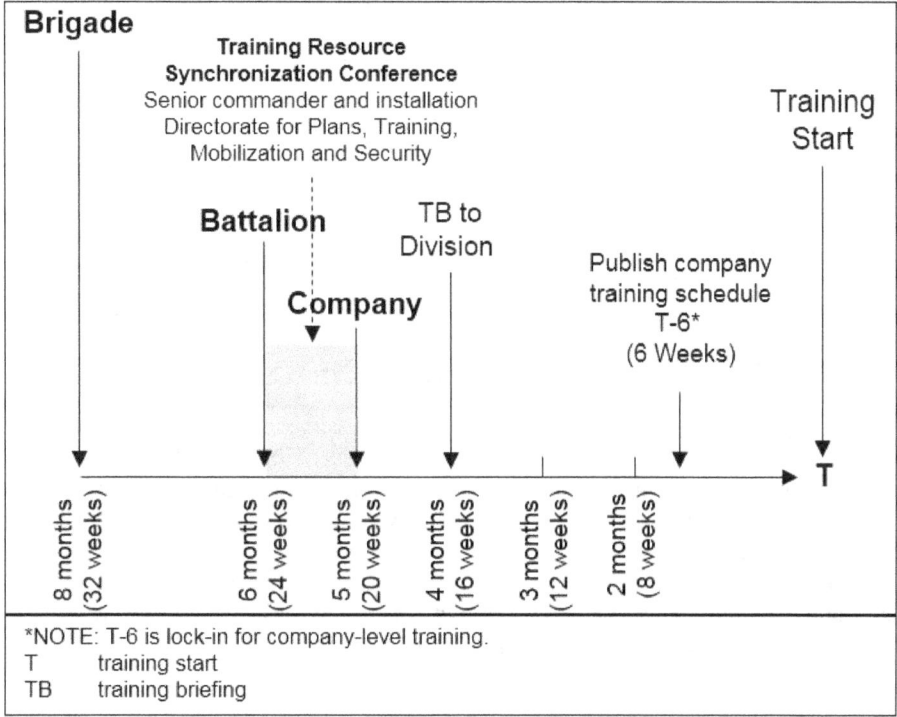

Figure 1-9. Notional training resource synchronization conference for a Regular Army brigade

Note. In figure 1-9, the installation training resource synchronization conference occurs within a planning and publication window that allows for validation of training resources no later than 5 months from the start of training and prior to the training briefing. For Reserve Component units, the coordination and synchronization of training resources require an understanding and visibility of training resource conferences all installations. This is key when Regular Army and Reserve Component installations and facilities provide training resources to support UTPs.

COMMANDERS' DIALOGUES

1-71. Units that train the way they fight establish and maintain planning horizons. When planning horizons are sound, units can deliver quality training and achieve training readiness. Commanders who train consistently and effectively conduct training meetings routinely from company to brigade levels. These commanders also conduct commanders' dialogues to maintain battle focus and keep training on schedule. The continuous process of planning, preparing, executing, and assessing each training event of the UTP requires commanders to lead and manage the frequent and recurring series of meetings.

1-72. Discussions and dialogues between the unit and higher commander occur throughout the training process. These recurring dialogues help ensure both commanders agree with the direction and scope of unit training. The dialogues also enable the higher commander to approve the training and to ensure the necessary resources are coordinated and available when training occurs.

1-73. Commanders' dialogues are truly dialogues and intended as points of discussion between the two commanders. These dialogues provide critical decision points for both commanders while planning,

Chapter 1

preparing, executing and assessing training. Commanders can adjust training plans at these decision points, if necessary, and verify that units have critical resources when and where they are needed to train. Table 1-3 illustrates when commanders' dialogues should occur.

Table 1-3. Commanders' dialogue at critical points in the training process

Commanders' dialogues take place...	*At this critical point...*
When mission-essential tasks are discussed	Mission analysis backbrief.
When the unit training plan is briefed to the commander two levels up	Training briefing.
During training meetings	Weekly training meeting at company and battalion; monthly at brigade.
During cyclical training briefings	Quarterly training briefing (Regular Army); yearly training briefing (Reserve Component).
During external evaluations	Before, during, and after external evaluations.

RESERVE COMPONENT TRAINING CONSIDERATIONS

1-74. When deployed for operations, the Army executes missions as one force in conjunction with joint forces, multinational forces, and interagency organizations. Both the Regular Army and Reserve Component share the same training doctrine and procedures and train to the same standard. However, in the training environment, the planning horizons differ somewhat for Reserve Component units as does the time available to train. Geographic dispersion of units also impacts Reserve Component training. An average reserve battalion can be spread over hundreds of miles increasing the complexity for these units to accomplish training. Additionally, many reserve units must travel many miles to the nearest training area, and individual Soldiers often travel extended miles to get to their training sites.

1-75. This manual notes the primary differences between Regular Army and Reserve Component training planning and activities where applicable. These differences are most evident in—

- Planning horizons.
- Resource coordination.
- Yearly training briefing.
- T-week concept.

PLANNING HORIZONS

1-76. The long-, mid-, and short-range planning horizons generally have a longer duration for Reserve Component units and typically span years. For example, the long-range planning horizon (and subsequent UTP) for a Reserve Component brigade may span up to 5 years. For a Regular Army brigade, this would typically be 1 year (see tables 1-1 and 1-2 on page 1-12).

RESOURCE COORDINATION

1-77. Ensuring the right training resources are available at the start of training can often be problematic for Reserve Component units. These units coordinate with their own as well as Regular Army installations for training resources, facilities, and support. Additionally, Reserve Component units also coordinate training plans with other Reserve Component units and Regular Army units. Understanding the training resource cycles and conferences that occur for Reserve Component and supporting Regular Army installations requires a knowledge of—and liaison with—multiple facilities and training areas. Refer to figure 1-9 on page 1-5 and corresponding note pertaining to Reserve Component units.

YEARLY TRAINING BRIEFING

1-78. To ensure that the UTP remains on track through the long-range planning horizon, Reserve Component units conduct yearly training briefings (YTBs) rather than quarterly training briefings (QTBs) conducted by Regular Army units. For briefings pertaining to Reserve Component units, see table 1-2 on page 1-12, paragraph 3-36, and appendix G.

T-WEEK CONCEPT

1-79. For Regular Army units, T-Week activities conform to a weekly schedule. Reserve Component units typically modify this construct and follow a monthly break out of specific company-level activities. Since units can tailor these timelines and activities to its needs, many Reserve Component units establish a T-*month* concept using the same methodology and procedures employed by Regular Army units, but on a monthly schedule. See paragraph 3-22 and appendix H for discussions of the T-Week concept.

1-80. To illustrate how available training time affects Reserve Component units and the associated activities affect planning, preparing, executing, and assessing training, see figure 1-10.

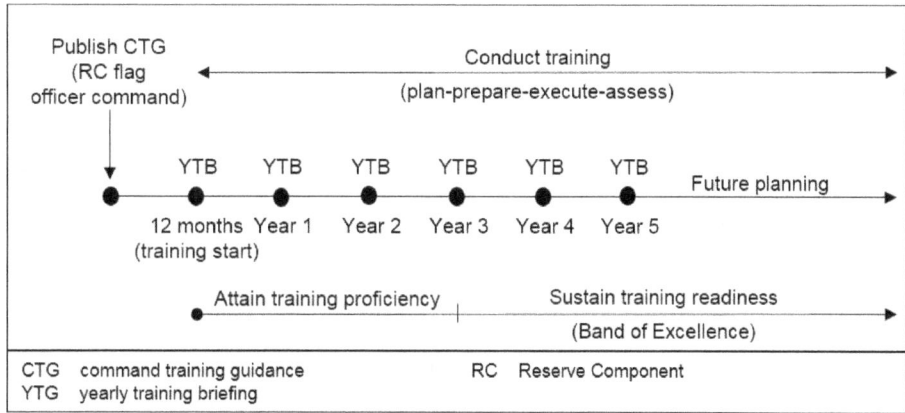

Figure 1-10. Notional Reserve Component unit training long-range planning horizons

PREMOBILIZATION AND POSTMOBILIZATION TRAINING

1-81. Mobilization is not the starting point for planning battle focused training. Reserve Component units have premobilization readiness and postmobilization training requirements. Units must develop premobilization training plans and receive approval for the current fiscal and training year. Units integrate postmobilization training plans with the premobilization training plans and then update and receive approval for each training year as well.

1-82. Premobilization training directly links to postmobilization training. A critical objective is to identify achievable, sustainable training requirements, which provide the focus for effective premobilization unit training. Reserve Component commanders train their units to standard on established premobilization tasks.

1-83. Postmobilization expands organizational training, raises the echelon trained, and increases the amount of multiechelon and combined arms training accordingly. Units create postmobilization plans at the same time as premobilization plans. Units update postmobilization plans regularly as premobilization training and revised commanders training assessments are completed.

PREMOBILIZATION TRAINING PLANS

1-84. Premobilization training focuses on company-level individual and collective tasks. Premobilization training plans identify training requirements, training events, equipment, and training support packages to attain and sustain task proficiency. The Reserve Component challenge in premobilization is to generate sufficient readiness to ensure as short a postmobilization period as possible. Sufficient readiness requires a clear linkage of tasks and time than the Regular Army. Proficiency in these tasks enables training to full METL proficiency when the unit is mobilized. The UTP includes focusing on METL tasks, to include preparation for and execution of annual training.

Postmobilization Training Plans

1-85. Postmobilization training focuses on company-level and above collective tasks. These plans identify training requirements, training events, equipment, and training support packages needed to train the unit to METL proficiency upon mobilization. Postmobilization plans are updated annually and reflect input from the execution of the premobilization plan. The commander approving the unit's METL and UTP also approves the postmobilization plan. The plan is then provided to the mobilization station commander where the postmobilization training will occur.

1-86. Installation commanders are responsible for supporting the execution of postmobilization training activities. They determine resource requirements and develop plans to support the unit to reach its deployment training requirements. Reserve Component commanders conduct periodic visits with the supporting installation commander to inspect training areas and facilities, identify and resolve support challenges, and clarify and refine training support requirements.

Chapter 2
Developing the Unit Training Plan

TRAINING READINESS

2-1. Training readiness stems from attaining proficiency in individual and collective tasks. To do that, unit commanders develop their UTP, focusing on the tasks to train, based on the higher commander's guidance. This is battle-focused training. Following the general framework of the military decisionmaking process (MDMP) (or troop leading procedures [TLP] for company and below), unit commanders begin the process to determine the METs—what to train. Training readiness is at the core of this determination—whether it is training to maintain and sustain certain capabilities or training to meet the requirements of an assigned mission.

2-2. The Army's training readiness is supported by training in the three training domains: institutional, operational, and self-development. The institutional training domain includes Army centers and schools that provide initial training and subsequent functional and professional military education for Army personnel. The operational domain encompasses training activities that unit leaders schedule, and that individuals, units, and organizations undertake. The self-development domain is completed by individuals as they pursue personal and professional development goals. See AR 350-1 for a discussion of training domains.

2-3. The process of determining essential tasks begins with receipt of guidance from the higher commander. (See figure 2-1.)

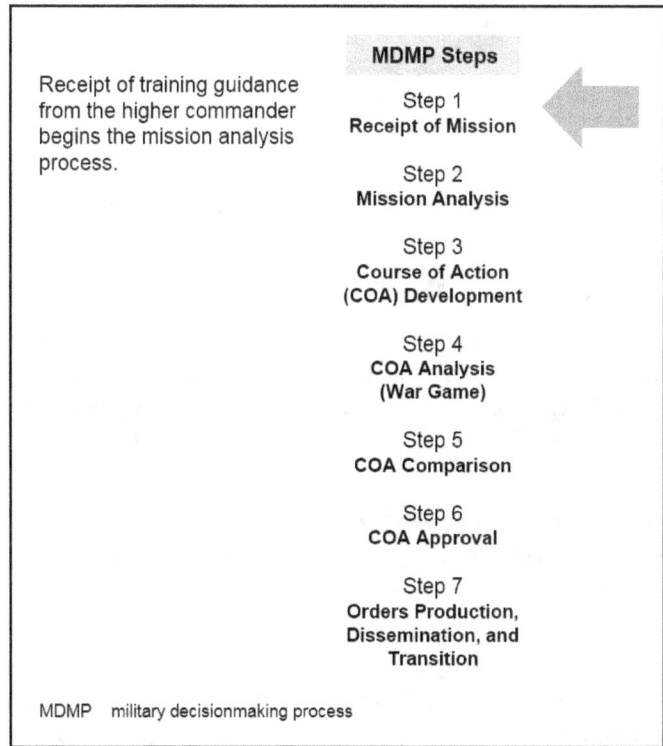

Figure 2-1. Receipt of training guidance begins the planning process

Chapter 2

THE ARMY OPERATIONS PROCESS

2-4. The Army uses the operations process of plan, prepare, execute, and assess as its training framework. Using this framework, the unit commander remains central to the training process in the same way the commander is central to the operations process. Planning, preparing, executing and assessing unit training does not significantly differ from performing these activities for an operation. Each unit commander begins the training cycle with top-down training guidance from the higher commander. The receipt of guidance begins a process of determining the correct collective tasks on which to train. The commander then develops a UTP to conduct that training in the time allotted. Planning for training follows the MDMP for battalion and above or TLP for company and below.

2-5. The resulting plan consists of training events that progressively develop task proficiency. Each training event follows a plan, prepare, execute, and assess cycle (see figure 2-2). Prior to the start of training, leaders verify availability of and coordinate for resources. Units execute training to standard, and leaders evaluate that training and determine if the unit meets proficiency standards. Leaders report to commanders on the unit's success for achieving proficiency. This bottom-up feedback provides commanders with complete information and data to accurately assess the unit and adjust training plans as necessary.

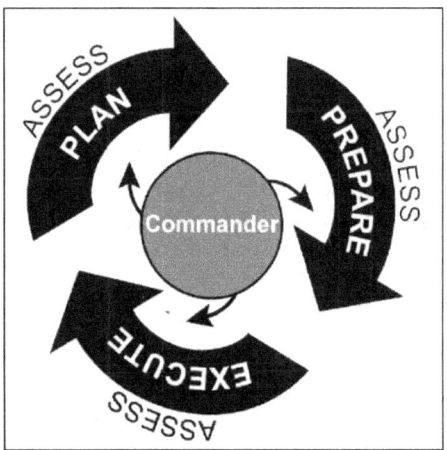

Figure 2-2. The Army operations process

COMMAND TRAINING GUIDANCE

2-6. Guidance from the higher commander to the subordinate unit commanders begins the training planning process. This top-down CTG communicates the higher commander's training priorities and helps provide a battle focus for the entire unit. Effective communication at each echelon ensures that subordinates understand the higher commander's guidance for training, that UTPs fully support the higher unit capability or mission, and that UTPs nest at each succeeding echelon.

2-7. In the CTG, the higher commander identifies—
- The unit's training focus, including its capabilities and mission.
- The desired readiness level down to brigade.
- The long-range planning horizon.
- The installation or command time management cycle.
- Brigade-level external evaluation (EXEVAL) dates and responsibilities by unit.
- Combat training center (known as CTC) rotation dates (by unit).
- Training environments in which to train.
- Other training guidance as necessary.

2-8. Division and higher commanders determine the desired readiness levels down to brigade. (See AR 220-1 for a description of readiness levels.) Due to the classification level of this information, the written CTG to subordinates does not include the desired readiness levels. Instead, the two commanders discuss and determine the desired readiness levels. This determination affects the installation-level resources priorities made by the senior commander as well as the installation time management cycle.

2-9. At division level and higher, the format of CTG is at the discretion of the commander. Many commanders use the memorandum format, while others use an OPORD format. At brigade to company level, a five-paragraph OPORD is used. Its training guidance is communicated in the UTP. See appendix F for a sample UTP order.

THE UNIT TRAINING PLAN

2-10. When the mission analysis backbrief is complete, the unit commander begins developing the UTP. This process begins with the development of training courses of action (COAs). Given the selected METs to train, the long-range planning horizon, training environments, and the higher commander's training guidance, planning can begin. Leaders first gather the information they know. Steps 3 through 6 of the MDMP provide a sequential and logical framework to develop a training COA. The resulting COA is approved by the next higher commander and becomes the UTP with a calendar.

COMPANY LEVEL UTP DEVELOPMENT

2-11. The UTP development at company level follows the same concepts employed at battalion and higher echelons. Companies use TLP that follow steps similar to the MDMP—used at battalion and higher with units with a coordinating staff. At the discretion of the battalion commander, company commanders—collaborating with the battalion staff (primarily the S-3 and S-4)—may develop an overarching battalion UTP rather than individual companies developing separate UTPs. In this instance, the battalion staff ensures that the COA development includes company training events integrated into the battalion UTP. The battalion staff ensures that time is available for individual company training events, company training objectives are identified, and company-level training resources are programmed and coordinated for as part of the battalion UTP.

MISSION ANALYSIS

2-12. On receipt of training guidance from the higher commander, the unit commander always conducts a mission analysis to understand the guidance given by the higher commander and to determine how the unit can best support that guidance. Mission analysis also starts the parallel and collaborative planning process within the command. Before beginning mission analysis, the unit commander gathers supporting references. These references provide the most current sources of information such as doctrine, technical manuals, unit SOPs, and on-line resources. Additionally, the unit commander gathers information on installation-level training resources to determine what they are, their availability, their location, and the requirements to secure them.

2-13. In conducting a mission analysis, the unit commander will—
- Identify and understand potential operational environments.
- Determine the METs to train.
- Assess the METs to train.
- Identify the long-range planning horizon.
- Identify training readiness issues.

2-14. Mission analysis provides the collective tasks on which the unit will focus its training. See figure 2-3 on page 2-4.

Chapter 2

Identify and Understand an Operational Environment

2-15. A major consideration in determining tasks to train, as well as building the necessary rigor into training, is identifying and understanding an operational environment. An *operational environment* is a composite of the conditions, circumstances, and influences that affect the employment of capabilities and bear on the decisions of the commander (JP 3-0). An operational environment is addressed in the higher commander's training guidance. An analysis and understanding of an operational environment will help determine not only tasks that the unit may need to train but also the correct conditions to replicate in training to ensure that units train the way they expect to fight. An effective training environment replicates an operational environment.

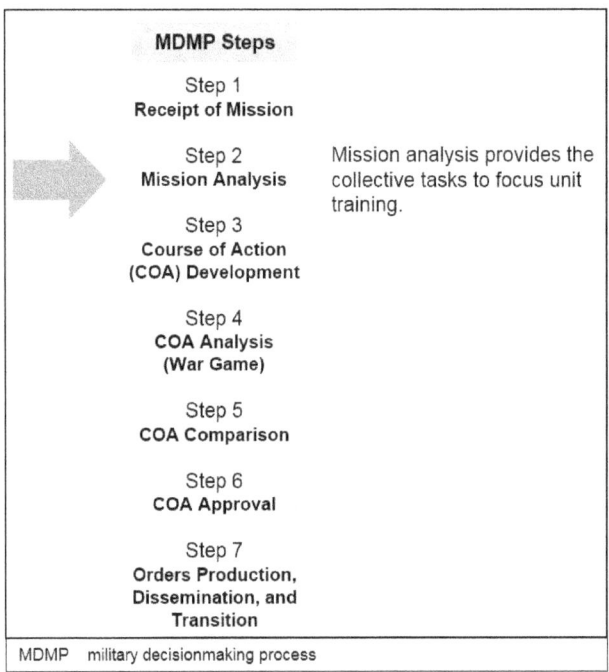

Figure 2-3. Mission analysis helps determine battle focus

Determine the METs to Train

2-16. The higher commander's training guidance provides the unit commander with capabilities or a mission to train. This is given as specific capabilities on which to train or as an assigned mission (who, what, when, where, and why) on which to train. In either case, the unit commander performs a mission analysis to determine the METs that best support the higher commander's guidance. Whether the unit trains directly against tasks from its METL or develops METs for an assigned mission, commanders with a standardized METL always report training readiness against that standardized METL. See AR 220-1 and DA Pam 220-1 for more information on reporting training readiness.

Train to Specific Capabilities

2-17. When the unit is not assigned a mission to train, the unit may be directed to train to specific capabilities. In this case, the commander prioritizes the METs on which to train. Commanders consider the following when determining the priorities:
- The higher commander's guidance.
- The tasks most likely to be assigned.
- The task most likely to have the lowest current assessment proficiency rating—untrained (U), marginally practiced (P-), practiced (P), and trained (T-).

Developing the Unit Training Plan

- Most likely operational environments for which to train.
- The long-range planning horizon (the time it will take to train).

2-18. For TOE units, commanders use the standardized METL as the primary source for selecting the priority of the METs to train. Figure 2-4 illustrates an example of how the priorities shift after a commander conducts a mission analysis. The unit's METL does not indicate which of these METs should be trained in priority. Following mission analyses, and based on current and projected task assessments and unit requirements, the commander determines the priority in which to train these tasks. In figure 2-4, the task "Conduct an Area Defense" is trained as the unit's first training priority.

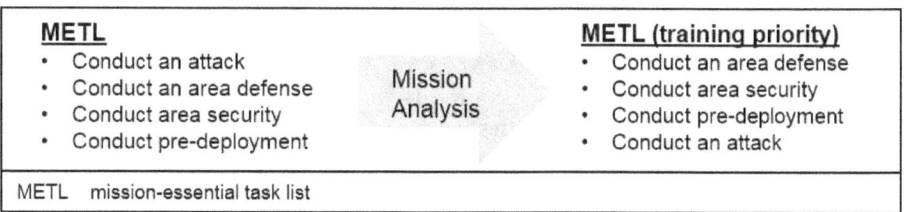

Figure 2-4. Notional mission analysis when prioritizing capabilities to train

Train to an Assigned Mission

2-19. When directed to train to an assigned mission, the unit commander identifies specified and implied tasks from the higher commander's CTG. From these tasks, the commander identifies unit essential tasks. The essential tasks then become the unit METs that focus training. A *specified task* is a specifically assigned to a unit by its higher headquarters (FM 6-0). The training guidance states specified tasks. An *implied task* is a that must be performed to accomplish a specified task or mission but is not stated in the higher headquarters' order (FM 6-0). A major consideration in determining implied tasks is identifying and understanding an operational environment on which to train. This understanding, along with an analysis of an operational environment may help determine additional implied tasks on which the unit may need to focus training. An *essential task* is a specified or implied task that must be executed to accomplish the mission (FM 6-0). In training, essential tasks for an assigned mission become METs.

2-20. Each identified essential task becomes a MET. The resulting list of tasks become the collective tasks on which the unit trains. (See figure 2-5 on page 2-6.) Commanders ensure that the assigned METL is not too broad in scope and that the METs are limited to those collective tasks that must be executed to accomplish the mission. An assigned METL based on an assigned mission that has an excessive number of METs only serves to diffuse the unit's battle focus.

2-21. The higher commander may assign a mission different from the subordinate unit's designed capabilities. In this instance, figure 2-5 on page 2-6 depicts that the METs on which the unit trains are determined through mission analysis in support of the assigned mission. To assist in that analysis, the unit commander refers to the METs and collective tasks of the type unit that does have the capabilities called for. Commanders also refer to the function CATS feature for useful information to help determine the correct collective tasks to train. Figure 2-6 on page 2-6 illustrates this process. In this scenario, an artillery unit receives an assigned mission focused on providing transportation support rather than providing fire support. Following mission analysis, METs are derived to support a transportation focus for the unit to train.

Assess Mission-Essential Tasks

2-22. After identifying the METs on which to focus training, the commander assesses the current task proficiency and the projected task proficiency. This initial assessment represents a current snapshot of the unit's training readiness. An early baseline assessment of METs enables the commander to begin considering the future scope of training. This assessment may provide useful information for the mission analysis backbrief between the two commanders at the conclusion of the mission analysis process. Using the proficiency ratings discussed in the discussion beginning in paragraph 1-6, the commander assesses each MET. The proficiency ratings are untrained (U), marginally practiced (P-), practiced (P), trained (T-), and fully trained (T). The commander enters these ratings in the DTMS.

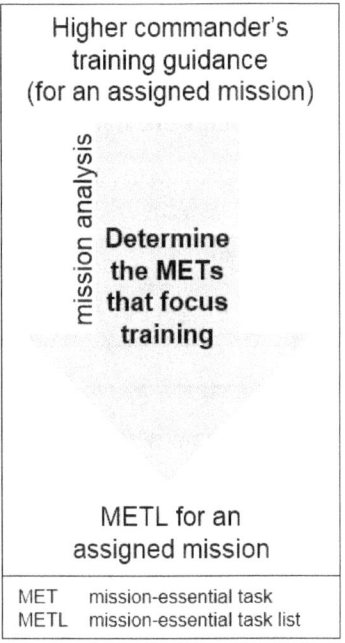

Figure 2-5. Development of a METL for an assigned mission

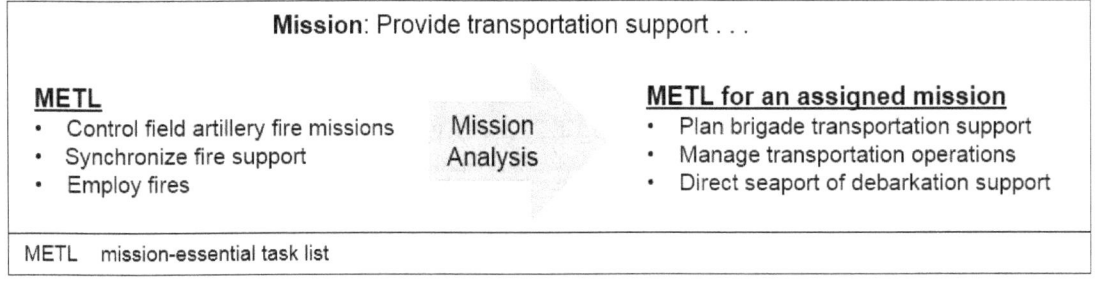

Figure 2-6. Development of a METL for an assigned METL with other capabilities

2-23. The commander also considers the assessments of the METs at the start of training. If given sufficient lead time between the beginning of training planning and execution, the assessments taken at the beginning of planning may significantly differ from the execution of training. The commander considers factors that might impact the unit's training proficiency when training starts such as personnel turnover, skill atrophy over time, and crew certification. Ideally, planning begins months before training begins. This means that some proposed METs may rate higher in proficiency at the start of training and others may atrophy to a lower proficiency rating during this period. (See figure 2-7.)

Developing the Unit Training Plan

METs	Current	Projected
Conduct an attack	T-	P
Conduct stability operations	U	P-

MET	mission-essential task	T-	trained
P	practiced	U	untrained
P-	marginally practiced		

Figure 2-7. Initial and projected start-of-training MET assessments

2-24. For the commander to make an informed and accurate start-of-training assessment, subordinates provide bottom-up feedback. The commander uses this feedback in the assessment. The best assessment of the unit's proficiency requires the commanders to be as objective as possible. An objective assessment helps inform the commander in the development of the UTP.

Identify the Long-Range Planning Horizon

2-25. The long-range planning horizon is provided in the higher commander's CTG. This horizon represents the time allocated for the unit to achieve and sustain training proficiency. Having a clear understanding of the time the unit has to train is essential to developing a successful training plan.

Identify Training Readiness Issues

2-26. During the mission analysis process, the commander may identify other training readiness issues. Some issues may necessitate a discussion between the unit commander and higher commander during the mission analysis backbrief. These issues range from the time available to train, resources available to train, or other concerns that the unit commander may want to discuss with the higher commander.

Conducts Mission Analysis Backbrief

2-27. The unit commander completes the mission analysis, selects the METs to train, and backbriefs the higher commander on the results of the analysis. (See figure 2-8 on page 2-8.) This backbrief is part of the commanders' dialogue process. The unit commander restates and verifies an understanding of the higher commander's training guidance.

2-28. During the mission analysis backbrief, the unit commander discusses proposed unit METs on which to train that support the higher commander's training guidance. They discuss the long-range planning horizon and training environments. They also discuss any other training issues related to the unit's ability to attain training proficiency in the time required. The higher commander approves or modifies the unit METs for training. The unit commander then begins to develop a UTP to train the unit on the selected METs.

2-29. Following the backbrief, the commander notifies subordinates of the results. At brigade and below, commanders use a warning order (WARNORD) format to communicate results. This order prompts subordinate commanders and leaders to begin their own mission analysis as well as to conduct parallel and collaborative planning. If the higher commander's training guidance included an assigned mission, the unit commander includes the unit's restated mission. In this mission of who, what, when, where, and why, the *what* covers the selected METs. If the training guidance did not include an assigned mission, the *what* becomes the prioritized METL tasks approved by the next higher commander. Figure 2-9 beginning on page 2-8 illustrates a notional scenario depicting a company conducting the mission analysis.

Chapter 2

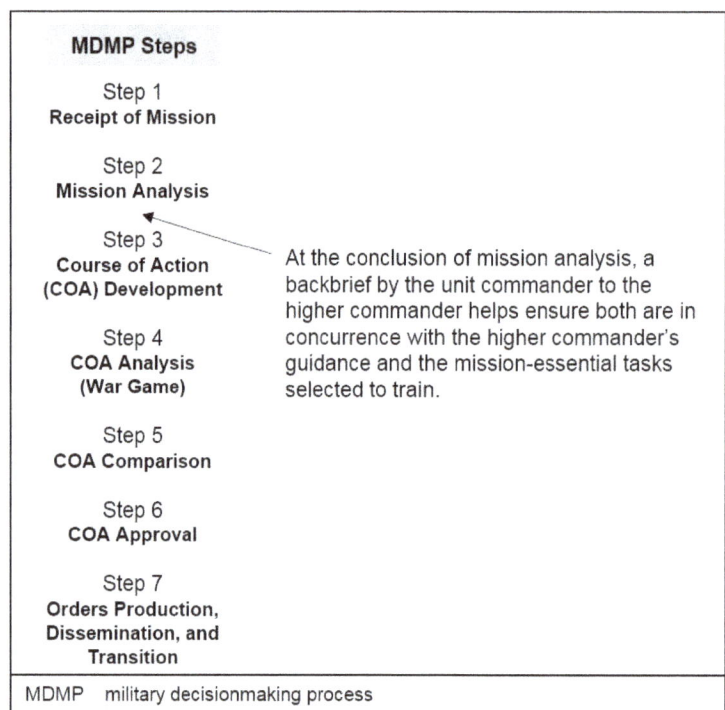

Figure 2-8. Mission analysis backbrief

After receiving the UTP from the infantry battalion commander, CPT Smith discusses the training guidance with the company first sergeant, platoon leaders, and platoon sergeants. Foremost in his mind, CPT Smith wants to understand how the company can best support the mission of the battalion. With the company leadership, CPT Smith begins a mission analysis of the battalion UTP. CPT Smith gathers the references and other tools that will help them through this process. The leaders review training doctrine (ADRP 7-0 and FM 7-0) and infantry doctrinal publications. They also review the CAT, company tactical standard operating procedures, training standard operating procedures, training resources on the ATN, and other documents.

CPT Smith and the other company leaders formulate how the company can best support the battalion training mission. They review the mission, the METs on which the battalion will focus training, the time available to train, training environments, and additional guidance from the battalion commander.

During mission analysis, CPT Smith and the other company leaders determine the specified and implied tasks to identify the essential tasks on which the company will focus training. CPT Smith and the first sergeant review the unit's standardized METL since this represents the capabilities that will most likely nest with the essential tasks to train. Since the battalion mission is to 'conduct an area defense' and 'conduct area security,' their analysis results in eight company collective tasks on which to train: employ obstacles, integrate direct fires, integrate indirect fire support, employ military deception techniques, conduct security patrol, conduct roadblock and checkpoint, secure routes, and secure civilians during operations.

Figure 2-9. Notional mission analysis vignette

Developing the Unit Training Plan

> As part of the analysis, the commander reviews the last assessments of the essential tasks to notate the company's current training readiness. This review helps the commander understand and visualize what the unit needs in time and resources to accomplish and support the battalion mission.
>
> Once the commander identifies the METs, CPT Smith and 1SG Jones verify that they understand the time the unit has to train. This understanding stems from their understanding of the battalion commander's end state for training and the commander's expectation when the unit will complete the training. They verify the potential operational environment for which to train. Then they formulate ways to best replicate that environment during training events with available training support system resources.
>
> After careful analysis and a discussion with 1SG Jones and the platoon leadership, CPT Smith contacts the battalion S-1 and makes an appointment with the battalion commander. The next day, CPT Smith backbriefs the battalion commander on the results of the company mission analysis.

Figure 2-9. Notional mission analysis vignette (continued)

2-30. Units based on a TDA—and other units without a standardized METL—perform a mission analysis to develop their METs and METL. TDA units are typically not deployable and perform their as-designed functions every day. Since TDA units do not have a standardized METL, their unit commanders develop many of the individual and collective tasks on which they train. Many of the tasks these units routinely perform are already established and published in the Army's training development capability database and accessible through ATN. Other tasks that are specific to the functions performed by the unit may need to be developed by the unit commander and approved by the higher commander. Table 2-1 illustrates sample tasks TDA commanders might consider as part of their mission analysis.

Table 2-1. Sample TDA collective tasks

- Provide installation resiliency services.
- Conduct training in general subjects (basic skills).
- Administer cadre training programs:
    - Certifications.
    - Professional development (faculty development programs).
    - Mandatory training (installation and local command requirements).
- Conduct administrative, logistic, and training operations in support of base operations.
- Provide installation predeployment and deployment services and operations.
- Provide installation railhead support.
- Train, support, and evaluate United States Army Reserve training units.
- Conduct installation and command physical fitness training and testing.

2-31. At the conclusion of mission analysis, the TDA commander determines which tasks are essential to the success of the unit. Following mission analysis—just as in a TOE-based unit—the unit commander backbriefs the higher commander to obtain approval of the TDA METL.

2-32. Following the mission analysis backbrief, the unit commander can begin formulating a UTP that supports the higher commander's guidance and supports training the unit on the selected METs. The mission analysis step is crucial to the entire process because it relies on an accurate determination and assessment of the METs selected to train. The conclusion of the mission analysis backbrief directly affects

Chapter 2

developing the training plan for the unit and ultimately affects unit training readiness over the long-range planning horizon.

COURSE OF ACTION DEVELOPMENT

2-33. Leaders first gather the information they know. Steps 3-6 of the MDMP provide a sequential and logical framework to develop a training COA. (See figure 2-10.) The resulting COA is approved by the next higher commander and becomes the UTP (which includes the UTP calendar).

2-34. When creating COAs, the primary goal is to develop a UTP that progressively develops MET proficiencies to an end state (when the unit is proficient) and beyond. This end state corresponds to the commander's visualized end state for training and directly supports the capability or mission on which to train. Developing training COAs accounts for the unit's current training proficiencies, the home station training environment, installation resource availability, and leadership knowledge and experience.

2-35. From company to brigade levels, developing the UTP calendar is fundamental to graphically developing training of COAs. (See ADRP 5-0 for developing COAs.) Often several possible best ways exist to train the unit. The development of several unit calendars allows the commander to choose the most viable ways to train the unit. The calendar graphically represents the unit's plan to train. Planners viewing the calendar framework generate options for analysis and comparison that satisfy the commander's guidance for training. As planners develop different COA options, they ensure each COA is—

- Feasible—doable.
- Acceptable—benefit is worth the cost.
- Suitable—appropriate.
- Distinguishable—not similar to another COA.
- Complete—no clear gaps.

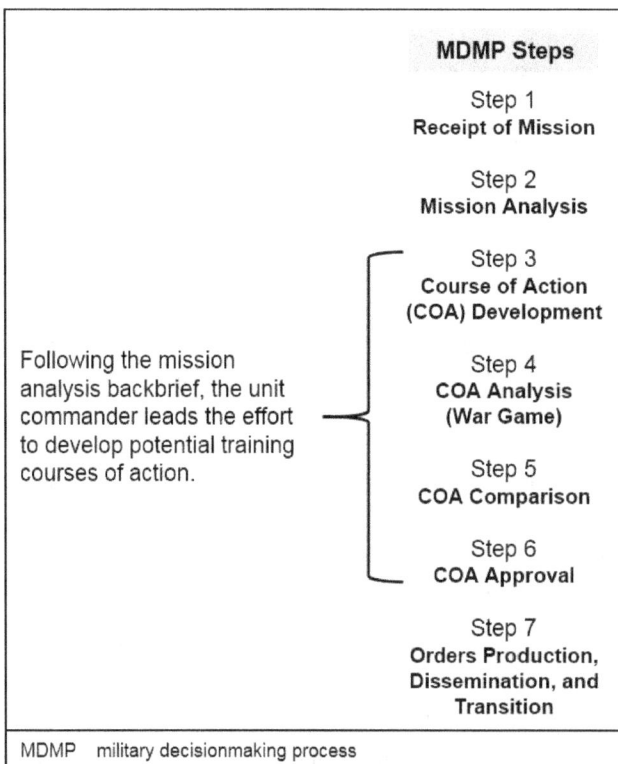

Figure 2-10. Steps 3-6 of the MDMP as it relates to unit training

2-36. Whether planning within the framework of the MDMP or TLP, planners consider the following planning concepts:
- Prepare the UTP calendar.
- Apply the command or installation time management cycle.
- Post the higher unit (multiechelon) training events.
- Determine unit training events.
- Identify training objectives for each training event.
- Use a backward planning approach using a crawl-walk-run methodology.
- Consider the training environment.
- Ensure time is programmed for subordinate units to train.

Prepare the Unit Training Plan Calendar

2-37. The UTP calendar is extremely important since it visually defines the time available to train. Once planners begin to apply the actual days available to train a COA, they will note that time is the greatest restricting factor to planning unit training. Planners have to contend with installation or command time management cycles, resources and facilities constraints, and limited classes of supply. Additionally, the unit competes with other units on the installation for the same limited resources. A simple calendar format depicting the planning horizon provides an excellent starting point for planners. The CATS planning tool in DTMS helps planners visualize the long-range planning horizon, too.

Apply the Command or Installation Time Management Cycle

2-38. Time management cycles create prime time training periods for subordinate organizations to achieve battle focus in training. At the installation level, the senior Army commander establishes a time management cycle to protect and prioritize training time and resources for installation units. Time management cycles help subordinate units identify, focus, and protect training periods and resources needed to support unit training. This cycle ensures that subordinate organizations can concentrate on executing their UTP. Subordinate units can publish additional time management cycles, but they must synchronize these additional cycles to support the command or installation cycle. UTPs and their supporting calendars identify time management cycles.

2-39. No matter the time management cycle that the senior commander establishes, all unit commanders must enforce it. Senior commanders must ensure that the planning and execution is highly disciplined and that all members of the command support and comply with training at designated times. Without the support and oversight of senior commanders, battalions, companies, platoons, and Soldiers will not be able to train to proficiency. Since specific activities vary among installations according to the local situations and requirements, the senior commander, in coordination with the installation staff, coordinates the unit's training requirements to protect unit training times.

2-40. One time management cycle used throughout the Army is the Green-Amber-Red cycle. Many units and installations employ this time management cycle or some variation of it. The commander employs the best method of a time management cycle based on the installation's readiness requirements, unit's readiness requirements, and resource allocations. Paragraphs 2-41 through 2-43 discuss what occurs in a Green-Amber-Red cycle. Figure 2-11 (on page 2-12), figure 2-13 (on page 2-15), and figure 2-15 (on page 2-16) illustrate time management cycles for different notional brigades. Note the distribution of crawl-walk-run events as they correspond to the appropriate Green-Amber-Red cycles.

Chapter 2

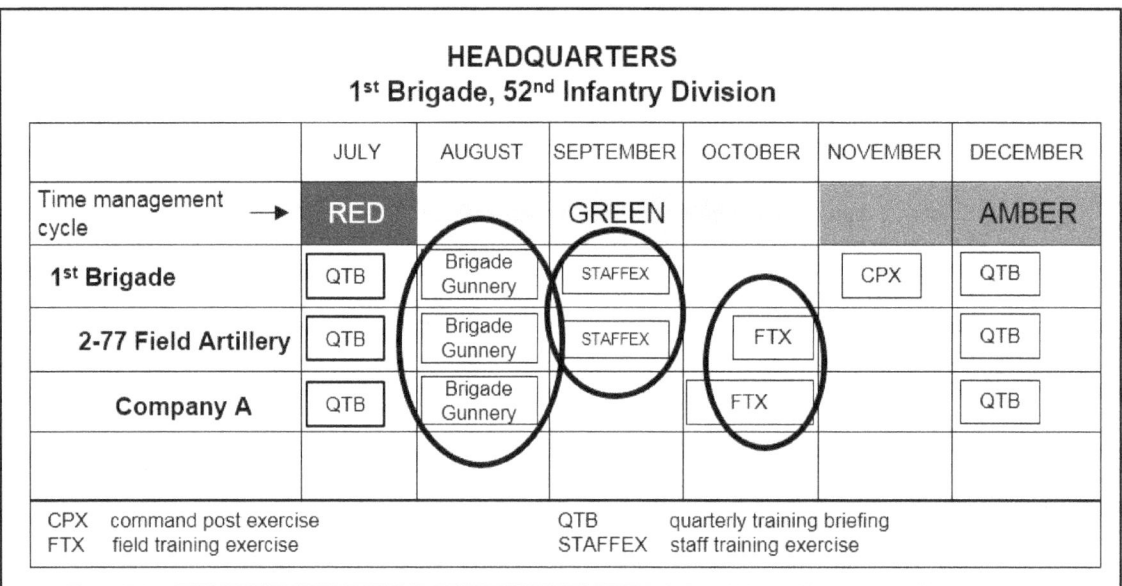

Figure 2-11. Multiechelon training events demonstrated in a notional UTP calendar

Green

2-41. Training is focused on multiechelon, unit collective tasks and on MET proficiency. Training is planned and synchronized with the availability of major training resources and key training facilities. Senior commanders ensure that subordinate organizations conduct training without distraction or unprogrammed external taskings. Training during these cycles—

- Requires maximum Soldier attendance at mission-essential training.
- Eliminates administrative and support requirements that prevent personnel from participating in training to the maximum extent possible.
- Limits leaves and passes.

Amber

2-42. Training is focused at the individual, leader, crew, and squad levels. Individuals maximize their own self-development by using installation education centers and distributed learning resources. Organizations are assigned support taskings beyond the capability of those units in the red cycle, but commanders strive for minimal disruptions to units in this cycle. Training during this cycle—

- Provides time for Soldiers to attend education and training courses.
- Enables some sub-organizations to schedule collective training.
- Diverts selected personnel to support requirements when all available personnel in organizations in the red period are completely committed to support requirements.
- Enables scheduling for periodic maintenance services.

Red

2-43. Training is focused to maximize self-development and individual task proficiency. Units in this cycle perform unit-level administrative requirements and allow the maximum number of Soldiers to take leave. More often, post support requirements take priority. During this cycle, leaders expand on providing additional mentoring, coaching, counselling to subordinates. Training in this cycle—

- Maximizes Soldiers' leaves and passes. When appropriate, unit schedules block leave.
- Coordinated and scheduled routine medical, dental, and administrative appointments with installation support facilities.

Developing the Unit Training Plan

Post the Higher Unit (Multiechelon) Training Events

2-44. Planners start by placing all multiechelon training events directed by their higher headquarters on the UTP calendar. Such training events include the higher unit's EXEVAL (such as a combat training center rotation and brigade field training exercise [FTX]).

2-45. COA development not only focuses on the METs selected to train, but is also developed around multiechelon training. Training more than one echelon deep (such as a company with platoons or a battalion with companies) provides a degree of realism not possible when training independent echelons. Training with other support elements—like medical support, engineer support, or military intelligence support—drives a more realistic training environment that replicates how the unit will actually operate. Each COA development is about training the entire organization to MET proficiency over the long-range planning horizon. COA development focuses on depicting only those training events in which subordinate units must participate.

2-46. Figure 2-11 demonstrates the building of multiechelon events from the top echelon to the bottom. Each headquarters develops the multiechelon training events that focus on attaining MET proficiency while preserving sufficient time on the UTP calendar for subordinates to plan and execute their own training.

2-47. Higher headquarter events affect subordinate unit planning as each unit develops COAs. A brigade that plans a minimum of brigade-level multiechelon events leaves time for the battalions to train. A brigade that plans too many brigade-level multiechelon events leaves less time for the battalions to train and even less time for companies and platoons to plan and execute their training in support of the brigade.

2-48. Following approval of the COA, other training activities—such as mandatory training, predeployment training, and installation support—can and should be included on the UTP calendar. This calendar provides the unit with a complete view of all training scheduled. When creating potential COAs and the UTP calendar, planners account for how the unit will achieve training proficiency.

Determine Unit Training Events

2-49. Commanders link training strategies to training plans by identifying and planning training events. Training events are the building blocks that are the foundation of a COA. During COA development, commanders and staffs broadly assess the number, type, and duration of training events that a unit may require to train the METs to proficiency.

2-50. Effective and realistic training events require commanders to analyze the tasks to be trained, the opposing force's (OPFOR's) counter tasks, and variables represented in a training scenario. Well-developed events incorporate conditions replicating an anticipated operational environment as much as possible. They place Soldiers and leaders in complex, ambiguous, challenging (morally and ethically), and rapidly changing conditions. Effective training includes events that require units and leaders to transition quickly between METs to develop adaptive and innovative leaders with decision-making agility.

2-51. METs are not trained in isolation. They are trained with their associated supporting collective and individual tasks during training events. Knowing what training events to train is an important first step in COA development. Ideally, the right series of training events will train multiple METs. Determining the right mix and sequence of training events ensures that units maximize valuable training time and resources and do not waste training time.

2-52. For TOE units, planners identify the training events by using the CATS. This strategy enables planners to develop training since it provides a proponent-recommended strategy. For TDA units and for units assigned to perform a functional mission, the CATS provides a wealth of information concerning tasks and training events. Planners consider carefully before modifying a CATS since it affects TDA and unit UTP development. The CATS shows recommended multiechelon events and identifies EXEVAL criteria. Effective planners start a unit UTP development by overlaying a CATS solution over known, actual calendar requirements.

2-53. All training events require training areas, facilities, and resources. Some events may require OPFORs, observer-controllers/trainers (OC/Ts), and role players. Other events may need training support system

Chapter 2

products and services, such as instrumentation and TADSS. Finally, a training event itself is only a tool to meet and sustain MET proficiency. Selected individuals evaluate all training events for their contribution to training readiness.

Identify Training Objectives

2-54. A *training objective* is a statement that describes the desired outcome of a training activity in the unit. Training objectives represent what the commander wants to achieve at the conclusion of each training event. Training objectives help chart the course for how training events contribute to MET proficiency. A training objective consists of the following:

- Task. A clearly defined and measurable activity accomplished by organizations and individuals.
- Condition. The circumstances and environment in which a unit is to perform a task.
- Standard. The minimum acceptable proficiency required in the performance of a particular training task.
- Training proficiency. This is the task proficiency rating that the commander expects the unit to meet at the conclusion of the event.

2-55. Training objectives are similar to tactical objectives in that they focus on the effects the commander wants to achieve. In this case, the effects focus on progressively (crawl-walk-run) mastering the METs. Training objectives help the unit focus on what it needs to accomplish during each event and how the event contributes to the overall attainment of the commander's visualized end state. A training objective can be a simple statement of goals for the event or as complex as aligning the METs being trained with the anticipated final assessment at the end of the event. Planners identify training objectives for each multiechelon training event that comprises COAs. Planners also develop and publish training objectives for each training event internal to the unit. Figure 2-12 illustrates a brigade training objective.

Task: Conduct an Attack, #07-6-1092

Conditions: The brigade is conducting operations independently and has received an operation order or fragmentary order to conduct an attack at the location and time specified. Coalition forces and noncombatants may be present in the training environment.

Standards:

1. Brigade leaders gain and or maintain situational awareness. Brigade commander and staff receive an order or anticipate a new mission and begin the military decisionmaking process. Brigade task-organizes forces within the brigade.
2. Staff obtains guidance from the commander. The staff plans, coordinates, and achieves the desired effects utilizing organic and attached assets.
3. Staff plans mobility, countermobility, and survivability; chemical, biological, radiological, and nuclear support; air defense support; and sustainment supporting operations.
4. Brigade commander and staff conduct risk management.
5. Brigade commander and staff conduct backbriefs and rehearsals to ensure that subordinates understand commander's intent and concept.
6. Brigade executes the attack and masses available combat power to destroy enemy in accordance with the commander's intent.
7. Brigade consolidates and reorganizes as necessary.
8. Brigade continues operations as necessary.

Training proficiency: The brigade is a 'T-' (trained) assessment for the task Conduct an Attack, task # 07-6-1092.

Figure 2-12. Sample brigade training objective

Developing the Unit Training Plan

Use a Backward Planning Approach

2-56. Backward planning is a simple technique that begins at the commander's visualized training end state. This end state is the point at which the unit expects to be trained to standard in the selected METs. The unit EXEVAL is the training event that normally culminates the end state on the UTP calendar (see figure 2-13 on page 2-16). The unit commander two levels up designs the EXEVAL to evaluate the unit METL and resources the EXEVAL so the unit commander has an opportunity to assess the unit. All units in the Army undergo an EXEVAL to validate a rating proficiency of trained or fully trained.

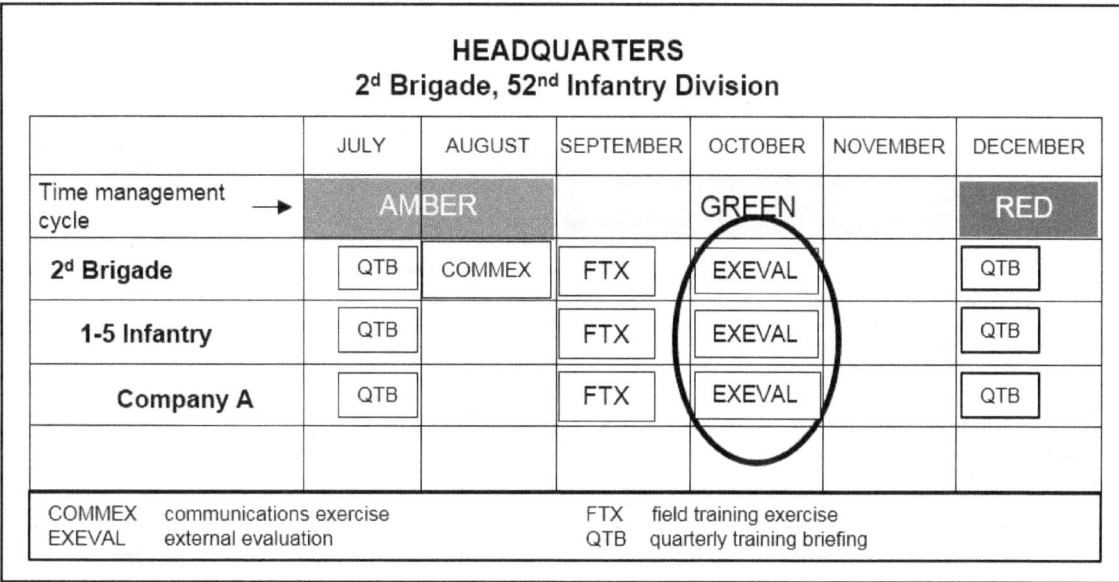

Figure 2-13. Example EXEVAL posted on a notional brigade UTP calendar

Use the Crawl-Walk-Run Methodology

2-57. Sequencing training events from simple to increasingly more complex events provides Soldiers, leaders, and the unit with the ability to build individual and collective task proficiencies as the UTP progresses (see figure 2-14). This approach ensures that task proficiencies progressively build on each other, laying a solid foundation before moving on to more complex tasks and events.

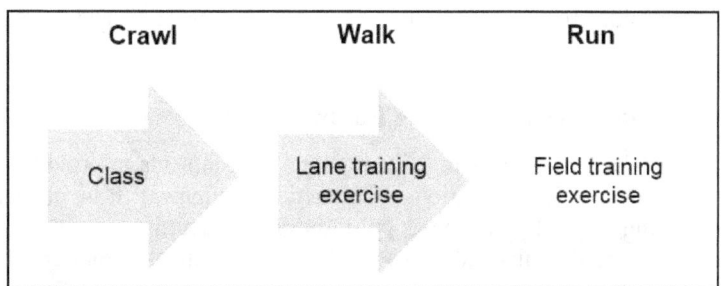

Figure 2-14. Sample of crawl-walk-run training events

2-58. CATSs indicate whether a training event is a crawl, walk, or run level event. In the crawl stage, the unit trains to first understand task requirements and standards (in figure 2-15 on page 2-16, the class scheduled for company A in August). In the walk stage, the unit trains the task with added realism by encountering changing conditions. Soldiers also begin to understand that tasks are not executed in or by themselves and to understand the linkages to other associated tasks (in figure 2-15 on page 2-16, the platoon situational training exercise scheduled in September). Soldiers also begin to work mutually as crews, teams, and small units. At the run stage, Soldiers train collectively to achieve task proficiencies under increasingly realistic conditions and to work mutually as effective and efficient teams (in figure 2-15, the company gunnery in October followed by the company FTX in November). This crawl-walk-run approach to planning and sequencing training events develops Soldiers, leaders, and units able to meet individual and collective task proficiencies in a reliable and predictable way.

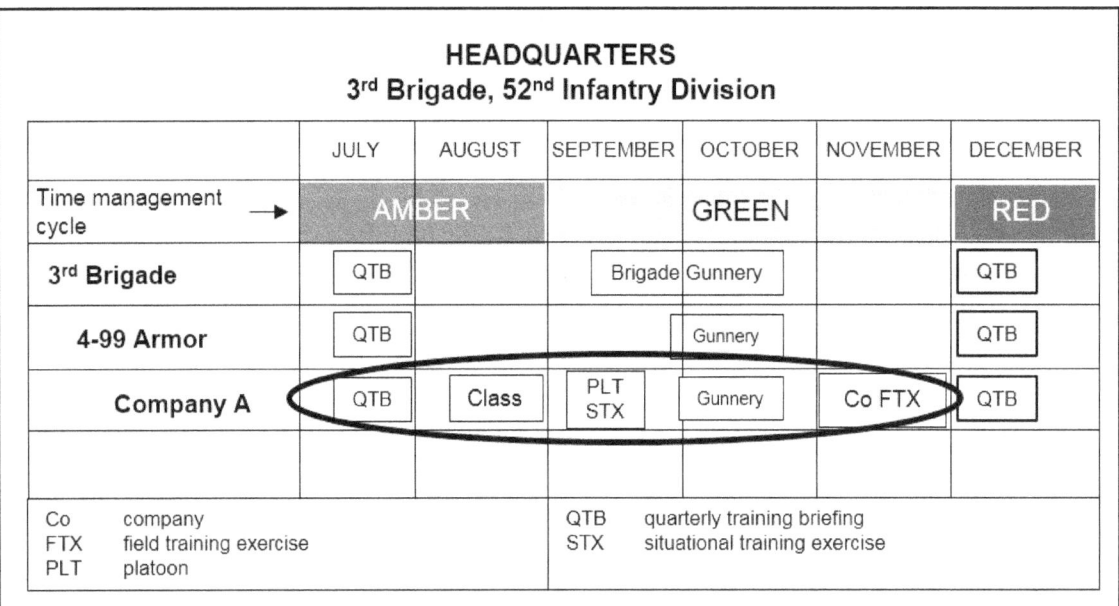

Figure 2-15. Company crawl-walk-run training events on the UTP calendar

Consider the Training Environment

2-59. The ability of a unit to conduct all training events in a live environment is impractical. The realities of limited training time and resources dictate that commanders, as stewards of the Army Profession, use creative and innovative means to conduct training in other-than-live training environments. Effective commanders and subordinate leaders plan and execute multiechelon training that combines required, needed, and optional training on several METs whenever possible. How units execute training events is an important consideration as COAs are developed. Ideally, with unlimited time and resources, all unit training is best executed when done in a live environment. However, this is not feasible due to limited time, resources, and safety considerations. Commanders leverage all the training support enablers available to get the best results possible.

Mix Live, Virtual, and Constructive Training Environments

2-60. The Army relies on a creative mix of LVC training environments to provide realistic training. Live training is training executed in field conditions using tactical equipment. It involves real people operating real systems. Live training may be enhanced by TADSS. Field training exercises, live fire exercises, deployment exercises, and battle drills under live conditions replicate an actual operational environment as closely as possible. Virtual training is executed using computer-generated battlefields in simulators with the approximate characteristics of tactical weapon systems and vehicles. Units use virtual training to exercise motor control, decision-making, and communication skills. Sometimes called human-in-the-loop training, it involves real people operating simulated systems. People being trained practice the skills needed to operate actual equipment, for example, flying an aircraft. Gaming is a subset of the virtual training environment. The military uses gaming technologies to create capabilities to help train individuals and organizations. Games support the development of individual-level tasks and skills and facilitate the assessments of small-unit or team collective task training. Gaming can operate in a stand-alone environment or be integrated with live, virtual, or constructive environments. Constructive training uses computer models and simulations to exercise command and staff functions. It involves simulated people operating simulated systems. Constructive training can be conducted by units from platoon through echelons above corps. LVC training is a broad taxonomy that covers the degree to which a training event uses simulations.

2-61. Units use virtual and constructive training environments to supplement, enhance, and complement live training. Virtual and constructive training environments help raise the entry level of proficiency for live training and reduce the time needed to prepare training. These environments also provide a variety of training environments, allowing training units to replicate multiple scenarios under different conditions. Based on training objectives and available resources—such as time, ammunition, simulations, and range availability—commanders determine the right mix and frequency of LVC training to ensure organizations use resources efficiently.

2-62. Commanders employ each training environment independently or combine two or more environments to meet the training objective. Employing a training environment independently is the easiest to plan and prepare. If using more than one training environment, leaders may use either a blended training environment (BTE) or ITE. An installation creates a fielding schedule for units to use an ITE.

Blended Training Environment

2-63. Blended training is unit training conducted concurrently within two or more training environments (live, virtual, or constructive simulation). Blended training lacks the sophisticated integrating technologies that allow the different environments to interact. When properly planned and resourced, blended training can include information systems that enable the unit commander and other leaders to receive a common operational picture or that enable the activity in one training environment to be used to stimulate reaction in the other. For example, if a company only has maneuver space for one live platoon, but wants to train the company headquarters and leadership in mission command tasks, then it can train two platoons in a tactical simulation or virtual environment and train the third platoon in a live training environment. In this example, the company leaders have the tactical challenge of commanding all three platoons and providing a more realistic training event than if only the live platoon were training. In contrast, the ITE is enabled by a sophisticated integrated architecture that allows full interaction between virtual and constructive environments, to include information systems. This architecture also allows limited interaction between live forces and virtual or simulated environments (for example, virtual and simulated artillery can cause casualties in live forces, if enabled, and support 'live' fire markers). The limitation of the ITE is its limited availability. A unit can plan, prepare, and execute blended training using ordinary computers with Internet access and using limited training space for concurrent live training. The disadvantage of blended training is that all planning and preparation are the unit's responsibility whereas integrated training requires only limited input from the unit (the tasks and training environment for which they want to train) and select system training for operators to enable effective, integrated training.

Integrated Training Environment

2-64. An ITE uses consistent (common TADSS enablers across installations) and continuous LVC training environments to stimulate information systems. An ITE uses correlated terrain databases in the TADSS and the Live, Virtual, Constructive—Integrating Architecture. This architecture—including standards, protocols, hardware, and software—enables seamless, synchronized integration among information systems and the simulations or simulators.

2-65. All training requires some form of training support—such as TADSS, facilities, services, ranges, and maneuver space. Planning and preparing a BTE and ITE is more complex than conducting simple maneuver or movement training. A BTE and ITE enable units to increase training opportunities with fewer resources. These environments enable units to customize the complexity of training conditions to make the training more challenging. Additionally, these environments enable units to assess and retrain quickly with a relatively low cost.

2-66. Training events that involve CATS often provide various live, virtual, or constructive options. For example, training often includes a walk-level (such as a situational training exercise) virtual event and a similar situational training exercise live event for the unit's crawl-walk-run level training.

Chapter 2

2-67. Just as leaders must understand an operational environment in combat, a leader must understand the training environment at home station. Competent leaders understand the training environment early in the process whether at home station or elsewhere. Specifically, leaders take initiative, quickly develop partnerships with the right personnel (for example staff from the Directorate of Plans, Training, Mobilization and Security; range control; or mission training complex), and familiarize themselves with training capabilities. Subsequently, unit leaders take subordinate leaders on a terrain walk of those capabilities.

2-68. Figure 2-16 depicts different training environments and their mixtures at different echelons in relation to the event level of training. There are several LVC options available; commanders determine the mix. For more information on the BTE and ITE, go to the ITE page on ATN.

Several Options: Commanders Determine the Mix

	Leaders			Staffs			Units		
	Crawl	Walk	Run	Crawl	Walk	Run	Crawl	Walk	Run
Brigade	L/V/C	L/V/C	L/V/C	L/C	L/C	L/V/C		L/V/C	L/V/C
Battalion	L/V/C	L/V/C	L/V/C	L/C	L/C	L/V/C		L/V/C	L/V/C
Company	L/V	L/V	L				L/V	L/V	L
Platoon	L/V/C	L/V	L				L/V	L/V	L
Crew/Squad	L/V/C	L/V	L				L/V	L/V	L
Individual	L/V/C	L/V/C	L	L/V	L/V	L	L/V	L/V	L

C constructive   L live   V virtual

Figure 2-16. Sample LVC training mix from brigade to individual Soldier

Ensure Time Is Scheduled for Subordinate Units to Train

2-69. Each headquarters ensures that it leaves available training time in its plan. Time must be allocated for subordinate units to determine and schedule their own training events. On the UTP calendar, this time is referred to as white space. White space is the open time on the training calendar for each subordinate unit to develop its own level of crawl-walk-run events. If each succeeding headquarters fills all the available training time, subordinate units will have no time available to plan training. For example, if a battalion accounts for all available training time in its UTP calendar, then its companies will have no time to develop and schedule the training they may need to plan and execute at their level.

COURSE OF ACTION ANALYSIS (WAR GAME)

2-70. Once multiple COAs are developed based on the higher commanders' training guidance, planners analyze them to identify difficulties, coordination issues, or resource issues as well as potential risks of potential planned events. Identification of major resources that may require immediate coordination and/or help from higher headquarters is important to prevent future training shortfalls. These adjustments may require decision points for the commander or adjustments to the events and their sequencing (see FM 6-0).

Developing the Unit Training Plan

2-71. Planners consider the following major resources:
- Land, facilities, and ranges.
- Ammunition and TADSS.
- Blended training environments and ITEs.
- Classes of supply (to include unit Class V allocations).
- OPFORs, role players, and master scenario events lists (MSELs).
- Resources not readily available at home station.
- Unit availability (Green-Amber-Red).

2-72. Commanders and staffs also use the CATS to better understand each training events requirements to include major classes of supply, TADSS, and other important planning factors.

COURSE OF ACTION COMPARISON

2-73. COA comparison is an objective process to evaluate COAs independently and against set evaluation criteria approved by the commander and staff. The commander and staff aim to identify the strengths and weaknesses of each COA, enable selecting a COA with the highest probability of success, and further develop that COA in an OPORD (UTP).

Compare Courses of Action

2-74. Comparison of the COAs is critical. The staff uses any technique that helps develop accurate and informed recommendations and assists the commander to make the best decision. A common technique is the decision matrix. This matrix uses evaluation criteria developed during mission analysis and refined during COA development to help assess the effectiveness and efficiency of each COA.

2-75. The decision matrix is a tool to compare and evaluate COAs thoroughly and logically. However, the decision matrix is also based on subjective judgments that may change during the evaluation. Values reflect the relative advantages or disadvantages of each criterion for each COA as initially estimated by a chief of staff or executive officer during mission analysis. At the same time, the chief of staff or executive officer determines weights for each criterion based on a subjective determination of their relative value. The lower values signify a more favorable advantage.

2-76. The decision matrix provides a very structured and effective method to compare COAs against criteria that, when met, suggest a likelihood of producing success. Staffs give specific broad categories of COA characteristics a basic numerical value based on evaluation criteria. They subjectively assign weights regarding their relative importance to existing circumstances. Then staffs multiply basic values by the weight to yield a given criterion's final score. A staff member then totals all scores to compare COAs. (See FM 6-0 for a discussion of the decision matrix.)

2-77. The staff compares feasible COAs to identify the one with the highest probability of success (MET attainment within the planning horizon). After completing the analysis and comparison, the staff identifies a preferred COA and makes a recommendation to the commander. If the staff cannot reach a decision, the chief of staff or executive officer decides which COA to recommend. (See ADRP 5-0 and FM 6-0 for discussions of COA comparison.)

Course of Action Decision Briefing

2-78. Once the staff chooses a training COA for execution, the staff then delivers a decision briefing to the commander. The chief of staff or executive officer highlights any changes to each COA resulting from war-gaming. The decision briefing includes—
- The commander's training guidance of the higher and next higher commanders.
- The training status of the entire unit (all subordinates).
- The current and projected proficiency rating of the METs—untrained (U), marginally practiced (P-), practiced (P), trained (T-), and fully trained (T).
- The COAs considered, including—

Chapter 2

- Assumptions used.
- Results of training estimates (as applicable).
- A summary of the war game for each COA, including critical events (such as long-range planning horizon, decision points, and availability of important training facilities and resources), modifications to any COA, and war-game results.
- Advantages and disadvantages (including risks) of each COA.
- The recommended COA. If a significant disagreement exists, then the staff should inform the commander and, if necessary, discuss the disagreement.

COURSE OF ACTION APPROVAL

2-79. At the conclusion of the decision briefing, the unit commander—with the advice of the staff, chief of staff or executive officer, and command sergeant major or first sergeant—determines which COA best supports unit training. The selected COA is briefed to the next higher commander for approval. See figure 2-17.

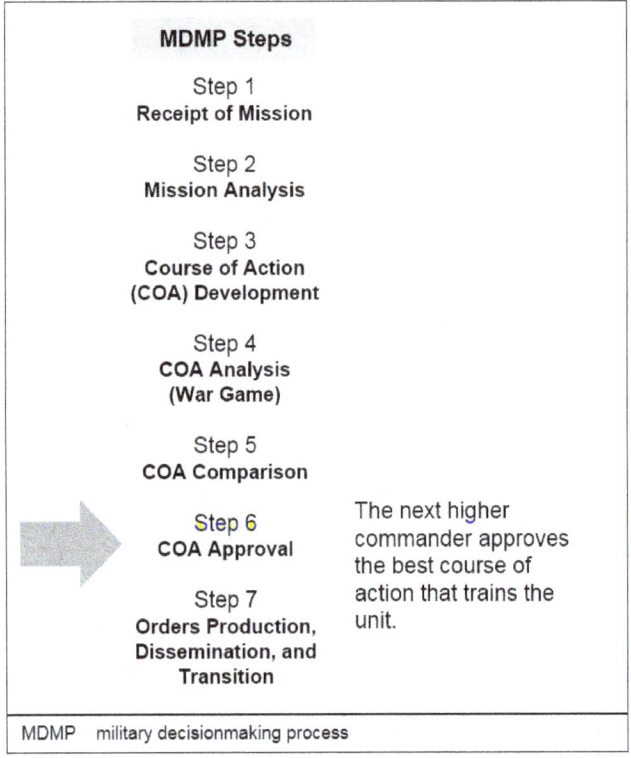

Figure 2-17. COA approval

PUBLISH THE UNIT TRAINING PLAN

2-80. Once the higher commander approves the COA, it ultimately becomes the UTP. The staff organizes the COA, the guidance given by the higher commander, and all additional clarifying information into a five-paragraph field order (brigade and below). When completed, the staff publishes it in accordance with the training guidance publication timelines found in tables 1-1 and 1-2 (on page 1-12) to subordinate and higher units as appropriate and posts it to DTMS. See figure 2-18. See appendix F for an example of a UTP and general content.

Developing the Unit Training Plan

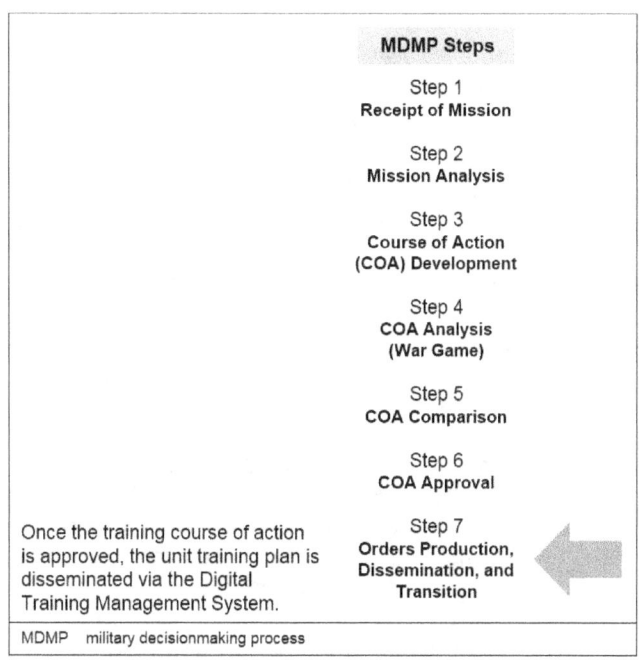

Figure 2-18. The approved COA becomes the unit training plan

2-81. While executing the UTP, the commander may direct changes to the base plan. At brigade and below, the commander communicates these changes to subordinates using fragmentary orders (FRAGORDs) that refer to the base UTP OPORD.

2-82. Subordinates receive the FRAGORDs and then begin to develop each of the UTP training events further. The subordinates employ the Army training model by planning for, preparing for, executing, and assessing each training event. They aim for the unit to train the METs to standard. In the development of the UTP and UTP calendar, the staff accounts for how the unit will achieve training proficiency to meet mission requirements.

2-83. After developing the training events, the staff publishes the UTP and UTP calendar. An effective UTP calendar includes internal training events such as mandatory training, predeployment training, and installation support. These details provide the unit a complete view of all training requirements during the planning horizons.

2-84. As the UTP is executed, unit commanders have a responsibility to minimize training distracters. A major training distracter occurs when the higher headquarters levies tasking requirements to subordinate units *after* training plans are approved and published. Taskings issued outside tasking policy timelines (refer to AR 350-1) contribute to training planned, but not conducted.

TRAINING BRIEFING

2-85. To ensure the division-level commander has visibility of, and concurs with the approved UTPs, the brigade commander conducts a training briefing (TB) with the division-level commander. The TB is a backbrief to the division commander of the overall unit long-range training strategy as described by the UTP.

2-86. Battalion commanders in separate brigades and regiments present the TB to corps major subordinate commanders. The TB for Reserve Component units is normally presented to the next higher commander. Separate Reserve Component battalion commanders and company commanders may also brief the next higher mission commander. See appendix G for sample briefing slides for TBs.

Chapter 2

2-87. The TB is hosted by the brigade commander who provides a brigade overview. Each subordinate battalion commander and command sergeant major briefs their individual unit UTPs. Home station and installation representatives (such as a representative from Directorate of Plans, Training, Mobilization and Security) attend. Figure 2-19 illustrates the TB process.

> The 2nd Brigade is conducting its TB for the division commander, MG Fredericks. Following the brigade training overview, each battalion commander and command sergeant major presents their UTP. In attendance are the division, brigade, and battalion primary staffs. Also in attendance are company commanders, first sergeants, and representatives from the Directorate of Plans, Training, Mobilization and Security. Two weeks earlier, the brigade and battalion S-3s attended the quarterly installation training resource synchronization conference to ensure planned and scheduled training areas, ranges, and facilities were locked-in.
>
> As the briefing progresses, the division commander comments and provides guidance to all commanders and leaders present. This briefing results in a contract between commanders: the brigade commander and battalion commanders agree to execute training as briefed or modified; the division commander agrees to support the plans with the necessary resources to support them.
>
> MG Fredericks will review the training progress of the brigade at the next scheduled QTB for the brigade.

Figure 2-19. Notional training briefing vignette

2-88. Periodic reviews and updates of UTP execution briefed during the TB are conducted during QTBs (for Regular Army units) or YTBs (for Reserve Component units). Paragraph 3-36 discusses the purpose and conduct of these important briefings.

Chapter 3
Conducting Training Events

OVERVIEW

3-1. Conducting training events encompasses all activities related to planning for, preparing for, executing, and assessing the training events that comprise the UTP. Commanders plan and coordinate training events in detail well before execution to synchronize METs and training objectives and to resource each event properly. Commanders use training meetings as the primary forum to ensure that coordination and planning for training events are on track.

3-2. All successful training requires resources coordination, rehearsals, and precombat checks before training. Effective training requires time locked in on the UTP calendar for units and individuals to retrain tasks as training occurs. If the unit fails to meet the training objectives for a specific training event, the unit allocates time to ensure that it can retrain the tasks before the event is concluded. A unit must be proficient in a failed task before it advances to more complex collective tasks.

TRAINING FRAMEWORK

3-3. Unit leaders use the basic Army operations process as the training framework (see figure 3-1 on page 3-2) for conducting each training event that comprises the UTP. Planning for training events does not significantly differ from planning for an operation. A commander's presence sends a message to Soldiers that training is crucial to unit success. It allows the commander to observe and assess the conduct of training, training effectiveness, resource utilization, leaders in action, the state of readiness, and individual morale. It also serves to strengthen mutual trust—trust between the leader and subordinates—that is integral to the chain of command. Preparing for operations (and training) under the philosophy of mission command requires trust up and down the chain of command and between individuals and units. Execution of training occurs with the resources available. Without the right resources available at the right time, meaningful and effective training will not occur and units will lose valuable, irreplaceable training time. The assessment of tasks and leader proficiency is a constant process as units plan and train. Evaluations of task performance and bottom-up feedback are key because they provide the commander the information necessary to make accurate and timely MET assessments.

WHERE TO START

3-4. The UTP identifies the multiechelon training events crucial to attaining task proficiency. It is the starting point for leaders to begin to assign planning responsibility and begin the process of determining and coordinating resources. It focuses on the multiechelon training events that train the METs such as a staff training exercise (known as STAFFEX), command post exercise, live fire exercise (known as LFX), or FTX. These training events require substantial resources, coordination, and facilities. Once multiechelon training events are accounted for and included in the UTP calendar, the unit adds other events like unit-conducted classes, mandatory training, and those training events supported by internal unit-provided resources and coordination for unit-wide visibility and action.

Chapter 3

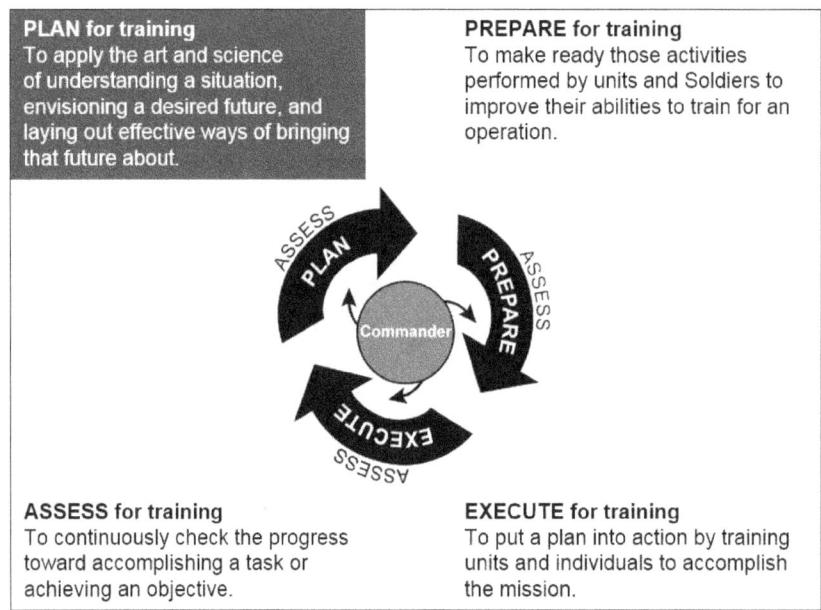

Figure 3-1. Plan phase of the operations process

PLAN

3-5. Following the operations process framework, the leader assigned as the primary planner for the training event reviews the initial training objectives for the event from the UTP. Following this review, the planner completes a mission analysis and confers with the commander for additional training guidance. Based on this discussion, the planner refines training objectives with additional details based on the guidance from the commander. (See the *Event Details* page found at the CATS Web site for major resources to assist the planner in mission analysis.) The planner uses T&EOs to identify other supporting collective and individual tasks that support higher collective tasks. Once planners identify these tasks, they determine all prerequisite tasks on which the unit must train prior to executing the event. CATSs help identify training gates for the event being planned.

3-6. Planners evaluate an operational environment to consider how to replicate it in the training environment. The higher commander's CTG identifies a potential environment to replicate in the training environment, including role players, type of visibility, types of terrain, and enemy forces. Using the objective task evaluation criteria matrix in the T&EO, planners identify the complexity of the training environment based on the commander's desired end state for task proficiency at the end of the training event. See appendix B for more on the objective task evaluation criteria matrix.

3-7. When no training environment is identified, the commander can create a training environment by using the decisive action training environment (known as DATE) available on the ATN Web site. This training environment is a composite model of the real-world environment. It provides a useful training planning tool to replicate an operational environment for training when one is not specified.

3-8. The creation of optimal training conditions results from several factors. Planners identify required resources early in the planning for a training event. Those same planners share knowledge of resource activities and their locations on the installation. Planners focus on creating a training environment that replicates an operational environment to the highest possible fidelity. Sometimes, planners combine LVC training environments to approximate an operational environment. (See AR 350-2 for the details on an operational environment and OPFORs resources.)

3-9. During the planning phase, the planner verifies the training venue (as live, virtual, or constructive) and locks in required resources. Ideally, the planners schedule these critical resources once the commander approves the COA to train. They reconnoiter the training site to ensure the unit can achieve the training objectives within the venue. Planners visualize the training event by drawing an event sketch and detailing how the unit will execute the training. They write a list of actions meet training objectives. They consider the time available to train versus the number of possible iterations to attain proficiency. This visualization serves as the concept for executing the training event. Once planners develop a sketch and visualized concept from start to end and the commander approves it, then additional resourcing for the event can begin.

3-10. Planners identify and request resources early and track their availability throughout the planning and preparation phases. Effective planners use the CATS, T&EOs, and unit historical records as a starting point to identify resources. Historical records typically document resources the unit needed and when it needed them. Successful planners know what resources they used previously for like training events. The event planner ensures the event resources—including any newly identified resources—are available. The DTMS has a checklist tool that allows users to set up and track the status of training resources associated within events.

3-11. An event administrative OPORD is required to execute the training and includes all necessary coordination. It explains the concept, resourcing, and responsibilities to execute the training event. Additionally, the plan identifies both tactical orders and OPFOR orders to drive the training and stimulate task execution.

8-STEP TRAINING MODEL

3-12. At the company and platoon levels, training models are developed and used as a simple and effective planning and execution tool for small-unit, individual training events. Training models do not provide a sufficient level of detail from which to develop a UTP, to fully develop training events, or to coordinate training events. Instead, they serve as a useful tool for subordinate leaders to ensure major activities and steps are accomplished. Training models help manage training events that are not complex in planning or execution. Units modify training models in the number of steps and procedures based on experience and the efficiencies gained by their use. One training model is the 8-step training model (see figure 3-2). The 8-step training model provides a flexible and reliable vehicle for creating continuity for planning and managing simple training events.

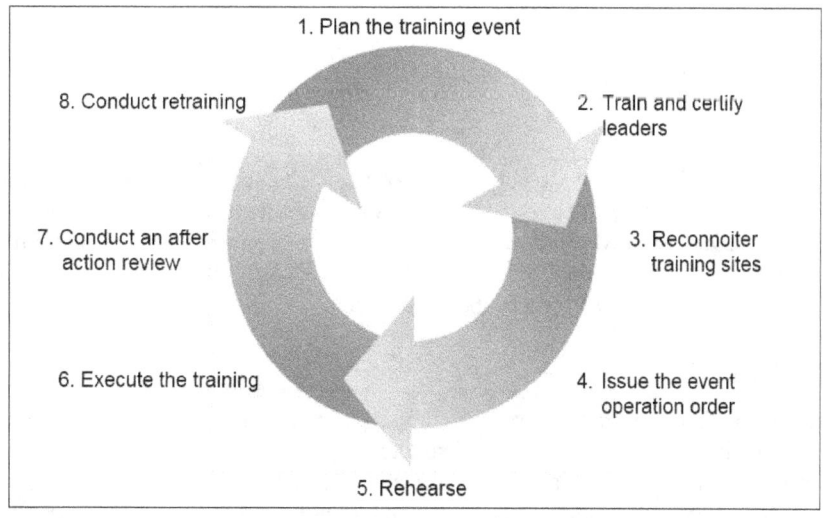

Figure 3-2. The 8-step training model

Chapter 3

Step 1 – Plan the Training Event

3-13. During step 1, leaders develop specific, obtainable, and measurable training objectives for the upcoming event based on guidance from the commander. Leaders allocate and ensure that there is adequate time scheduled for the event and it is indicated on the unit's training schedule. They create scenarios and instructions to support the training objectives. Leaders identify required resources, including necessary training areas and possible trainers. They identify hazards and eliminate or mitigate associated risks. Lastly, leaders develop training support and assessment plans, thereby establishing the groundwork for high-quality training.

Step 2 – Train and Certify Leaders

3-14. Step 2 involves training and certifying leaders. Leaders consist of officers, NCOs, civilians, and Soldiers. Qualified leaders train and certify other leaders. Qualified personnel are knowledgeable of the training subject matter and have performed the task themselves to standard. The train-the-trainer concept ensures that those responsible for training can provide proper instruction and certification to the unit. This step also includes training and certifying OPFOR leaders and training role players for the training environment.

Step 3 – Reconnoiter the Training Site

3-15. Leaders reconnoiter proposed training areas and facilities. Leaders verify that the location can adequately support the proposed training and enable the unit to accomplish training objectives. During step 3, leaders check that all resources, training areas, and training support plans are properly coordinated and prepared for execution. They make contact with support site personnel and review scheduling and coordination issues. If necessary, leaders modify the training event plan during step 3 to accommodate training site requirements and maximize training opportunities. Effective units do not perform training when training is not planned, coordinated, and supported properly with adequate resources.

Step 4 – Issue the Event Operation Order

3-16. Commanders and leaders ensure subordinates have all available information to perform the training. Through the OPORD, the commander clearly identifies the tasks to be trained, training objectives, and a clear mission statement. The commander also defines the scope of the training, how it will be conducted, and the tasks to train. A successful training event relies on all leaders understanding the expected outcome of the training, focused on the commander's training objectives.

Step 5 – Rehearse

3-17. Rehearsals are critical to the execution of any plan whether for operations or training. All those involved in the training event conduct rehearsals to ensure understanding, synchronization, and preparation of tactical actions. Leaders supervise rehearsals to ensure that those responsible for the training are prepared to conduct efficient, organized, and effective performance-oriented training. This step includes conducting the rehearsals necessary for OPFOR leaders and personnel.

Step 6 – Execute the Training

3-18. Commanders ensure the training event occurs as planned and on schedule. A training event requires maximum participation, minimum training distracters, and leaders checking and supervising where necessary. Trainers train Soldiers and ensure standards are met. To the greatest extent possible, commanders avoid planning training and not conducting it; they conduct every training planned. Commanders also minimize training distracters that interfere with training.

Step 7 – Conduct an After Action Review

3-19. During and after training, commanders review the tasks trained, assess the unit's training level in respect to the objectives, and obtain lessons learned to improve the training and unit's tactics, techniques, and procedures (TTP). Commanders record these assessments in DTMS for future use in other training events or to include these in unit SOPs.

Step 8 – Conduct Retraining

3-20. Units never depart a training event with tasks not trained to standard and training objectives not met. Units retrain tasks as necessary until they achieve the standard before they conclude the training event. Too often, units neglect this step because of limited time, limited resources, or other pressing requirements. However, step 8 is often the most critical step. Training instills competency and confidence in units, leaders, and Soldiers and enables the unit to develop task proficiency. Commanders honestly and objectively assess their units and ensure the unit meets task standards.

T-WEEK CONCEPT

3-21. The T-Week concept provides a logical, backward planning approach for developing training events. It provides detailed, chronological, and specific considerations for the planning and coordination necessary for each training event. The T-Week concept helps ensure that commanders consider and complete all significant actions necessary to execute training in a timely manner. Leaders use the concept as a guide for developing training events for the short-range planning horizon.

3-22. The T-Week concept ensures that units or individuals complete all critical actions before and after the training event. Leaders have to start early enough in the planning cycle to ensure the unit has all the resources to train when training begins. Unless the staff properly plans and prepares before training events, the unit may fail to attain the MET proficiencies that the commander envisioned during training execution. Additionally, commanders and leaders must thoroughly understand the home station's available training resources and facilities. See appendix H for an extensive discussion of the T-Week concept.

> *Note.* Reserve Component units operate in a monthly cycle, so the Regular Army's T-Week construct may not work. They may need to implement a monthly concept to consolidate weeks into months. Reserve Component units only need to replace T-Week activities with the corresponding activities associated with the month. For many Reserve Component units the requirement to begin and plan initial UTP training events could be years.

PREPARE

3-23. Preparing for training involves those activities performed prior to training to improve the unit's abilities to train effectively. (See figure 3-3 on page 3-6.) Preparing for training starts with ensuring trainers are subject matter experts in the tasks and the events trained. Trainers demonstrate task proficiency before teaching a task to others. Training and certifying leaders are critical in delivering quality, effective training to the unit. They ensure adequate preparation time and resources are available to conduct training. Preparation includes final coordination for training resources scheduled and programmed earlier in the plan phase. This preparation ensures that training resources are available when training begins.

3-24. Every training event is an opportunity for leader training. Each event gives senior leaders the opportunity to coach and mentor subordinates. Senior leaders actively develop subordinate leaders during preparations and develop specific leader training objectives for each training event.

3-25. Preparing for training also includes preexecution checks. Preexecution checks are the informal coordination measures conducted prior to conducting training events and must not be confused with precombat checks. Often, preexecution checks are tied to administrative resourcing or tasks that were identified within the event administrative OPORD. Leaders continuously track and conduct preexecution checks. Some informal coordination measures might include checking that—

Chapter 3

- The OPFOR has been equipped and trained.
- Leaders are certified to conduct range operations.
- All identified classes of supply and materials were requested in accordance with the administrative OPORD and have arrived by the request suspense.

Leaders use the DTMS to assist in tracking preexecution checks throughout the preparation process.

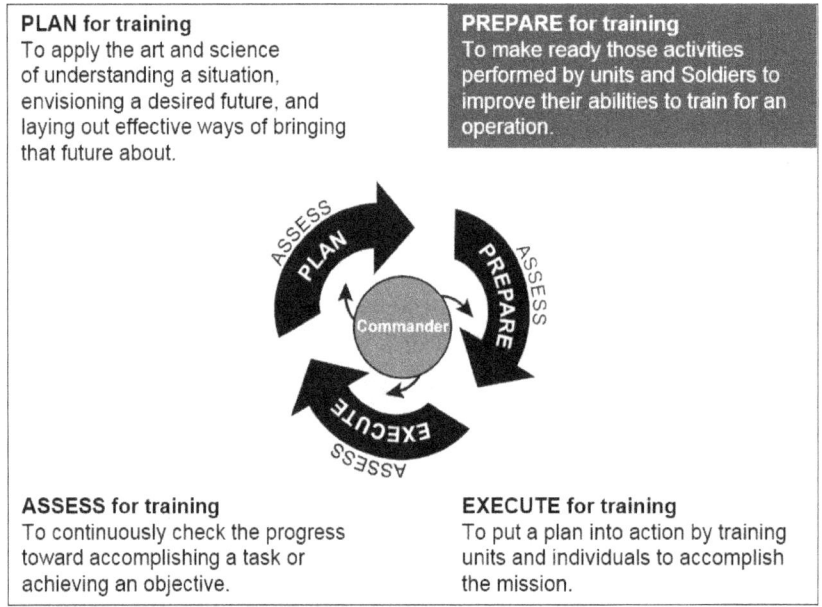

Figure 3-3. Prepare phase of the operations process

3-26. Preparing for training includes having units rehearse anticipated actions during the training event. Rehearsals provide a means of ensuring units synchronize and execute actions to standard during training. The OPFOR also rehearses its plan before executing the training event. The OPFOR rehearsal ensures this force understands its plan and can effectively stimulate quality training. Additionally, units rehearse lane training exercises to synchronize timing and actions associated with the tactical situation. Rehearsals are essential for an effective and realistic training experience.

3-27. Prior to training, leaders and planners prepare and develop an assessment plan. This plan captures unit performance as it is executed and enables leaders and trainers the opportunity to evaluate the unit as action unfolds. This plan also includes OC/Ts walking training areas to ensure that as the unit executes tasks, OC/Ts observe task execution.

3-28. When preparing for training, planners ensure final preparations are complete. The commander approves all required resources when training schedules are published and six weeks before the unit executes the training. The commander protects approved and scheduled training from taskings and distracters. If taskings and distracters put training at risk, the commander engages the higher commander to mitigate if necessary. As the event nears, planners ensure delivery of resources to the training site. Leaders check that TADSS are functional and that Soldiers know how to install and use them. Planners ensure the training site is set up in accordance with the administrative OPORD. Finally, they make final checks before the training event begins.

EXECUTE

3-29. Units execute training when they put a plan into action to meet the training proficiencies and training objectives specified by the commander. (See figure 3-4.) Commanders establish measurable and attainable training objectives that develop and demonstrate collective task proficiencies. Well planned and communicated training guidance, well-developed plans, and maximized opportunities and resources enable units to execute quality training.

3-30. During execution, leaders and OC/Ts perform evaluations using T&EOs to record a unit's performance as training is executed. Leaders conduct on-site, informal AARs during training, where training occurs to correct deficiencies in observed task execution. Trainers objectively measure unit training against published Army standards (found in the T&EOs). (See appendix A for a discussion on realistic training and appendix E for lane training.) When standards are not met, the unit retrains tasks to meet the standard.

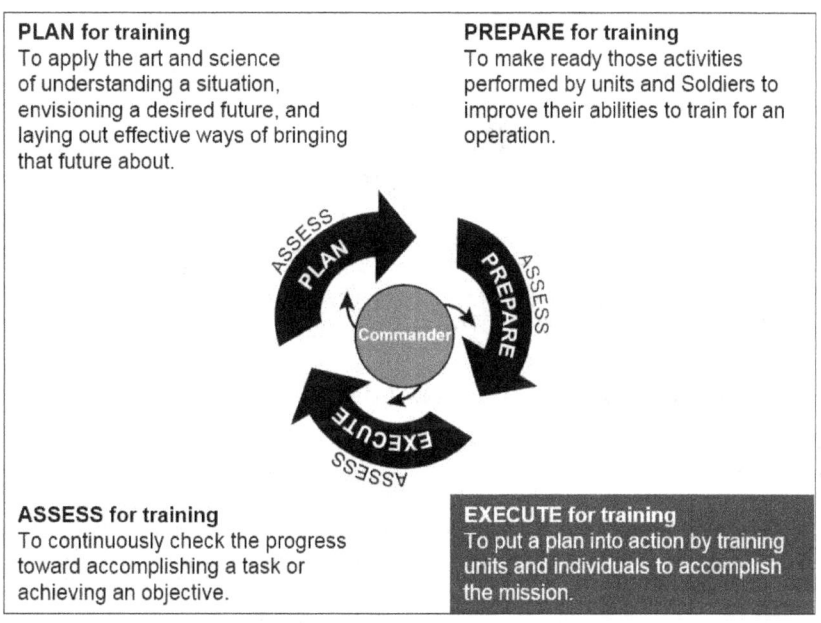

Figure 3-4. Execute phase of the operations process

ASSESS

3-31. Leaders assess training by continuously checking progress toward task achievement or training objectives. (See figure 3-5 on page 3-8.) Training events provide the venue for commanders and leaders to evaluate and measure the effectiveness of the collective tasks selected to train. The training objectives—determined and published by the commander for each training event—communicate the task, condition, standard, and expected training proficiencies for the collective tasks selected. Leaders use the assessment plan developed during preparation to evaluate unit performance. During execution, leaders use T&EOs to record a unit's performance every time it attempts a collective task. Evaluators—using the objective task evaluation criteria matrix on the T&EO—objectively record the proficiencies noted as the unit completes tasks. At the training meeting following the training event, evaluations are aggregated bottom-up, so the commander can assess whether the unit met the training objectives. The training meeting occurs the week following the start of training (T+1 per the T-Week concept). Using the training proficiency ratings discussed in chapter 1, the commander completes the assessments and subsequently records them into DTMS. Training meetings conducted routinely by echelon are critical to the assessment process.

Chapter 3

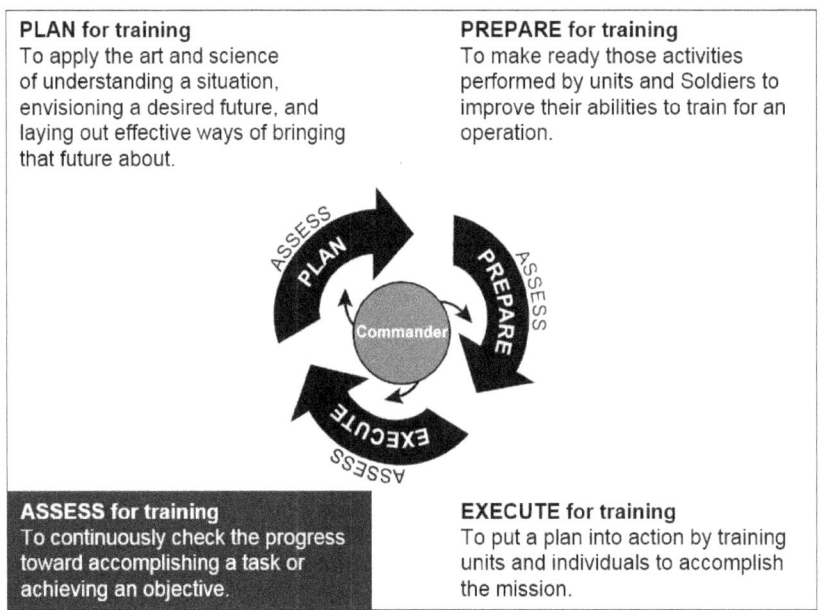

Figure 3-5. Assess phase of the operations process

TRAINING MEETINGS

3-32. Training meetings provide the commander and unit leaders a forum to meet periodically to assess past, current, and future training. Training meetings are among the most important meetings a unit conducts. Brigades conduct training meetings monthly whereas battalions and companies conduct them weekly. At company training meetings the commander assesses training just conducted based on the bottom-up feedback provided by evaluators. At brigade and battalion levels, training meetings focus on overall long- and mid-range planning progress and ensuring that training resources for subordinate units are coordinated for within the command and at the installation level. Training meetings also provide a forum for the commander to track and assess UTP progress and direct modifications to the plan, as needed.

Battalion and Brigade Training Meetings

3-33. In support of company-level training, battalions and brigades also conduct training meetings. These focus on overall UTP progress and more critically, on ensuring that training resources for subordinate companies are coordinated for and available when training begins. The brigade is responsible for interfacing with agencies in the installation training support system (typically, the installation Directorate of Plans, Training, Mobilization and Security). Training meetings occur weekly at the battalion level and monthly at brigade level. At battalion and brigade levels, attendees include—

- Commander.
- Deputy commander (at brigade-level).
- Executive officer.
- Command sergeant major.
- Battalion commanders and command sergeants major (at brigade-level); company commanders and first sergeants (at battalion level).
- All primary coordinating staff (such as the S-1, S-2, and S-3).
- Key staff officers and NCOs.
- Supporting and supported unit representatives.

3-34. The agenda topics covered at brigade and battalion training meetings include—

Conducting Training Events

- Training just completed (last month). This is the forum for the commander, based on bottom-up feedback (such as AARs and T&EOs) to assess the METs trained in this period.
- Training scheduled but not conducted (and why).
- Training highlights (to include event training objectives for the next 45 days down to company level).
- Installation training resource synchronization conferences scheduled for the next 60 to 90 days and the status of unit training resource requests.

Company Training Meetings

3-35. At company training meetings, the T-Week concept (see appendix H) drives the discussion for the detailed planning of each training event. Also at the company level, bottom-up feedback from subordinate leaders and evaluators provide the necessary input to objectively assess training conducted. See figure 3-6 for a hypothetical company training meeting. (See appendix C for a details on company training meetings.)

On Tuesday at 1300, B Company conducts its recurring training meeting. In attendance is the company commander, first sergeant, executive officer, supply sergeant, and platoon leaders and platoon sergeants. The company commander, CPT Angela Hawkins, begins the meeting on time following a set agenda. She and the executive officer also keep the meeting from straying to other tangents and focus the meeting solely on company training.

Last week, the company conducted a FTX. During this event, the company focused one of its training objectives on the collective task 'Occupy an Assembly Area.' CPT Hawkins indicated that this task was previously assessed as a P- rating. The commander wanted to use the FTX to improve this assessment to a T- rating. During the training meeting, the commander reviews the bottom-up feedback from the platoon leaders, the T&EOs provided by observers from company A, and her own observations. Based on this feedback, she assesses the company as a T- rating for this task. The executive officer updates the task 'Occupy an Assembly Area' from a P- rating to a T- rating.

Platoon leaders and sergeants stated that they conducted hip-pocket training during the FTX. They acknowledge the unit still needs to use available down time to work on Warrior tasks and battle drills identified by the commander and first sergeant. CPT Hawkins emphasizes that leaders need to take every available opportunity to train Soldiers to improve individual skills. She states that with limited training time, company leaders need to take advantage of available time to improve on these Soldier-level skills.

Attention now turns to the coordination for upcoming events within the next six weeks. The executive officer pulls up the UTP calendar from the DTMS to review these future events. The commander sees that the company is at T-Week 5 for an M4 qualifying range. She asks the executive officer if the DA Form 581 (*Request for Issue and Turn-In of Ammunition*) request for ammunition is approved and if convoy clearances and driver certifications for the pick-up at the ammunition holding area are on track. The executive officer indicated that approvals, clearances, and certifications are in and that 1LT Johnson and SSG Rolf are the range officer and NCO in charge of the range. The commander asks them both for an update on range safety and the plan to run each platoon through a virtual weapons trainer prior to the range.

Figure 3-6. Notional company training meeting vignette

Chapter 3

> Looking beyond 6 weeks at the mid-range planning horizon, the commander reviews the training objectives for each major training event to make sure that the company stays on track with the UTP. She provides additional planning guidance at this time and emphasizes to the platoon leaders that resource planning is vitally important at every step in the T-weeks leading up to any event.
>
> At 1430 hours, the commander concludes the company training meeting.

Figure 3-6. Notional company training meeting vignette (continued)

QUARTERLY AND YEARLY TRAINING BRIEFING

3-36. QTBs (for Regular Army) and YTBs (for Reserve Component) are periodic UTP updates to the commander two echelons above. These briefings support the TB that is briefed prior to the start of training. Similar to the TB, the brigade commander provides the brigade training overview, and battalion commanders and command sergeants major brief the current status of UTP progress. Battalion commanders in separate brigades and regiments present the QTB to corps major subordinate commanders. The YTB for Reserve Component units is normally presented to the next higher commander. The YTB is conducted prior to the start of the fiscal year in Reserve Component units. Separate Reserve Component battalion commanders and company commanders may also brief the next higher commander. Some Reserve Component units may not be able to conduct in-person briefings. In those cases, commanders must use other means such as messages or mail. Ideally, installation training resource conferences should occur just prior to the QTBs or YTB to provide the most current and accurate information relating to the installation training resources and facility scheduling. See appendix G for details concerning QTBs and YTBs.

ASSESSING TRAINING

3-37. An *assessment* is determination of the progress toward accomplishing a task, creating a condition, or achieving an objective (JP 3-0). Commanders determine training readiness using evaluations and assessments. Evaluations are based on the performance of tasks measured against an established standard under set conditions. Evaluations are recorded using T&EOs for collective and individual tasks. Users access T&EOs on ATN, CATS, DTMS, and the CAR. These Web sites are the Army's only sources that provide the prescribed training tasks, conditions, and standards for all Army individual and collective tasks.

Objective Considerations

3-38. To enable unit leaders and commanders to evaluate proficiency of collective tasks objectively, they use established task proficiency criteria and standards. Task proficiency criteria and standards differentiate the level of training a unit has achieved using the proficiency ratings. See the discussion beginning in paragraph 1-5 for Army task rating proficiency standards.

3-39. Evaluations of task performance steps—documented within a task performance measure of the task T&EO—are objective evaluation ratings assigned directly to demonstrated task proficiency. Evaluators observe performance of the tasks measures and grade the performance steps either as GO or as NO-GO.

3-40. Evaluators use the objective task evaluation criteria matrix found on every collective T&EO to help evaluate performance of collective tasks (see figure 3-7). By considering certain execution criteria—like the training environment and day or night conditions—the evaluator or unit commander can record a more accurate and objective evaluation of task performance. An accurate and objective evaluation yields a more objective assessment of task performance. See appendix B for details on objective task evaluation criteria matrixes and specific T&EO completion instructions. Evaluators for the Organizational Inspection Program also complete checklists. See appendix I for potential questions.

Subjective Considerations

3-41. While the T&EO and task proficiency standards provide objective criteria for determining task proficiency, assessments allow leaders to take into account the subjective nature of training. Leaders' assessments combine their professional observations with other information to develop an overall assessment of the unit's ability to accomplish its mission. Final authority of a unit's assessment lies solely with the commander. Commanders and leaders might consider the following information in their assessments:

- Assessment and feedback from higher.
- AARs.
- Subordinate leader and Soldier feedback.
- Evaluator and OC/T comments.
- Personal experience and observations.

Plan and Prepare							Execute					Assess
Operational Environment			Training Environment (L/V/C)	% Leaders present at training/authorized	% Present at training/ authorized	External evaluation	Performance measures	Critical performance measures	Leader performance measures		Task assessment
SQD and PLT	CO and BN	BDE and above									
Dynamic (single threat)	Dynamic and complex (4 + OE variables and hybrid threat)	Dynamic and complex (all OE variables and hybrid threat)	Night	≥85%	≥80%	Yes	≥90% GO	All	≥90%		T
				75-84%			80-90% GO		80-89%		T-
Static (single threat)	Dynamic (single threat)	Dynamic and complex (all OE variables and single threat)		65-74%	75-79%	No	65-79% GO				P
				60-64%	60-74%		51-64% GO				P-
	Static (single threat)	Dynamic & complex (< all OE variables and single threat)	Day	<60%	<60%		<51% GO	<All	<80%		U

BDE	brigade	OE	operational environment	T	fully trained	
BN	battalion	P	practiced	T-	trained	
C	constructive	P-	marginally practiced	U	untrained	
CO	company	PLT	platoon	V	virtual	
L	live	SQD	squad			

Note: The percentages used in this figure are for illustration only. See the collective task's published training and evaluation outline for the applicable percentages.

Figure 3-7. Objective task evaluation criteria from a training and evaluation outline

Chapter 3

Evaluations

3-42. Evaluations can be executed using internal assets or by an external agency. Normally commanders evaluate tasks during the execution phase of training events, but they also evaluate tasks during the planning and preparing phases of events. Leaders use evaluations as an opportunity to coach and mentor subordinates. Evaluations may be informal, formal, internal, external, or any combination of these. (See figure 3-8 for evaluation types.)

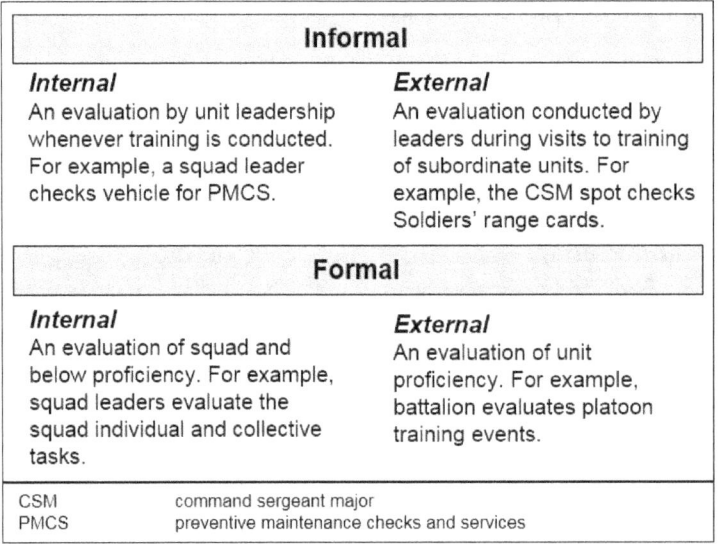

Figure 3-8. Formal and informal evaluations

3-43. When evaluating individual and small-unit training events, evaluators normally include every Soldier and leader involved in the training of the tasks. For large-scale training events, evaluators sample a number of individuals and subordinate organizations to determine proficiency in individual and collective tasks.

3-44. During and after formal evaluations, evaluators prepare their findings and recommendations in reports. Evaluators provide reports to the evaluated unit commander and higher commanders as required by the headquarters directing the evaluation. Evaluation documentation can range from an annotated individual training record or T&EO for an internal training evaluation to a comprehensive report on Reserve Component units during annual training.

3-45. The completed T&EOs—including written comments, AAR comments, and coaching and mentoring comments—provide leaders and Soldiers with immediate and documented feedback on their performance. Commanders use evaluator input as a significant source of input for each MET or collective task when scoring training proficiency. However, the objective task evaluation criteria matrix is the primary input in determining the overall task proficiency assessment.

Informal Evaluation

3-46. Informal evaluations are conducted by leaders either internal, or external to the unit. They occur as training, or unit activities are executed. They are conducted on the spot and require little to no supporting resources. They provide a quick and informal means of providing immediate feedback to individual Soldiers or small units on their performance to sustain or improve that performance.

Formal Evaluation

3-47. Formal evaluations are conducted by leaders either internal or external to the unit. Evaluations can be scheduled or conducted without notice to evaluate training proficiency or to evaluate specific unit activities. Formal evaluations typically require supporting resources to conduct. Resources range from facilities to conduct in/out briefings to facilities to conduct AARs to video devices to record task execution. Formal evaluations enable recording and providing feedback to units on their proficiency and performance. Evaluators provide the results to sustain or improve the performance to the unit commander.

Internal Evaluation

3-48. Internal evaluations are conducted by unit leaders when training or when a unit conducts activities. They evaluate the unit's ability to perform specific tasks or activities. They can be either informal or formal in nature. The results of formal internal evaluations are provided to the unit commander. The commander then determines whether to either sustain or improve performance.

External Evaluation

3-49. EXEVALs are unit proficiency evaluations. They are formal in nature and conducted external to the unit. The EXEVAL provides commanders with an objective way to evaluate their unit METs or selected collective task proficiencies. All units in the Army undergo an EXEVAL to validate fully trained (T) or trained (T-) task proficiency ratings.

3-50. An EXEVAL includes the following key requirements:
- The higher commander two levels up approves and resources it (for example, a brigade approves and resources a company-level EXEVAL).
- The commander resources it to achieve a minimum of T or T- task proficiency rating.
- The higher commander (one or two levels up) trains and certifies external OC/Ts. The senior OC/T can be from an adjacent unit within the higher command of the unit evaluated.
- The higher commander trains and evaluates METs and battle tasks (to include battle drills).
- T&EOs are the objective basis of the evaluation.
- The higher commander two levels up supervises the final AAR.
- The formal commander (one level up) discusses with the unit commander the expected proficiency levels for METs and battle tasks (to include battle drills) and overall level of proficiency for readiness reporting units (see AR 220-1).

3-51. Immediately following an EXEVAL, the unit commander and the next higher commander formally discuss the unit's proficiency on METs or collective tasks as well as on the unit's overall training readiness assessment based on the EXEVAL. This discussion—
- Ensures both commanders objectively consider the EXEVAL, personal observations, and the experience of the next higher commander before the unit commander formally assesses the unit's training proficiency.
- Provides an opportunity for commanders to coach and mentor subordinates.
- Uses TBs to result in a training contract or agreement between the senior and subordinate commander for the way ahead.
- Provides an understanding of priorities and the resources required to either improve or sustain training proficiency.

The end state for the EXEVAL commanders' dialogue is for the two commanders to agree on the units training proficiency and overall training readiness.

Assessments

3-52. Assessments provide a final graded determination on an individual's, a leader's, or a unit's ability to perform a task to the published standard.

3-53. At the individual level, leaders observe Soldier task performance. They record the results of this performance using individual task T&EOs. Leaders also use the results of these assessments to counsel Soldiers to sustain or improve task performance.

3-54. In the assessment of leaders, commanders consider subordinate leaders' proficiency. An effective commander deliberately observes and assesses subordinate leaders. The commander pays particular attention to assessing the character, competence, and commitment of subordinate leaders. These three criteria are the certification criteria for all Army professionals. Training provides excellent opportunities to grow and develop leaders throughout the unit. Commanders exercise mission command; they create an environment that encourages on-the-job learning and encourages leaders to take prudent risks and make honest mistakes. To assist senior leaders in the assessment of subordinate leaders, leader development plans are an essential tool. Refer to appendixes A and H for more on leader development planning.

3-55. At the unit level, leaders analyze and correlate observations and evaluations of observed unit performance. The resulting assessment is based on an aggregate of these many inputs. From company level and higher, these unit assessments form the basis of recording unit training readiness, which contributes to a unit status reporting.

3-56. As part of the UTP, commanders ensure the assessment planning—
- Fixes responsibility within the staff and subordinate units for gathering and analyzing evaluation data and preparing recommendations.
- Concentrates on effective leader and unit training.
- Uses the command sergeant major, first sergeant, and other senior NCOs to gather feedback on individual, crew, and team training.
- Allows the higher commander to monitor outcomes and take action to reshape priorities, policies, or plans to overcome training weaknesses and sustain strengths.

3-57. Commanders assemble as much information as they can about a unit's performance and its ability to perform selected METs or collective tasks. Staff compile these tasks following a combat training center rotation or from other units if the unit conducts training at home station. Combat training center packages are an excellent source of feedback. Other important sources of feedback for the senior commander's assessment of the unit's ability to accomplish missions include—
- Personal observations of training.
- Deployment exercises.
- Assessment and feedback from higher.
- Maintenance and log evaluations.
- Staff visit reports.
- Inspector general and special inspections.
- Unit status reports.
- Army Audit Agency reports.
- TBs and QTBs or YTBs.
- Warrior tasks and battle drills.

AFTER ACTION REVIEW

3-58. An AAR includes a facilitator, event participants, and other observers. It is an event used to analyze an organization's performance, during and at the conclusion of a training event or operation. The goal of an AAR is to improve a unit's future performance. Using AAR as a structured review process allows training participants to discover for themselves what happened, why it happened, and how they can perform the task better. For more detailed descriptions and discussions for conducting an AAR, see appendix D.

Appendix A
Realistic Training

GOALS OF REALISTIC TRAINING

A-1. Realistic training is a deliberate practice of conducting individual and collective tasks to enable tactical and technical proficiency. This proficiency supports mission accomplishment in a training environment that approximates an operational environment in both sufficient complexity and substance. Realistic training incorporates the human, cultural, and political aspects of armed conflict to reflect the feeling of persistent danger in complex training environments. Realistic training also develops cohesive teams of Army professionals who can improve and thrive in ambiguous, complex, and challenging situations. Effective realistic training focuses on improving team and individual performances and decision making.

A-2. To win in a complex world, leaders work to enhance training realism in every training event. Leaders ensure that units and Soldiers train to attain more than technical and tactical proficiency. Realism involves robustly representing the complexities of variables in an operational environment as well as their posed physical, mental, and ethical challenges.

A-3. Ultimately, realistic, well-planned, and executed training aims to produce Soldiers, leaders, and units with the right capabilities to win in a complex world. Realistic training develops and hones these capabilities. First, the training builds unit proficiencies in tasks. Second, a unit that sustains proficiency in tasks often operates in complex and stressful training environments successfully. When training concludes, the leaders and Soldiers in a unit are confident and able. They perform tasks to standard under dynamic and complex conditions with skill and determination. To sustain that task proficiency, units continue to provide training environments that are well planned, well resourced, and led by trained officers and NCOs. See figures A-1 and A-2 (on pages A-2 and A-3 respectively) for a training event planning scenario.

CHARACTERISTICS OF REALISTIC TRAINING

A-4. The characteristics of quality training become evident once training is planned, prepared for, and in the process of execution. The best training events enable units and individuals to attain training objectives, positively improve individual and collective task proficiency, and build Soldier confidence. Soldiers and leaders know when quality training is conducted; they fully embrace realistic training that challenges them. They also know when training is poorly planned, prepared for, and executed. The following highlights a few of the primary characteristics of realistic, quality training:

- All leaders are present and engaged.
- Unit effectively leverages training resources.
- Leader development is a priority.
- Leader protects training from distracters.
- Units and Soldiers train with those they operate.
- Training environment replicates an operational environment.
- AARs are integral.
- Training challenges units and Soldiers intellectually and physically.
- Training is performance oriented.
- Training is tailored to drive initiative and adaptability.
- Training provides continually changing conditions.

- Units train one level down and evaluate two levels down.
- Units and Soldiers train repetitively.

MAJ Jordan, an experienced multi-tour combat veteran and newly assigned S-3 for the 1-22nd Infantry Battalion, is planning a battalion-level, home-station training event for the MET, "Conduct an Attack." The training event focuses on several collective tasks, battle drills, and individual tasks including—

- Plan an attack at battalion level.
- Conduct an assault at company level.
- Conduct an assault at platoon level.
- Evacuate casualties.
- Treat casualties.
- Execute fire support.
- Synchronize close air support.

In preparing for the training event, MAJ Jordan faces some challenges to make the training as realistic and demanding as possible. First, he determines how to represent joint forces, civilians on the battlefield, and a complex urban environment to the appropriate fidelity. Second, he checks if the battalion or higher headquarters has the ability to provide an OPFOR with overmatch in selected niche capabilities without significant external support. Third, he determines how the battalion will integrate fire support and close air support with appropriate simulated effects.

MAJ Jordan also recognizes the need to add more realism to casualty identification, assessment, and care under simulated battlefield conditions. In short, he needs to determine training events that address these challenges to better replicate—with the highest level of fidelity, complexity, and rigor that exist—an actual operational environment to meet training standards.

Additionally, MAJ Jordan considers how to adequately engage, motivate, and challenge leaders and Soldiers during this training event, especially those with combat experience. He determines if the supporting infrastructure adequately delivers and can sustain the training enablers and products required for realistic training. MAJ Jordan ascertains methods to enhance current training capabilities to replicate the physical and intellectual hardships Soldiers faced in recent combat better. He then specifies the necessary tools and processes needed for more effective and efficient unit training in this realistic training.

Figure A-1. Realistic training vignette

ALL LEADERS ARE PRESENT AND ENGAGED

A-5. Quality training is commander-driven, but all unit leaders have a direct responsibility to train their organization. Leaders must be present, visible, engaged, and fulfilling their role at training. If it is their training event, then they command it. At a subordinate's event, they assess it. At a higher organization's event, they support it. Commanders and leaders actively display the behaviors that they require of their subordinates. While commanders are the unit's primary trainer, subordinate leaders are responsible for the proficiency of their respective organizations and subordinates.

UNIT EFFECTIVELY LEVERAGES TRAINING RESOURCES

A-6. Good trainers and leaders know and use all available training resources. These resources include training doctrine, proponent publications, Army training support system resources, ITE enablers, and the

Realistic Training

ATMS. The ATMS consists of the ATN, the CATS, and the DTMS. To train effectively with limited time and resources, trainers leverage every available resource to maximize training proficiencies. For example, the platoon training a task that cannot be fully performed in a live environment due to training area restrictions considers using virtual or constructive training environments.

Concept of Operations: The 1-22nd IN BN conducts an attack to clear the mountainous area and foothills overlooking Mega City. Objective 1 requires A Co. and B Co. to block enemy forces from fleeing to Mega City and occupying structures. Objective 2 requires C Co. and D Co. to destroy or push enemy forces deeper into the mountain range. Fire support and close air support are available via C Co. fire support team with joint terminal attack controller (known as JTAC) attached.

The battalion S-3, a combat veteran, has identified key shortfalls to train for tactical and technical proficiencies in these tasks under conditions that more accurately represent the stressors and complexities of an operational environment:

1) Replicated joint, interagency, and multinational assets, an urban area with civilian population, and other aspects of an operational environment.
2) A hybrid OPFOR with overmatch in selected niche capabilities to include cyber and space.
3) Realistic wraparound to account for mission command requirements up two echelons (division) and adjacent units.
4) Tactical aircraft with appropriate ordnance, given limited availability of those assets.
5) Realistic tactical combat casualty identification, assessment, and care.

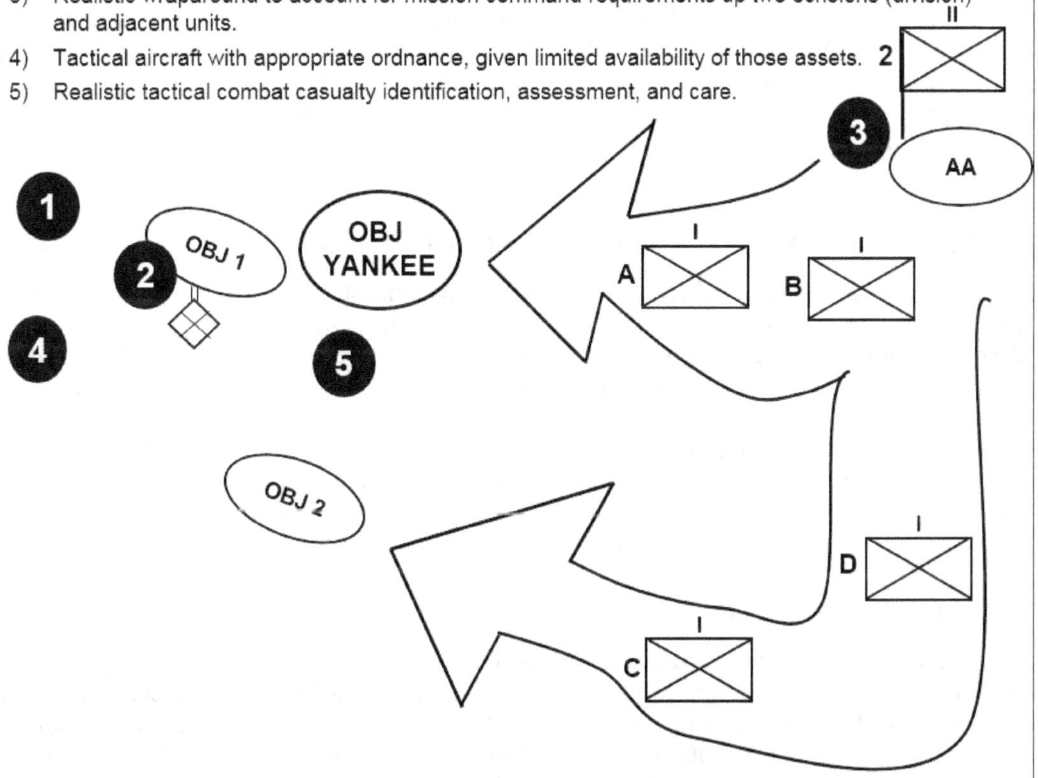

AA	avenue of approach	IN	infantry
BN	battalion	OBJ	objective
Co.	company	OPFOR	opposing force

Figure A-2. Graphic for realistic training vignette

LEADER DEVELOPMENT IS A PRIORITY

A-7. Leader development occurs in all three training domains: institutional, operational, and self-development (see AR 350-1). In the operational training domain, leader development is more progressive and battle focused. As the unit trains, a leader's honest mistakes can be made without prejudice. Training is

Appendix A

also the venue for leaders to try again. Leaders who fail at the first attempting a task can retrain the task as necessary. Sometimes leaders develop other methods and techniques that may prove more effective. Once a leader displays task proficiency, the trainer increases the difficulty level. The increased difficulty induces a positive learning environment and builds the leader's confidence to master tasks under changing and more challenging conditions. Senior leaders actively plan and monitor subordinate leaders' progressive development. They underwrite honest mistakes and provide timely coaching and mentoring during the entire training process.

LEADER PROTECTS TRAINING FROM DISTRACTERS

A-8. Once commanders lock in the training, approve the UTP calendar, and publish the training schedule, the training must not change. Senior commanders provide the necessary resources to train—including time—and protect subordinate units from unprogrammed taskings or other training distractions. Commanders establish and enforce a command climate that creates stability and predictability throughout the organization by protecting approved training. There is nothing more disruptive to unit training readiness than training planned, but not conducted because of unscheduled requirements.

UNITS AND SOLDIERS TRAIN WITH THOSE THEY OPERATE

A-9. Effective collective training is best conducted with higher, lower, and all supporting and supported elements available. Multiechelon and combined arms training consists of collective training performed simultaneously by all engaged echelons. This method of training optimizes the use of time, resources, and personnel while supporting a more realistic training environment. For example, to train to "Conduct a Combined Arms Breach of an Obstacle," an infantry unit requires artillery, engineer, and other functional support.

TRAINING ENVIRONMENT REPLICATES AN OPERATIONAL ENVIRONMENT

A-10. A training environment replicates an operational environment as much as possible. There is no better means of preparing Soldiers and units than making the training environment as realistic as possible. Units and Soldiers thrive on complex, dynamic, challenging, and realistic training that is well planned and well led. That training requires commanders to diligently ensure that resources to make training realistic and challenging are available when needed and to know how to leverage LVC training environments. Since units complete most training time at home station, commanders strive to make that training environment as realistic as possible. Realistic training creates units that are operationally adaptable and can quickly adjust to changing conditions. Ultimately, this type of training saves lives in actual operations because units are already familiar with the stress and demands of the training environment.

AFTER ACTION REVIEWS ARE INTEGRAL

A-11. AARs are well planned, resourced, and facilitated throughout the entire training process. These reviews do not just occur at the conclusion of a training event. Informal AARs also occur as training unfolds and when required. The best training ensures that leaders identify faulty execution early enough in an event to be corrected on the spot. No units or Soldiers should depart a training event without the confidence that they can execute tasks to the published standard. Facilitated AARs require detailed planning and are always led by competent, knowledgeable, and engaged leaders. AARs promote and enhance development of individual leaders within training events.

TRAINING CHALLENGES UNITS AND SOLDIERS INTELLECTUALLY AND PHYSICALLY

A-12. Training is intellectual and physical in nature. Training challenges Soldiers intellectually because it requires them to demonstrate an extensive amount of unique expertise to conduct military operations. It challenges Soldiers physically as they use strength, endurance, and physical skills to apply force to defeat an opponent. Combat operations are tough, stressful, and unforgiving. Commanders create the right conditions, difficulty, and intensity for every training event. This tailoring includes unexpected changes in conditions that require subordinates to apply initiative and adaptability.

A-13. Realistic training must mentally challenge Soldiers and leaders to keep them engaged and motivated. Challenging training develops character, competence, commitment, and self-confidence in the individual while building mutual trust and cohesion in the unit as Soldiers share sense of accomplishment. Training accomplishments have the added benefit of strengthening personal morale and enhances unit ésprit de corps. It inspires excellence by fostering initiative, enthusiasm, and an eagerness to learn.

TRAINING IS PERFORMANCE ORIENTED

A-14. Training is performance oriented. Performance-oriented training is hands-on and experiential; units and Soldiers train the task under conditions and to the standard specified. Units and Soldiers learn best through repetition, using a hands-on approach. As conditions in operational environments can and do change so do conditions in a training environment. Once a unit or Soldiers achieve task proficiency, training then includes variations of conditions. Soldiers train better, faster, and to a higher degree of proficiency when they know the task, conditions, and standards.

TRAINING IS TAILORED TO DRIVE INITIATIVE AND ADAPTABILITY

A-15. Training conditions that include unexpected changes require subordinates to apply initiative and adaptability. Effective training experiences, coupled with organized and timely candid feedback, build leaders' and subordinates' competence and trust. Leaders build unit, staff, and Soldier trust when they consistently demonstrate competence under unpredictable, changing, and stressful conditions. Together, character, competence, and commitment build the necessary trust that enables Soldiers and leaders to be agile, adaptive, and innovative.

TRAINING PROVIDES CONTINUALLY CHANGING CONDITIONS

A-16. Once proficiency is achieved under the task's published conditions, leaders continually change the conditions. They change the tactical scenario, higher and subordinate unit participation, the physical environment, and time of day. Such varied conditions provide the unit or Soldier the opportunity to perform the tasks under increasingly complex and challenging situations. Changes in leadership can also produce more adaptive performance, just as in real operations. When leaders cannot perform their role, subordinates must step in and lead. By continually changing the conditions, the unit becomes more confident in its ability to perform the task under increasingly more stressful situations.

UNITS TRAIN ONE LEVEL DOWN AND EVALUATE TWO LEVELS DOWN

A-17. Commanders directly oversee the training of a subordinate unit one level down as they plan, prepare for, execute, and assess their training events. When they oversee these units, commanders also actively evaluate units two levels down. This level of command oversight helps ensure that subordinate units adhere to training plans and the battle focus of the higher unit and to demonstrate task proficiencies.

UNITS AND SOLDIERS TRAIN REPETITIVELY

A-18. Practice makes perfect. The more units or Soldiers train a task to standard, the more proficient the units or Soldiers become. To master a task, units or Soldiers perform the task consistently and instinctively under various conditions. This is true from individual Soldier tasks to the more complex unit collective tasks. Units and Soldiers that train on tasks repeatedly and under increasingly more difficult conditions grow more comfortable and confident in their ability to perform the task. Leaders strive to train units and Soldiers to exceed the minimum standard, especially when units and Soldiers will perform the tasks in real world conditions that are complex and ambiguous.

This page intentionally left blank.

Appendix B
Training and Evaluation Outlines

OVERVIEW

B-1. The T&EO is the Army's source for individual and collective task training standards. The T&EO consists of the major procedures (steps or actions) a unit or individual must accomplish to perform a task to standard. A collective task also describes the performance required of a unit under the conditions of the training environment. **The *training and evaluation outline* is a summary document that provides information on individual or collective task training objectives, resource requirements, and evaluation procedures**. T&EOs are developed, approved, and published by the responsible proponents. This appendix focuses on collective task T&EOs.

B-2. During training events, leaders strive to achieve the Army standard for tasks trained. During training events, leaders and evaluators use T&EOs to measure observed task proficiency. Completed T&EOs form the backbone of bottom-up feedback that company commanders and first sergeants review at the weekly training meeting (see figure B-1). The T&EOs provide the commander the necessary objective evaluations to assess unit training proficiency and ultimately to assess training readiness.

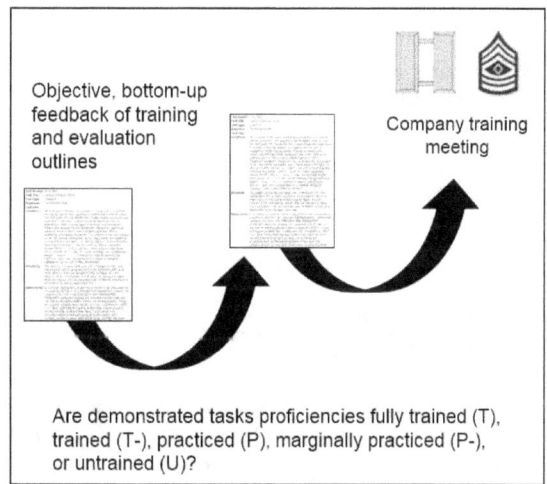

Figure B-1. Bottom-up feedback of task evaluations

REPOSITORIES

B-3. The Army has several official repositories that contain T&EOs. Users can access T&EOs at—
- The ATN.
- The DTMS.
- The CATS.
- The CAR.

Users access the DTMS, CATS, and CAR via the ATN. Users accessing T&EOs through the ATN do not require additional privileges to view and print the T&EOs.

Appendix B

ELEMENTS

B-4. Collective task T&EOs have the same basic elements in their outline. This appendix focuses on those elements that are crucial to conducting the evaluation and recording observed task performance. These elements include—

- Task number.
- Task title.
- Distribution restriction.
- Destruction notice.
- Foreign disclosure.
- Supporting references.
- Condition.
- Standard.
- Live fire.
- Notes.
- Performance steps.
- Performance measures.
- Task performance and evaluation summary block.
- Prerequisite collective tasks.
- Supporting collective tasks.

B-5. Figure B-2 illustrates a sample first page of a T&EO that a user might see when accessing it an official repository.

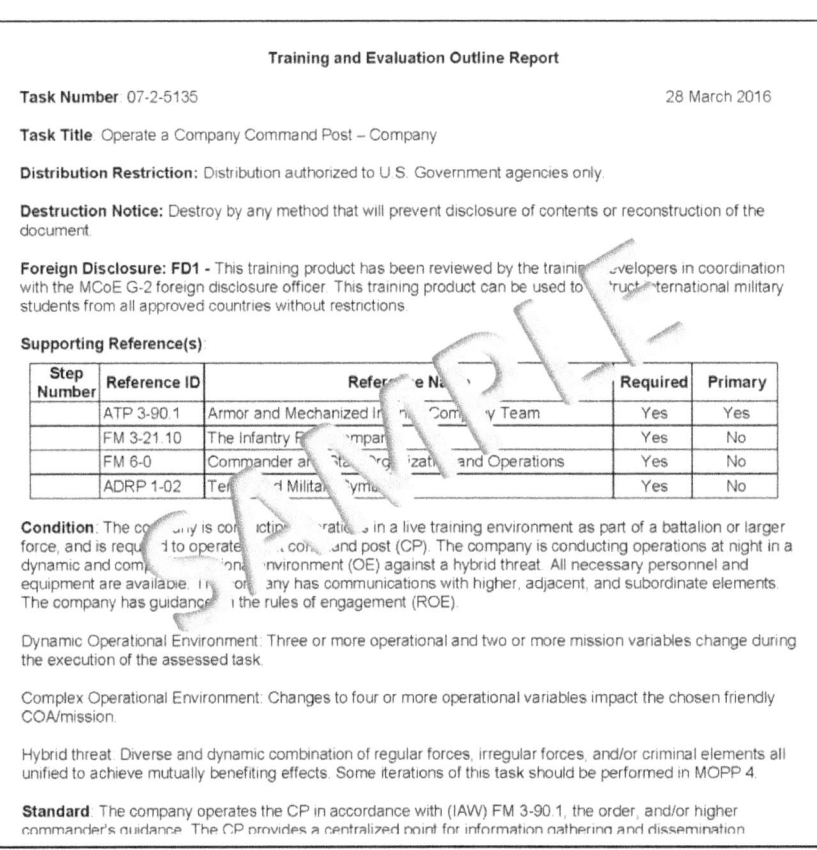

Figure B-2. Sample training and evaluation outline

TASK NUMBER

B-6. A task number is a unique identifier specifying an individual or collective task. The individual task number system differs from that for collective tasks. For collective tasks, the task number consists of three groups of numbers separated by hyphens.

B-7. The first two numbers indicate the school or proponent code (see table B-1). An example of a task number is 07-2-5135. In this example, the first two digits, **07**, indicates an infantry task. A proponent is an Army organization or staff that has been assigned primary responsibility for material or subject matter in its area of interest.

Table B-1. School and proponent codes

Code	School or Proponent	Code	School or Proponent
01	Aviation	27	Judge Advocate (military law)
02	Music	30	Military Intelligence
03	Chemical Biological, Radiological, and Nuclear	31	Special Operations
05	Engineers	33	Military Information Support Operations
06	Field Artillery	34	Combat Electronic Warfare and Intelligence
07	Infantry	40	Space and Missile Defense
08	Medical	41	Civil Affairs
09	Ordnance (missile and munitions)	42	Supply
10	Quartermaster	43	Maintenance (except missile)
11	Signal	44	Air Defense Artillery
12	Adjutant General	45	Public Affairs
14	Finance	46	Public Information
16	Chaplain	55	Transportation
17	Armor	63	Combat Service Support*
19	Military Police	70	Acquisition, Logistics and Technology
21	Individual Soldier	71	Combined Arms
* Combat Service Support is known as Sustainment			

B-8. The second number of the task number indicates the echelon for which the collective task applies. In the example of 07-2-5135, a **2** applies to a company (troop, battery, or detachment) level. See table B-2 for echelon codes. Echelon codes indicate the level of command for which the T&EO is applicable.

Table B-2. Echelon codes

TOE Units		TDA Units	
1	Battalion (squadron)	11	Army Command
2	Company (troop, battery, or detachment)	12	Command or agency
3	Platoon	13	School or center
4	Squad or section	14	Activity
5	Crew or team	15	Department, directorate, or division
6	Brigade (group or regiment0	16	Branch
7	Division	17	Detachment, facility, office, or team
8	Corps	18	Garrison or installation
9	Echelons above corps		
TDA table of distribution and allowances		TOE table of organization and equipment	

B-9. The school or proponent assigns the last set of four digits of the task number. These four digits are unique to the particular task and echelon. In the example of 07-2-5135, the **5135** is the given example.

Appendix B

TASK TITLE

B-10. The task title includes both the task evaluated and the echelon to which it applies. If a task applies to multiple unit types at the same echelon, the title only lists the echelon (like company). In the example in figure B-2 on page B-2, the task number 07-2-5135 identifies the infantry task: Operate a Company Command Post – Company.

DISTRIBUTION RESTRICTION

B-11. The distribution restriction identifies any restrictions to distribution. The restriction is specified by the proponent.

DESTRUCTION NOTICE

B-12. The destruction notice identifies special destruction guidance. Usually the destruction notice correlates with a certain distribution restriction. The proponent includes any destruction instructions here.

FOREIGN DISCLOSURE

B-13. The foreign disclosure identifies any restrictions imposed when sharing the T&EO with foreign sources. The proponent provides any foreign disclosure instructions here.

SUPPORTING REFERENCES

B-14. The supporting references element identifies the supporting references for each performance step. The table for the supporting references lists the step number, reference identification, reference name, required, and primary reference source.

CONDITION

B-15. A task condition statement provides the general information required to allow multiple units to perform a task to standard based on common doctrine. The condition statement identifies the situation and training environment in which the unit should be able to perform the task to standard. See the sample text in figure B-2 on page B-2.

STANDARD

B-16. The task standard statement provides the criteria for determining the minimum acceptable proficiency of task performance under operating conditions. Users reference the objective task evaluation criteria matrix (see figure B-3) for minimum acceptable standards. The school or proponent specifies and modifies the matrix based on the requirements of the task, unit type, and echelon.

OBJECTIVE TASK EVALUATION CRITERIA MATRIX

B-17. The objective task evaluation criteria matrix as seen in figure B-3 enables unit leaders to evaluate unit task proficiency more accurately and more objectively. When the commander assesses unit task proficiency, and the unit has not performed the task at echelon (as an entire unit), the commander can then consider proficiency of subordinate units on the task. In this case, the commander's assessment of task proficiency should be no higher than the lowest task proficiency assessment of any subordinate unit. After commanders consider T&EOs and other sources of bottom-up feedback, commanders can subjectively upgrade or downgrade an assessment of a unit's MET proficiency.

Training and Evaluation Outlines

Plan and Prepare				Execute						Assess
Operational Environment			Training Environment (L/V/C)	% Leaders present at training/authorized	% Present at training/authorized	External evaluation	Performance measures	Critical performance measures	Leader performance measures	Task assessment
SQD and PLT	CO and BN	BDE and above								
Dynamic (single threat)	Dynamic and complex (4 + OE variables and hybrid threat)	Dynamic and complex (all OE variables and hybrid threat)	Night	≥85%	≥80%	Yes	≥90% GO	All	≥90%	T
				75-84%			80-90% GO		80-89%	T-
Static (single threat)	Dynamic (single threat)	Dynamic and complex (all OE variables and single threat)		65-74%	75-79%		65-79% GO			P
				60-64%	60-74%	No	51-64% GO			P-
	Static (single threat)	Dynamic & complex (< all OE variables and single threat)	Day	<60%	<60%		<51% GO	<All	<80%	U

← Task Dependent → ← Task Independent →

BDE	brigade	OE	operational environment	T	fully trained
BN	battalion	P	practiced	T-	trained
C	constructive	P-	marginally practiced	U	untrained
CO	company	PLT	platoon	V	virtual
L	live	SQD	squad		

Note: The percentages used in this figure are for illustration only. See the collective task's published training and evaluation outline for the applicable percentages.

Figure B-3. Objective task evaluation criteria matrix

TERMS OF REFERENCE

B-18. Proponents use several terms of reference for the objective task evaluation criteria matrix.

Appendix B

Operational Environment

B-19. The proponent describes the variables of an operational environment in the condition paragraph of the T&EO. The school or proponent builds a near-peer competitor into the training scenario. It uses the following terms:

- **Static**—A static training environment has aspects of operational variables needed to stimulate mission variables that are fixed throughout the unit's execution of the task.
- **Dynamic**—A dynamic training environment has operational variables and threat TTP for assigned countertasks that change in response to the execution of friendly force tasks.
- **Complex**—A complex training environment requires a minimum of four—terrain, time, military (threat), and social (population)—or more operational variables; brigade and higher units require all eight operational variables to be replicated in varying degrees based on the task being trained.
- **Single threat**—A single threat in a training environment is a conventional force, irregular force, criminal element, or terrorist force.
- **Hybrid threat**—A hybrid threat in a training environment uses diverse and dynamic combination of conventional forces, irregular forces, terrorist forces, and criminal elements unified to achieve mutually benefitting effects.

Training Environment

B-20. The proponent sets training environment conditions. The three training environments consist of live training, virtual training, and constructive training.

B-21. Live training is training executed in field conditions using tactical equipment. It involves real people operating real systems. Units can use TADSS to enhance live training.

B-22. Virtual training is training executed using computer-generated battlefields in simulators with the approximate characteristics of tactical weapon systems and vehicles. Sometimes called human-in-the-loop training, it involves real people operating simulated systems. Virtual training is used to exercise motor control, decision-making, and communication skills. Virtual training can involve learning the skills to operate actual equipment, for example, flying an aircraft. Gaming is a subset of the virtual environment. The military uses gaming technologies to create capabilities to help train individuals and organizations. Gaming supports the development of individual-level tasks and skills. Gaming also facilitates assessments of small-unit or team collective task training. Units can operate gaming in a stand-alone environment or integrate it with live or constructive training environments.

B-23. Constructive training uses computer models and simulations to exercise command and staff functions. It involves simulated people operating simulated systems. Constructive training can be conducted by units from platoon through echelons above corps.

Percent of Leaders Present

B-24. The unit records the percent of unit key leaders present at the training event. The objective task evaluation criteria matrix compares the number present against the numbers identified in the TOE, modified TOE, or TDA that authorized unit strength.

Percent Present for Training

B-25. The unit records the percent of the unit's members present at the training event. The objective task evaluation criteria matrix compares the number present against the numbers identified in the TOE, modified TOE, or TDA that authorized unit strength.

External Evaluation

B-26. An EXEVAL is an evaluation planned, coordinated, and executed by an organization outside the unit two levels up. The evaluating unit can be one level up or another like-type unit or echelon. All readiness reporting units in the Army undergo an EXEVAL to achieve and validate fully trained (T) or trained (T-) task proficiency standards.

Performance Measures

B-27. The proponent defines the performance measures for each task. The proponent identifies the performance measures in the applicable T&EO for the task.

Critical Performance Measures

B-28. The proponent defines critical performance measures for each task. The unit gets these measures in the applicable T&EO for the task.

Leader Performance Measures

B-29. The proponent defines the leader performance measures for each task. The proponent identifies the performance measures in the applicable T&EO for the task.

Task Assessment

B-30. The overall task assessment is determined by the highest assessment level of the lowest rated category. Once the evaluator has tallied up the GO and NO-GO performance steps and measures, the evaluator circles those measures on the objective task evaluation criteria matrix (see figure B-3 on page B-5). Present with other criteria that is aggregated across the matrix, the evaluator makes an objective task assessment using the highest level assessment of the lowest rated category. In figure B-3 on page B-5, all items except *Leader performance measures* were rated as *fully trained (T)*. Since the evaluator scored the performance measure as 80-89%, the *Task assessment* is scored as a *trained (T-)*.

LIVE FIRE

B-31. The proponent will indicate any requirements or specifications for live fire associated with the task.

SAFETY RISK

B-32. This is the risk level for any identified hazards that may be associated with the conduct of the task. ATP 5-19 identifies these risk levels as extremely high (EH), high (H), medium (M), and low (L).

CUE

B-33. A cue is a task condition that indicates why the unit performs the task. A cue also clarifies the aiding and limiting factors that set the stage for the conduct of the task.

DANGER, WARNING, AND CAUTION NOTICES

B-34. Users determine if the training warrants danger, warning, or caution notices. Users rate the risk and complete the appropriate box. See also ATP 5-19 for risk assessments.

REMARKS

B-35. This element provides space for the school or proponent to add additional clarifying details as necessary.

NOTES

B-36. The notes element clarifies the objective task evaluation criteria matrix standards. The school or proponent identifies leader tasks (conducted by a leader or leaders) with an asterisk (*). The school or proponent identifies critical steps or child steps with a plus sign (+). Proponents specify the GO and NO-GO criteria for both leader and critical steps.

Appendix B

PERFORMANCE STEPS

B-37. Performance steps are the major actions a unit must accomplish to perform a collective task to standard. Performance steps provide a sequential, step-by-step description of the discrete actions that compose a task. The steps are broken into plan steps, prepare steps, and execute steps. In each of these groups, the steps are numbered and in sequential order. A unit must perform each step. Some steps have no sub steps, and other steps have multiple sub steps. For instance in figure B-4, performance step #6 is "+The company commander issues an OPORD. Ensures that subordinates, attachments (as applicable), and staff section representatives(s) are present for the OPORD issuance." The performance step falls under the plan portion (not shown). In this example, step #6 has no sub steps but is a critical step (shown with the plus sign). Under the prepare step, step #8 reads "*Company leaders prepare for command post operations in coordination with the higher headquarters." This step has several sub steps and is conducted by a leader (shown with the asterisk). Each numbered performance step becomes a performance measure.

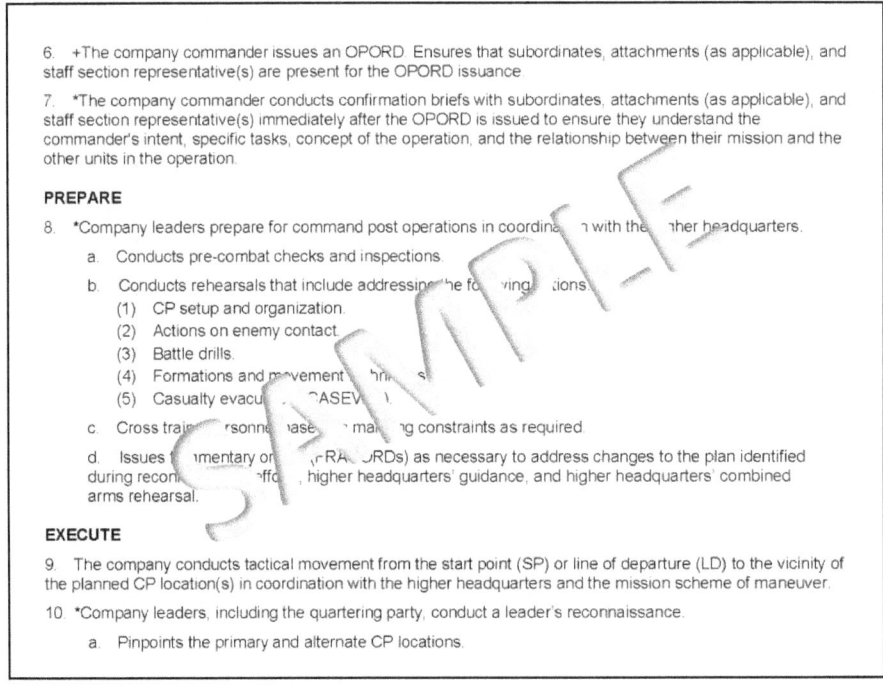

Figure B-4. Sample extract from T&EO illustrating performance steps

PERFORMANCE MEASURES

B-38. Performance measures are actions that are objectively observable, qualitative, and quantitative. Critical steps (or leader steps) are notated with a plus sign or an asterisk respectively. Evaluators and leaders use performance measures to determine if a unit satisfactorily achieves a performance step or sub step. Evaluators rate a unit's performance as GO, NO-GO, or N/A (for *not applicable*) measure (see figure B-5). If the performance step of a task was performed to standard, a GO is assessed for the associated performance measure. If a particular performance step in the task was not performed to standard, a NO-GO is assessed. If the measure does not apply at a particular echelon or is not observed during training of a particular unit, the evaluator can designate this in the N/A column so as not to affect the GO or NO-GO status of the unit.

Training and Evaluation Outlines

PERFORMANCE MEASURES	GO	NO-GO	N/A
1. The company gained and/or maintained situational understanding.	✓X		
2. +The company commander received the mission requiring operation of a command post and began execution of troop leading procedures.	✓X		
3. * The company commander issued the warning order (WARNORD).	✓X		
4. *The company commander coordinated with higher headquarters.	X	✓	
5. +The company commander conducted mission analysis focusing on the directed mission, enemy forces and their capabilities, terrain and weather effects, troops available, time available to execute the operation, and civil considerations (METT-TC) and developed a tentative plan.	X	✓	
6. +The company commander issued an OPORD.	X	✓	
7. *The company commander conducted confirmation briefs with subordinates immediately after the OPORD was issued to ensure subordinates understood commander's intent, specific tasks, concept of the operation, and the relationship between their mission and the other units in the operation.	✓X		
8. * Company leaders prepared for command post operations.	✓X		
9. The company conducted tactical movement from the start point (SP) or line of departure (LD) to the vicinity of the planned CP location(s).	X	✓	
10. *Company leaders, including the quartering party, conducted a leader's reconnaissance.		✓ X	
11. *The company commander or designated representative positioned the CP.	✓X		
12. +The company established security and conducted operations.	✓X		
13. * The company commander decided based on higher headquarters' OPORD and guidance whether to displace the command post.	✓X		
14. The company submitted SITREPs IAW the higher headquarters order.	X	✓	

TASK PERFORMANCE / EVALUATION SUMMARY BLOCK

ITERATION	1	2	3	4	5	M	TOTAL
TOTAL PERFORMANCE MEASURES EVALUATED	14	14					28
TOTAL PERFORMANCE MEASURES GO	8	13					21
TRAINING STATUS GO/NO-GO	NO-GO	GO					

ITERATION: 1 (2) 3 4 5 M
COMMANDER/LEADER ASSESSMENT: T (T-) P P- U

FRAGORD	fragmentary order	HQ	headquarters
M	mission-oriented protective posture	OPORD	operations order
P	practiced	P-	marginally practiced
T	fully trained	T-	trained
U	untrained		

Figure B-5. Sample extract from T&EO illustrating performance measures

TASK PERFORMANCE AND EVALUATION SUMMARY BLOCK

B-39. This block provides the evaluator a means of recording GO and NO-GO observed performances based on the iterations conducted (times the task was attempted). In the T&EO, the task performance and evaluation block provides a table of spaces that evaluators use to total the number performance measures evaluated, total the number of performance measures that scored a GO, and total the number of units with a GO or NO-GO training status. In figure B-5, the unit evaluated conducted 2 iterations of this particular task. The evaluator recorded a total of 28 performance measures observed, 21 of these recorded as GO. Only the recorded performance for the final iteration is carried over to the objective task evaluation criteria matrix (see figure B-3 on page B-5). In this example, the performance recorded in the final iteration was 12 of 14 measures recorded as a GO. The resulting percentage of 85% is circled in the corresponding percentage block of the performance measures column of the objective task evaluation criteria matrix.

Appendix B

ITERATION

B-40. This block provides a space for the evaluator to record the number of iterations (task attempts) the unit being observed performs. The 'M' column records an iteration performed while the unit was in mission-oriented protective posture (MOPP).

COMMANDER/LEADER ASSESSMENT

B-41. Since the final iteration performed is recorded in the objective task evaluation criteria matrix, the commander/leader records the corresponding performance rating here.

Mission(s) Supported

B-42. The proponent indicates any specific missions with which this task may be associated.

Mission-Oriented Protective Posture 4

B-43. This block indicates if the task must be performed under a specific MOPP. It will also include any additional instructions for the conduct of the task in the MOPP.

Mission-Oriented Protective Posture 4 Statement

B-44. If the task is to be performed specifically in MOPP 4, the proponent identifies any additional performance requirements or limitations for task execution.

Night Vision Goggles

B-45. This block indicates if this task must be performed under conditions of limited visibility and if night vision goggles (known as NVGs) are required in the execution of the task.

Night Vision Goggles Statement

B-46. The proponent specifies any additional instructions or limitations in the use of night vision goggles that are used in the performance of the task.

PREREQUISITE COLLECTIVE TASKS

B-47. Prerequisite collective tasks are tasks that have a first-order effect on setting the conditions for the task. Prerequisite collective tasks apply to the majority of the population trained.

B-48. For several tasks on the T&EO, evaluators record each step number, each task number, the title of the task, the proponent of the task, and the status of the unit evaluated. The step number is the performance step (discussed in paragraph B-37) and its associated title. The task number is the number that leads the T&EO (discussed in paragraph B-6). The task title is the title of the task number (discussed in paragraph B-10).

OPPOSING FORCE TASKS

B-49. OPFOR tasks are tasks that list any OPFOR tasks required in support of the task trained.

SUPPORTING COLLECTIVE TASKS

B-50. A supporting collective task is a task that supports another collective task.

SUPPORTING INDIVIDUAL TASKS

B-51. Supporting individual tasks are tasks performed to enable the successful performance of the supported collective task. The individual must perform the individual task so the unit can accomplish the collective task. Proficiency must occur at the individual task level before it can occur at the collective task level.

SUPPORTING DRILL TASKS

B-52. Supporting drill tasks are any drill tasks associated with the task trained. Supporting drills enable the successful performance of the supported collective task.

SUPPORTED UNIVERSAL JOINT TASK LIST TASKS

B-53. If the task is linked to or associated with a universal joint task list (known as UJTL) task, note the task here.

TRAINING AIDS, DEVICES, SIMULATORS, AND SIMULATIONS

B-54. TADSS includes a list of any TADSS that units may use in support of the task trained.

EQUIPMENT AND MATERIEL

B-55. Equipment and materiel lists the resources relevant to the task trained. For collective tasks, users limit the inclusion of equipment and materiel items to those relevant to the target population trained.

Equipment

B-56. Equipment includes those items that are relevant to the task being trained. These are identified by the equipment's line item number (known as LIN). For collective tasks, the inclusion of equipment is limited to that which is relevant to the target audience trained.

Materiel

B-57. Materiel includes those items that are relevant to the task being trained. These are identified by the materiel's national stock number (known as NSN). For collective tasks, the inclusion of materiel is limited to that which is relevant to the target audience trained.

ENVIRONMENT

B-58. The proponent states specific environmental protection requirements for the task.

SAFETY

B-59. The proponent states any additional safety risk requirements associated with the task in accordance with ATP 5-19. These are in addition to the safety risk level noted in paragraph B-32.

This page intentionally left blank.

Appendix C
Company Training Meetings

PURPOSE

C-1. Training meetings provide the commander and unit leaders with visibility of the current state of unit training readiness and are the key to keeping the UTP on course. Accordingly, they are a recurring entry on the company's weekly training schedule. Training meetings also facilitate the top-down/bottom-up flow of training information and coordination. The T-Week concept provides the general framework and guide for planning and coordination of training events during training meetings (see appendix H).

> *Note.* Although this appendix focuses on the company level, training meetings held at battalion and brigade are no less important and are equally vital to ensuring unit training proficiency. Training meetings at all echelons apply the basic ideas discussed in this appendix.

C-2. Feedback is an important aspect of training meetings and is used to refine the UTP as it progresses. Feedback takes many forms including personal observation, AARs, and informal evaluations. Subordinates provide their bottom-up feedback when they assess the training proficiency needs of the unit and individual Soldiers. Leaders provide top-down feedback when they conduct training meetings. The agenda of a training meeting includes reviewing past training, identifying and planning necessary retraining, planning and preparing future training, and exchanging timely training information between leaders. A training meeting is a forum for discussing training assessments and unit, leader, and task proficiencies.

C-3. Training meetings are not a forum for discussion of administrative operations or activities not related to training. Training is the sole topic. Training meetings have three goals:
- Review past training (previous week) to include—
  - Training scheduled but not conducted and the reason why it was not conducted.
  - The commander's review of bottom-up feedback and assessment of tasks trained. After the assessment, commanders record them in DTMS.
- Review future training events (to T-Week 5) to include—
  - Re-confirming the training focus and training objectives for future events. Validate tasks (collective and individual) to train focusing on the METs.
  - Ensuring training resources are coordinated and locked in for each event as well as resolving resource discrepancies.
- Ensure that face-to-face cross-communication between leaders occurs and that they discuss and resolve training issues. Subordinate leaders provide assessments of proficiencies as well as ensure tasks trained at platoon, squad, and individual levels are executed and assessed to standard and support the tasks the company must train.

C-4. Successful training meetings—
- Validate the tasks (collective and individual) to train for upcoming events, focusing on the METs.
- Synchronize unit METs with training events.
- Delegate and confirm responsibilities critical to executing events.
- Review and confirm resource requirements and statuses.
- Ensure communication between leaders.
- Refine the training focus—METs and training objectives—for upcoming events.

C-5. Leaders alternate training events with training meetings. After a unit executes tasks during a training event, the leader assesses the unit's performance of the training event. The unit continues to retrain the MET to standard until it attains proficiency. When an external trainer makes an assessment, the commander records the unit proficiency in the DTMS. See figure C-1.

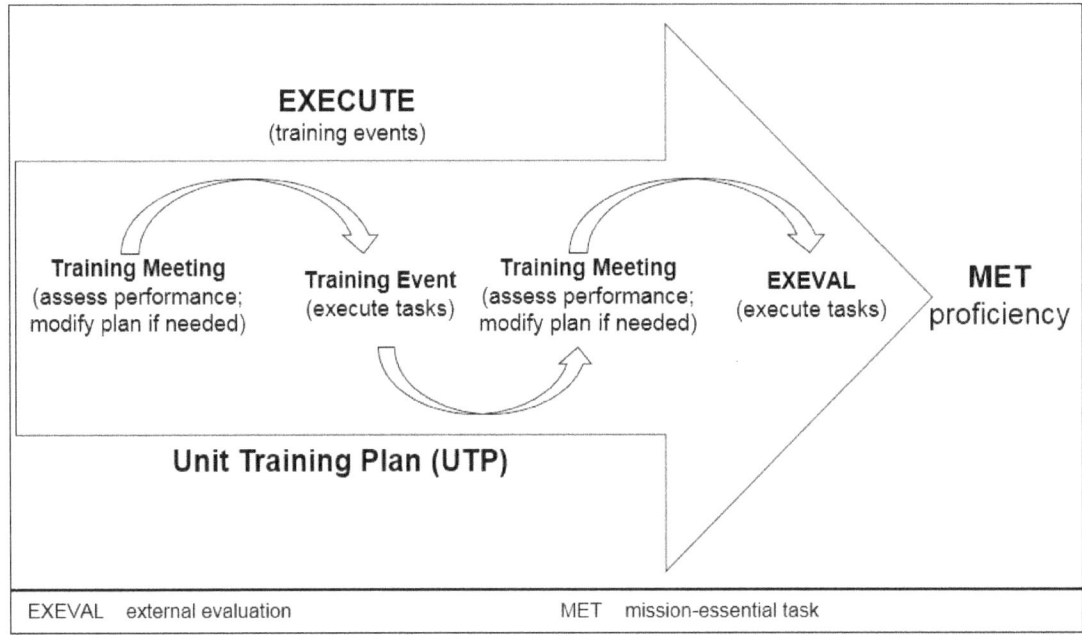

Figure C-1. UTP processes from execution to MET proficiency

C-6. Commanders individually manage and coordinate each training event to ensure the UTP is executed as designed. If the staff needs to modify the UTP based on the unit achieving (or not achieving) specific, published training objectives, then the staff uses the commander's guidance given during training meetings. This guidance drives future training event planning, and ultimately, the UTP.

PARTICIPANTS

C-7. Leader participation is essential for a successful company training meeting. The commander determines the participants to attend. Paragraphs C-8 through C-17 lists suggested participants to attend company training meetings and their responsibilities.

COMPANY COMMANDER

C-8. The commander (known as CO) runs the training meeting and is responsible for following the agenda. Prior to the meeting, the commander updates the training estimate of the company's proficiency to meet UTP training objectives. The commander reviews the assessment of the collective tasks to train, the UTP calendar, upcoming training schedules, and upcoming training event OPORDs. The commander then provides guidance for upcoming events and adjusts the focus for future training events' based on this review. Next, the commander confirms the status of resource requests and their requirements. The commander updates the training estimate—to include collective task assessment, training risk status of external resources, and status of trainers—and specifies the individual Soldier tasks for hip-pocket training with advice from a company first sergeant.

EXECUTIVE OFFICER

C-9. The executive officer (known as XO) runs the training meeting in the commander's absence and coordinates training for all the Soldiers in sections or attachments without platoon leaders or platoon sergeants. The executive officer reviews the current assessment for METs and supporting collective tasks. The executive officer provides the status of resources to support upcoming events and identifies resource issues affecting upcoming training. Additionally, the executive officer identifies and consolidates new resource requirements based on an adjustment of tasks to train for upcoming events.

FIRST SERGEANT

C-10. The first sergeant (known as 1SG) is the senior enlisted advisor to the commander on all issues that affect not only individual training in the unit but also collective training. The first sergeant provides an assessment of individual and collective tasks as well as on training of key warrior tasks and battle drills that support the company's collective tasks to train. The first sergeant provides guidance and advice on training plans and reviews preexecution checks discussed during the training meeting. Additionally, the first sergeant helps in the leader development of officers and NCOs by actively participating in forming effective training plans for platoons (tasks to train and identification of resource requirements). The first sergeant advises the commander on the selection of individual Soldier tasks for hip-pocket training.

PLATOON LEADERS

C-11. Based on training conducted, platoon leaders brief on their assessments of collective tasks and on training of key leader tasks, warrior tasks, and battle drill proficiency of their platoon. Platoon leaders recommend adjusting training focus (tasks to train) for upcoming events based on their assessments. Additionally, they confirm previously submitted resource requirements for upcoming events, or they identify new resource requests based on a change to the training focus for an upcoming event.

PLATOON SERGEANTS

C-12. Platoon sergeants provide their assessment of section- or crew-level and individual tasks based on training conducted. They observe and receive feedback from squad leaders on the status of individual training conducted and support the company's collective tasks. Platoon sergeants brief the status of specific essential preexecution checks—including the status of trainer, resources, tasks to train, or site reconnaissance—for upcoming events. Additionally, platoon sergeants provide input to any changes—such as collective tasks, warrior tasks, battle drills to train, and resource requirements—to upcoming events.

KEY STAFF NONCOMMISSIONED OFFICERS

C-13. Master gunners and other key staff NCOs attend training meetings and advise the commander on the status of specialized training. For example, the master gunner works with the first sergeant to track individual and crew-served weapons qualifications and helps leaders with gunnery training assessments. Other key NCOs identify and advise leaders on opportunities to integrate specialized training into upcoming events. Additionally, they advise leaders on specialized resource requirements for upcoming events.

SUPPORTING MAINTENANCE PERSONNEL

C-14. Supporting maintenance personnel coordinate the maintenance efforts of the company and work with the commander and executive officer to ensure timely support is provided. Supporting maintenance personnel provide input on the status of maintenance training in the company, recommend maintenance-related training, and inform the commander of scheduled services and inspections that will impact training. These personnel identify any issues that will impact upcoming training events. Additionally, they may advise the commander on maintenance training requirements based on an assessment of training previously conducted.

Supply Sergeants

C-15. Supply sergeants provide input to the commander on supply-related issues, inspections, and inventories. Supply sergeants also work with the executive officer and first sergeant to coordinate necessary support from outside sources. They assist the executive officer and first sergeant in identifying,

Appendix C

coordinating, and resourcing logistic support requirements—internal and external—for future training events.

Master Gunners

C-16. Unit master gunners (if applicable) provide the status of training and requirements for gunnery for the entire unit. They continually coordinate and update this information with the company executive officer and first sergeant prior to the training meeting.

Attached and Other Support Leaders

C-17. Other leaders attend training meetings to coordinate their training efforts with those of the company. For example, a commander for an artillery battery with an attached target acquisition radar section may attend the meeting. These leaders provide their assessment of tasks and battle drills previously trained. They confirm the tasks to train and the status of resource requirements for upcoming events. Commanders must fully integrate and support the training of all habitually associated units. Reserve Component companies may have personnel associated with the Regular Army attend the training meetings. These personnel bring valuable experiences and the latest training techniques from Regular Army units.

ROUTINES FOR TRAINING MEETING

C-18. Company training meetings have set routines. They occur at a regular time and place while following a set agenda. Company training meetings include updating company METs and coordinating for training. Lastly, training meetings include a review of preexecution checks as well as a plan for future training.

TRAINING MEETING RECURRENCE TIME

C-19. Generally, leaders conduct training meetings on the same day and time each week. This regularity provides a degree of battle rhythm in training, consistency, and predictability. Leaders can conduct training meetings using collaborative electronic means, like a video teleconference (commonly known as VTC), or a teleconference as necessary.

C-20. Leaders consider several factors before selecting a time to conduct training meetings. Main considerations include—
- Enabling leaders to attend.
- Minimizing training disruptions.
- Allowing subordinate leaders time to prepare.
- Local policy.

C-21. Reserve Component company commanders encounter more challenges when scheduling training meetings. They have three alternatives:
- Conduct the meeting during a regularly scheduled drill period.
- Conduct the meeting during an additional training assembly.
- Conduct the training meeting during a "for points only" or non-paid assembly.

TRAINING MEETING AGENDA

C-22. The agenda is keyed to the T-Week concept (see a detailed discussion in appendix H). There are three phases to company training meetings. The first is used to assess previous training (T-Week +1). The second phase is used to coordinate upcoming events (T-Week 5 through T-Week 1). The final phase is used to plan training for future training events (T-Week 7 and T-Week 6). The agenda maintains a focus for all to see, understand, and follow. Staffs post the agenda prior to the meeting.

Agenda Items

C-23. In the first phase of the training meeting agenda, the commander reviews the previous week's training:
- Update the platoon or subordinate element assessments, to include collective and individual tasks, warrior tasks, and battle drill training (T-Week +1).
- Identify training not conducted.
- Update company assessments (METs).
- Identify retraining required.
- Identify DTMS database update requirements and responsibilities.

C-24. In the second phase of the training meeting agenda, the commander coordinates by—
- Reviewing FRAGORDs that include new or updated command guidance.
- Conducting preexecution checks T-Week 5 through T-Week 1.
- Identifying any changes to upcoming events (tasks to train).

C-25. In the third phase of the training meeting agenda, the commander discusses future planning:
- Review battalion and company UTP calendar for adjustment as needed.
- Provide commander's updated planning guidance for events (adjust training focus of events).
- Demonstrate how platoon tasks support the company METLs (from the company UTP).
- Review the draft training schedule for T-Week 6 and T-Week 7.
- Review the major T-Week milestones for T-Week 8 through UTP publication, assign responsibility for the tasks, and receive updates.
- Confirm and identify additional resource requirements.

Time Requirements

C-26. Training meetings should not last more than an hour and a half if well organized. The intent is for the commander to achieve the meeting objectives as quickly and efficiently as possible. See table C-1 for an approximate times for each phase of a training meeting.

Table C-1. Times for training meeting agenda

Action	Time
Review of previous week's training	30 Minutes
Preparation for T-5 through T-1 training	30 Minutes
Future planning (T-7 and T-6), including a review of major milestones (T-8 through UTP publication)	30 Minutes
T training week UTP unit training plan	

Review Last Week's Training

C-27. Commanders begin the meeting by discussing the training just completed. The bottom-up input by the platoon leaders and platoon sergeants is critical to assessing collective, leader, and individual training proficiency of the unit. Company leaders discuss the agenda items listed in paragraphs C-28 through C-31. Commanders then record the assessments in DTMS.

Platoon Assessment

C-28. Platoon leaders and platoon sergeants assess collective and battle task proficiency ratings and Soldier proficiency ratings since the last training meeting. The sources of the platoon assessment may be formal or informal and based on the task T&EO. A platoon assessment includes—

Appendix C

- Collective tasks, battle tasks, leader tasks, Soldier tasks, warrior tasks, and battle drills.
- The proficiency rating—fully trained (T), trained (T-), practiced (P), marginally practiced (P-), and untrained (U)—of all training conducted by the platoon assessments from T&EOs (also GO and NO-GO results from the performance steps, as necessary).

Training Shortfalls

C-29. As each platoon completes the training assessment, leaders address training shortfalls. A training shortfall occurs when a unit plans training but does conduct it. Platoon leaders must explain to the commander the reasons for not executing training and the plans to reschedule the missed training. A training shortfall also occurs when a unit fails to meet training objectives. If a unit fails to meet objectives, it must retrain on those tasks until it earns a fully trained (T) or trained (T-) proficiency rating score. Commanders record training shortfalls that include—

- Training planned but not conducted (include discussion of tasks not trained).
- The reason for not executing training.
- A retraining plan, if needed.

C-30. Assessment of completed training may reveal training that is incomplete or not conducted to the Army standard. Leaders conduct retraining at the first opportunity, ideally during the same training period. However, when this cannot happen, leaders may need to adjust subsequent training events (adding or subtracting tasks to train) to retrain on those tasks that the unit failed to train to standard. Staff then adjust the UTP for future events.

C-31. In reviewing retraining requirements, company leaders consider several factors:

- The number of Soldiers or elements involved.
- The sequential order of retraining with other planned training. Leaders determine if one task needs to be trained before proceeding to a future task.
- Resource availability (such as ranges, instructors, and logistics).
- Original planning and modification for the task, as necessary.
- The time and place to conduct rescheduled training at the first available opportunity.
- The resources available, in particular the resources needed to retrain a task. Retraining takes priority over training new tasks.

UPDATED COMPANY MISSION-ESSENTIAL TASK ASSESSMENTS

C-32. Once subordinates have provided their assessments, the commander and first sergeant provide their input to training conducted and identify any training shortfalls. This process not only ensures a common understanding of the commander's training end state (based on the unit mission and guidance) for the unit but also develops subordinate leaders. Through this open dialogue, commanders hold their subordinate leaders responsible for training their respective organizations. This is a critical aspect of the process as it is imperative that leaders develop subordinates.

C-33. After all platoons complete their training assessments and discuss any training shortfalls, the commander—with input from the first sergeant, platoon leaders, and executive officer—ensures that company MET assessments are updated in DTMS.

COORDINATION FOR SHORT-RANGE TRAINING

C-34. Coordination for training (T-Week 5 through T-Week 1) requires a review of command guidance and preexecution checks.

Review of Command Guidance

C-35. During a review of command guidance, the unit reviews FRAGORDs or any other new or updated command guidance that will impact training (T-Week 5 through T-Week 1). The guidance could be either externally directed or based on the commander's assessment of the unit. Commanders convey the purpose of the training and the desired end state, but exercising mission command, they leave the how to achieve the results to subordinates. This latitude allows subordinates to use their critical and creative thinking to support the commander's guidance and vision. Additionally, leaders understand and assess the impact of this command guidance on the current training plan, discussing this impact and its associated risks.

C-36. Leaders identify training events that the staff will modify to incorporate the tasks previously identified during the assessment of last week's training. Again, leaders discuss the adjustments to the current training plan to understand clearly their impact on the commander's end state for upcoming training. Once leaders understand the training focus for the upcoming events, the company leadership reviews key aspects of the preexecution checks for these events.

Preexecution Checks

C-37. Preexecution checks are procedures, usually using checklists, employed to ensure all planning and prerequisite training (collective, Soldier, and leader) has been conducted prior to the execution of training. These are not precombat checks. A critical part of the training meeting is the discussion of preexecution checks. Preexecution checks are developed by the chain of command, and responsibility for their execution is fixed to ensure training is resourced and conducted properly. As units develop training schedules more fully, these checks become increasingly detailed. Preexecution checks provide the attention to detail that units need to use time and other resources efficiently.

C-38. Units modify and refine their lists based on their specific organization and mission. See figure C-2 on page C-8 for sample questions for the preexecution checks. Units strive to answer each question with a yes. If a unit fails to answer in the affirmative, then it has failed to meet that requirement.

C-39. By reviewing preexecution checks, the commander ensures training events are fully planned and coordinated with all elements of the company. The time for the company to complete the checks depends on unit and organization SOPs. It is imperative the company commander understands the resource timeline requirements. Regular Army commanders plan one to six weeks out (or even further based on requesting timelines for resources) when reviewing preexecution checks. Reserve Component commanders plan for three months. Within these training windows, commanders review preexecution checks in reverse order. Commanders start at the last week (for Regular Army) or last month (for Reserve Component) and work down until the next training period is covered in detail. Preexecution checks should be a part of the unit's SOP for training.

C-40. The primary trainer indicated on the training schedule briefs preexecution checks. If the primary trainer is the platoon sergeant, then the platoon sergeant briefs the preexecution checks during the training meeting. For almost every training event for platoon and below, the platoon sergeant is the key coordinator. The platoon sergeant coordinates the efforts of other NCOs in the platoon and ensures that training is thoroughly prepared.

Appendix C

- Has unit integrated the lessons learned since the last time they conducted training?
- Is the opposing force equipped and trained (if applicable)?
- Has unit integrated attached elements into planning and execution of training?
- Has unit completed a DD Form 2977 (*Deliberate Risk Assessment Worksheet*)?
- Do the trainers have the list of tasks to be trained?
- Have leaders identified prerequisite tasks for the training event? Are Soldiers trained on prerequisite tasks prior to the event?
- Does unit have leaders certified to conduct range operations?
- Are trainers identified and available for training?
- Do trainers have training and evaluation outlines for all tasks to be trained?
- Do trainers have a copy of the operation order?
- Has unit programmed rehearsal time for trainers?
- Has unit requested training ranges, facilities, and training areas?
- Has unit conducted a reconnaissance?
- Does unit have range or maneuver books on hand?
- Has unit submitted and received approval for convoy clearances?
- Has unit identified, requested, and approved training aids, devices, simulators, and simulations (TADSS)?
- Can trainers properly operate all TADSS?
- Has unit requested Class I (food)?
- Has unit requested and picked up Class II (fuel)?
- Has unit requested and picked up Class V (ammunition)?
- Has unit requested transportation?
- Does unit have sufficient expendable supplies on hand?
- Has unit deconflicted external taskings and appointments?
- Has unit scheduled time for retraining as necessary?
- Has unit specified the recovery plan in the operation order?
- Has unit scheduled time for an after action review?
- Has unit coordinated the backbrief for the chain of command?

Figure C-2. Sample preexecution checks questions

PLAN FOR FUTURE TRAINING

C-41. In the third phase of the training meeting, the commander discusses future planning. Agenda items for this phase include the following:

- Review battalion and company UTP including its calendar for adjustments.
- Provide the commander's updated planning guidance for events (training objectives).
- Demonstrate how platoon tasks support company METs.
- Review draft training schedule for T-Week 7 and T-Week 6.
- Confirm and identify additional resource requirements.
- Identify individual tasks for hip-pocket training.

C-42. The company commander must check the battalion UTP. Events indicated on the battalion UTP calendar or found in the UTP are put on the company training schedule first. After these events are posted, the commander issues guidance (company tasks to train and the end state of training) for these future events. These tasks support the company's METs from the UTP and the battalion's training focus for the event. The commander's guidance starts the planning process to support the company's training focus, identify tasks, and develop preexecution checks to fix responsibilities.

HIP-POCKET TRAINING

C-43. Hip-pocket training usually consists of individual tasks on which the unit can train when it experiences inactive periods during scheduled training. Ideally, leaders train these selected tasks in 15 to 30 minutes since more time may not be available. It is another technique for managing sustainment training. Normally, the company commander selects tasks for this type of training. Commanders can use training meetings to obtain input from subordinates on what training needs to be sustained. Hip-pocket training gives leaders confidence in their abilities to train and results in more efficient use of Soldiers' time. Initial training or collective task training ordinarily requires more time and resources than will be available for short notice, unscheduled training. Figure C-3 illustrates implementing hip-pocket training.

Prior to going to the range, SGT Smith checked her squad's individual proficiencies using the DTMS. She noticed there were two tasks on which she could focus hip-pocket training to improve squad proficiencies: Employ Hand Grenade (#150-AWT-1002) and Perform First Aid for an Open Chest Wound (#081-831-1026). Knowing that there was most likely an opportunity for down time at the range, she printed out the T&EOs for these tasks.

SGT Smith and her squad are participating in the company hand grenade range. The squad has an hour until it goes to the firing line. With this downtime before engaging targets with grenades, SGT Smith recognizes a good opportunity to train.

She goes through the tasks with her squad. She first reads the task title, conditions, and standards of each. She then demonstrates executing each task, focusing on the performance step and measures to do each task correctly. She then has the squad members perform the task individually, noting their performance on the corresponding T&EO. After each squad member performs the tasks multiple times, SGT Smith is satisfied that they perform these two tasks to the stated standard. She conducts an informal AAR, reviewing what each individual was supposed to do, getting them to describe what they actually did, and as a group getting them to discuss how they could perform these two tasks better.

Just as SGT Smith completes the AAR, the range NCO in charge calls the squad to the firing line. When they redeploy to garrison, SGT Smith records not just their range results but also the results of their hip-pocket training in each Soldier's individual training record within DTMS.

Figure C-3. Notional hip-pocket training

PLATOON LEADER AND PLATOON SERGEANT INPUT

C-44. Based on their training assessments, platoon leaders and platoon sergeants review current events identified in the company UTP and validate tasks to train to improve training proficiency. Additionally, these leaders discuss resource requirements. Platoon leaders and platoon sergeants brief the resulting plans (adjusted training focus for future events) to the commander during the training meeting.

TRAINING SCHEDULE DEVELOPMENT

C-45. Commanders receive input from all platoons and other elements of the company before formulating the draft training schedule. Because of support limitations or other conflicts, the commander may have to disapprove a training event that a platoon requested or move it to another week (Regular Army) or month (Reserve Component).

This page intentionally left blank.

Appendix D
After Action Reviews

PURPOSE

D-1. An *after action review* is a guided analysis of an organization's performance, conducted at appropriate times during and at the conclusion of a training event or operation with the objective of improving future performance. It includes a facilitator, event participants, and other observers. The AAR provides valuable feedback essential to correcting training deficiencies. Feedback must be direct, immediate, and standards-based.

D-2. The AAR is a professional discussion that requires the active participation of those being trained. AARs enable units or Soldiers to discover for themselves what happened and then develop a plan for improving performance. These reviews provide candid insights into strengths and weaknesses from various perspectives and feedback, and focus directly on the commander's guidance, training objectives, and standards. Leaders know and enforce standards for collective and individual tasks. Task standards are performance measures found in the respective T&EOs.

D-3. Leaders avoid creating the environment of a critique during AARs. A critique only gives one viewpoint and frequently provides little opportunity for discussion of events by participants. The climate of the critique, focusing only on what is wrong, prevents candid and open discussions of training events and stifles learning and team building. Since Soldiers and leaders participating in an AAR actively self-discover what happened and why, they learn and remember more than they would from a critique alone. Unlike a critique, an AAR—

- Focuses directly on training objectives.
- Emphasizes meeting the Army standard on collective and individual tasks rather than judging success or failure.
- Uses leading questions to encourage participants to self-discover important lessons from the training event.
- Allows a large number of Soldiers and leaders (including OPFORs) to participate so that more of the training can be recalled and more lessons learned can be shared.
- Assigns responsibility for a timeline to improve performance improvement measures.

D-4. Leaders make on-the-spot corrections when training Soldiers and units. These corrections occur when leaders understand the commander's guidance as well as the tasks to be trained to improve Soldier, leader, and unit performance. Units that conduct AARs and empower subordinates to make on-the-spot corrections are more effective.

D-5. Effective AARs reflect the commander and the commander's active role in unit training. AARs foster an environment of trust, collaboration, initiative, and cohesion necessary among Soldiers and leaders in decentralized operations. Soldiers learn and understand the commander's guidance and act decisively while accepting prudent risks.

TYPES OF AFTER ACTION REVIEWS

D-6. There are two types of AARs, formal and informal. A formal AAR is resource-intensive and involves planning for and preparing the AAR site, supporting training aids, and supporting personnel. Informal AARs require less planning and preparation. Any AAR—formal or informal—also analyzes any moral-ethical decisions that the unit made during the execution of a task. Both AARs involve all Soldiers and focus on what was planned, what happened, what worked, and how to improve performance and increase complexity within the commander's guidance. See table D-1 one page D-2 for a comparison of.

Appendix D

FORMAL

D-7. Leaders plan formal AARs at the same time they finalize their training plan (six to eight weeks before execution). Formal AARs require more planning and preparation than informal AARs. They require site reconnaissance and selection, coordination for training aids (such as terrain models or map blow-ups), and selection, set up, and maintenance of the AAR site.

D-8. During formal AARs, the AAR facilitator—unit leader or OC/T—identifies and facilitates a discussion of specific events based on training objectives, performance measures, the commander's guidance, and a plan to achieve it. The facilitator provides an overview of the training events plan (what was supposed to happen) and facilitates a discussion of actually what happened during execution, identifying strengths, weaknesses, and issues. Participants then identify what retraining needs to be conducted and how to conduct the tasks differently to achieve the desired outcomes. The facilitator concludes the AAR by reviewing key points, reviewing issues, summarizing observed strengths and weaknesses, and restating the participants' identification of how to improve performance to meet the commander's guidance.

INFORMAL

D-9. Leaders conduct the informal AAR after previously identified events or as on-the-spot coaching while reviewing unit and Soldier performance during training. Due to time constraints and other limitations, conducting informal AARs at appropriate times as the training event progresses allows for on-the-spot corrections that enable immediate improved performance. Informal AARs—with immediate correction and retraining—also enable overall improved unit performance as the unit concludes its training event or scenario. Informal AARs provide immediate feedback to Soldiers, leaders, and units during training. Ideas and solutions gathered during informal AARs can be put to use as the unit continues its training.

D-10. Informal AARs require fewer training aids than formal AARs. For example, after destroying an enemy observation post during a movement to contact, the squad leader conducts an informal AAR to make corrections and reinforce strengths. Using nothing more than pinecones to represent squad members, the squad leader and squad members discuss the contact from start to finish. The squad quickly—
- Identifies what was supposed to happen.
- Establishes what happened from all levels.
- Evaluates performance against the Army standard (as stated in the task's T&EO).
- Identifies strengths and weaknesses.
- Identifies opportunities to improve performance within the commander's guidance when training continues.

Table D-1. Comparison of formal and informal after action reviews

	Formal	Informal
Conductor	Conducted by either internal or external leaders and external OC/Ts	Conducted by internal chain of command and internal OC/Ts
Duration	Takes more time to prepare	Takes less time to prepare
Aids	Uses complex training aids	Uses simple training aids
Schedule	Scheduled—leaders identify events and tasks beforehand	Unscheduled—conducted as needed, primarily based on leader assessment
Location	Conducted where best supported	Conducted at the training site
OC/T observer-controller/trainer		

FUNDAMENTALS OF TRAINING AFTER ACTION REVIEW

D-11. AARs have the following fundamentals characteristics. They—
- Are conducted during or immediately after each event.
- Focus on commander's guidance, training objectives, and standards.

After Action Reviews

- Focus on Soldier, leader, and unit performance.
- Involve all participants in the discussion.
- Use open-ended questions.
- Encourage initiative and innovation in finding more effective ways to achieve standards, to meet training objectives, and to meet the commander's guidance.
- Determine strengths and weaknesses.
- Link performance to subsequent training.

AGENDA FOR TRAINING AFTER ACTION REVIEW

D-12. AARs conducted during training follow the same agenda as AARs conducted during operations:
- Review what was supposed to happen.
- Establish what happened.
- Determine what was right or wrong with what happened.
- Determine how to perform the task differently next time.

D-13. A training AAR begins with a review of what was supposed to happen. A facilitator (sometimes called an evaluator), along with participants, reviews what was supposed to happen. This review is based on the commander's guidance, training objectives, and tasks to train. An OPORD or the training schedule typically contains information that states what was supposed to happen. This information is repeated in the training plan. The facilitator also reviews the UTP, training objectives, applicable individual training records, and T&EOs. Ideally, the leader of the evaluated unit conducts the AAR with assistance from an evaluator or OC/T.

D-14. The training AAR continues as the evaluator establishes what happened. The facilitator and participants determine what actually occurred during the training event, phase, or operation. The leader attempts to gather as many views or perspectives—such as from the OPFOR, squad leader, team leader, or rifleman—as feasible. These views help to establish a common understanding of the operation or event. Leaders then understand the complexity of an event and work to solve complex, ill-defined problems quickly. An effective AAR requires an accurate account of events. The evaluator and participants determine what actually happened during performance of the task. The discussion that follows is only as good as the accuracy of the events. For force-on-force training, OPFOR members assist in describing the flow of the training event and both the evaluated unit and OPFOR discuss training outcomes from their respective points of view.

D-15. After establishing the events, the AAR covers what was right or wrong with what happened. Participants identify the strong and weak points of their performances based on the commander's guidance and performance measures. The facilitator guides discussions to ensure maximum input that is operationally sound and relevant to the training event. Effectively guided discussions reach conclusions that are doctrinally sound, consistent with Army standards, and relevant to the unit mission. Participants and evaluators assess and candidly discuss what happened in terms of whether actions and decisions were ethical, effective, and efficient.

D-16. A training AAR concludes as the participants determine how the unit should complete the task differently next time. The facilitator guides the unit in self-determining how it might perform the task more effectively in the future. The unit identifies problems and provides solutions as well as identifies who is responsible for making the recommended changes. Additionally, the facilitator guides the discussion to determine a more effective way to train the tasks to achieve the commander's guidance. The evaluator or OC/T assists the chain of command undergoing the training to lead the group in determining exactly how participants will perform differently the next time the unit attempts the task. Ideally, this assistance motivates units and Soldiers to conduct future sustainment training to standard.

STEPS OF AFTER ACTION REVIEW

D-17. Effective AARs, formal or informal, require leaders to plan, prepare for, execute, and assess. AAR planning is part of each training event. Successful training leaders understand the unit's mission and the

Appendix D

commander's guidance for the training event. During planning, commanders identify opportunities to conduct AARs, assign OC/T responsibilities, and lock in allocated time and resources to conduct AARs. As leaders conduct training, subordinate leaders assess unit and leader proficiency on collective and individual tasks, conduct on-the-spot coaching, and lead informal AARs. These tasks require that leaders understand the commander's guidance, concept of operations, and tasks to be trained during a training event.

D-18. The amount and level of detail needed during the planning and preparation processes depend on the type of AAR to be conducted and available resources. The AAR process has four steps:
- Plan.
- Prepare.
- Execute.
- Assess.

STEP 1: PLAN THE AFTER ACTION REVIEW

D-19. The AAR plan provides the foundation for successful AARs. Commanders provide their guidance to develop an AAR plan for each training event. Subordinates then determine how to achieve the commander's guidance. The guidance applies to formal and informal AARs and identifies—
- Who will conduct the AAR.
- Who will provide information.
- Aspects of the operation an AAR evaluates.
- Who will attend the AAR.
- When and where the AAR occurs.

D-20. Leaders or OC/Ts use the AAR plan to identify critical places and events to observe to provide the unit a timely and valid assessment. Critical places can include unit maintenance collection points, passage points, and unit aid stations. The AAR plan identifies responsible persons who (either internal or external to the unit) facilitate the AAR for a particular event. The leader or OC/T is the individual tasked to observe training, provide control for the training, and lead the AAR.

Selecting and Training Observer-Controllers/Trainers

D-21. When planning an AAR, commanders select leaders and OC/Ts—
- Who demonstrate proficiency in the tasks to be trained.
- With knowledge of the duties they are to observe.
- With knowledge of current doctrine and TTP.

D-22. When using external OC/Ts, ideally they are at least equal in rank to the leader of the unit they will assess. If commanders must choose between experience and an understanding of current TTP or rank, they should go with experience. A staff sergeant with experience as a tank platoon sergeant is a better platoon OC/T than a sergeant first class who has no platoon sergeant experience. Commanders are responsible for training and certifying OC/Ts to include providing training on how to conduct an AAR. Ideally, inexperienced OC/Ts should observe properly conducted AARs before acting as an OC/T.

Reviewing the Training and Evaluation Outline

D-23. When planning the AAR, units review applicable T&EOs for understanding performance measures and steps for all individual and collective tasks. T&EOs state the Army performance standards for these tasks. Units and Soldiers access T&EOs through the ATN at https://atn.army.mil via the DTMS and the CATS. The commander specifies the guidance for the event along with the objectives and tasks to be trained. The commander also states the training environment for the training event and the focus of the tasks trained. Leaders review the T&EOs that lists the conditions and standards for the respective individual or collective tasks. Leaders use the individual training records and T&EOs to measure unit and Soldier performance.

D-24. Leaders and OC/Ts review the tasks to be trained as specified in the commander's guidance for an upcoming event. The T&EO states performance measures and the order specifies the commander's guidance. The respective T&EOs are not only provided to remaining OC/T team members but also to the Soldiers in the unit. All members of the unit review these documents to gain a complete and mutual understanding of the critical places and phases to assess task performance.

Schedule Stopping Points

D-25. When planning the AAR, commanders schedule the time and place to conduct it as an integral part of training events. Commanders plan for AARs during and at the end of each critical phase or major training event. For example, a leader may plan a stopping point after issuing an OPORD, upon the unit's arrival at a new position, or after consolidation on an objective.

D-26. Commanders plan for 30 to 45 minutes for platoon-level AARs, 1 hour for company-level AARs, and about 2 hours for battalion-level and above AARs. Training to standard takes priority over training to time. Soldiers receive better feedback on their performance and remember the lessons longer as result of a quality AAR.

Determining Attendance

D-27. The AAR plan specifies who attends each AAR. At each echelon, an AAR has a primary set of participants. At squad and platoon levels, everyone attends and participates. At company or higher levels, it may not be practical to have everyone attend because of continuing operations or training. At company or higher levels, unit and OPFOR commanders, unit leaders, and other key players may be the only participants. Leaders or OC/Ts may recommend additional participants attend based on specific observations.

Choosing Training Aids

D-28. The AAR plan specifies training aids. Effective training aids directly support the discussion of the training and promote learning. The local training support center catalogs available training aids. Home station training support center support and training aids are available within the Army training support system.

D-29. Under the right conditions, dry-erase boards, video equipment, digital maps, terrain models, and enlarged maps support AAR discussion. For example, if reconnaissance reveals no sites provide a view of the exercise area, the AAR facilitator can use a terrain table or digital map.

D-30. When choosing training aids in the AAR plan, leaders consider terrain visibility, group size, suitability to task, and availability of electrical power. Leaders need only use a training aid if it makes the AAR better.

Reviewing the After Action Review Plan

D-31. The AAR plan is only a guide. Commanders issue their guidance, and subordinates determine how to achieve that guidance. Commanders, leaders, and OC/Ts regularly review the AAR plan during training meetings to ensure the training meeting stays on topic and the plan meets the unit's training needs. Commanders, leaders, and OC/Ts can adjust the plan as necessary, but changes take preparation and planning time away from subordinate leaders or OC/Ts. The AAR plan aims to allow OC/Ts and leaders as much time as possible to prepare for the AAR.

STEP 2: PREPARE THE AFTER ACTION REVIEW

D-32. Preparation is the key to the effective execution of any plan. Preparing for an AAR begins before the training and continues until the actual event.

Appendix D

Review Guidance and Supporting Documentation

D-33. The commander's guidance and training objectives are the basis for observations and the focus of the AAR. When preparing for an AAR, leaders and OC/Ts review the commander's guidance, OPORD, training objectives, and T&EOs. These reviews occur before training and immediately before the AAR. Leaders and OC/Ts review current doctrine, technical information, and applicable unit SOPs to ensure they have the tools to observe unit and individual performance properly. Leaders and OC/Ts read and understand all WARNORDs, OPORDs, and FRAGORDs that the unit issues before and during training to understand what is supposed to happen. The detailed knowledge that OC/Ts display during these reviews adds credibility to their assessments.

Identify Important Training Events

D-34. Based on the commander's guidance, leaders or OC/Ts identify which training events—MET or as identified by the commander—are critical. Leaders or OC/Ts also identify that training events are positioned in the right place at the right time to observe the unit's actions. Critical events can include—
- Training events that demonstrate MET proficiency.
- The issuance of OPORDs and FRAGORDs.
- The issuance of the MDMP or TLP.
- Contact with OPFORs.
- Resupply and reconstitution operations.
- Passage of lines.

Identify After Action Review Facilitators

D-35. AAR facilitators are either internal or external evaluators. Internal leaders participate in the training and are part of the organization whereas external evaluators—typically OC/Ts—do not participate in the training. Both evaluators have the requirement to make and consolidate insights, observations, and lessons to facilitate the discussion of what happened. OC/Ts accurately record what they see and hear to prevent loss of valuable information and feedback. These records include events, actions, and observations by time sequence. OC/Ts can use any recording system—such as notebooks, mobile devices, prepared forms, or index cards—as long as it is reliable and sufficiently detailed (identifying times, places, and names). A recording system notates the date-time group of each observation so evaluators can easily integrate their observations with observations of other OC/Ts. This collection of observations provides a comprehensive and detailed overview of what happened. When OC/Ts have more time, they review the notes and fill in any details not written down earlier.

D-36. Leaders actively participate in the event and facilitate the AAR. They listen to professional discussions, feedback, and the participants in the AAR. The observations of participants during the event enable leaders to understand the execution of the tasks as well as the impact of the training environment. When participants share their observations, Soldiers and leaders develop mutual trust as they gain a common understanding of the unit's strengths and weaknesses.

D-37. One of the most difficult OC/T tasks involves determining when and where to observe training. The best location is where the OC/T can observe the performance of critical tasks and the overall flow of unit actions. The OC/T does not always need to stay close to the unit leader. The OC/T's position avoids distracting training participants. OC/Ts also avoid compromising the unit's location or guidance by being obvious. They are professional, courteous, and as unobtrusive as possible at all times. They look and act like a member of the unit. For example, OC/Ts use individual and vehicle camouflage, movement techniques, or cover and concealment.

Select After Action Review Sites

D-38. AARs occur at or near the training exercise site. During formal AARs, leaders identify and inspect designated AAR sites and prepare a site diagram showing the placement of training aids and other equipment. Designated AAR sites allow pre-positioning of training aids and rapid assembly of key personnel, minimizing wasted time.

D-39. Leaders often conduct informal AARs at or near the training site. The primary difference from formal AARs is that informal AARs use minimal training aids that facilitators often find on the ground (such as rocks or twigs). Based on the commander's guidance, leaders determine the time and location of the AAR site when they prepare for the AAR.

D-40. An effective AAR site allows Soldiers to see the terrain where the exercise or training took place. If this is not possible, the trainer finds a location that allows them to see the terrain where the most critical or significant actions occurred. Time and resources determine the type and complexity of the terrain model, enlarged map, sketch, or copy of the unit's graphics.

D-41. The leader or OC/T enables Soldiers attending the AAR to get as comfortable as reasonably possible. Leaders invite participants to remove helmets, find shelter from the elements, and have some refreshments such as coffee and water. Ideally, participants face away from the sun and key leaders sit up front. A comfortable environment enables participants to focus on the AAR without distractions. Additionally, when leaders prepare an AAR, they move vehicle parking and equipment security areas far enough away from the AAR site to prevent distractions.

Collect Observations

D-42. Leaders and senior OC/Ts need a complete picture of what happened during the training to conduct an effective AAR. Leaders and OC/Ts implement the Army problem solving process to establish the base logic for gathering information and observations.

D-43. During an informal AAR, the leader or facilitator can rely upon the input from the unit during the AAR or gather observations from subordinates and OPFOR (if applicable). The observations gathered assist the leader with gaining an understanding of the operation from subordinate leaders that will help drive the AAR.

D-44. During a formal AAR, the senior OC/T receives input from subordinates, supporting units, and adjacent units. This combined input provides the senior OC/T with a comprehensive review of the observed unit and its impact on the higher unit's mission. The senior OC/T also receives input from OPFOR leaders, players, and OC/Ts. The OPFOR perspective is critical in identifying why a unit was or was not successful. During formal AARs, the OPFOR leader briefs the OPFOR plan and guidance to set the stage for a discussion of what happened and why.

Organize the After Action Review

D-45. OC/Ts gather all the observation information and organize notes in a chronological sequence to understand the flow of events. The leader or OC/T selects and sequences key events of the operation in their relevance to the commander's guidance, training objectives, tasks to train, and key discussion or teaching points.

D-46. Leaders and OC/Ts then organize the AAR using one of three techniques: chronological order of events, warfighting functions, or key events, themes, or issues. The chronological order of events technique is logical, structured, and easy to understand. It follows the flow of training from start to finish. By covering actions in the order they took place, Soldiers and leaders can better recall what happened. The warfighting functions technique structures the AAR using the warfighting functions. The AAR focuses on the warfighting functions and their associated systems (people, organizations, information, and processes) and links to the commander's guidance and training objectives. Participants can identify strengths and weaknesses across all phases and can recommend solutions. This technique is useful in training staff sections. The last technique focuses on key events, themes, or issues. This technique focuses on critical training events, which directly support training objectives. This technique is effective when time is limited.

Appendix D

Rehearse

D-47. Facilitators and OC/Ts rehearse delivery of the AAR during preparation. This rehearsal includes considering the possible questions or issues that participants may broach. Effective rehearsals include all the training resources that will be used in the actual AAR.

Formal After Action Reviews

D-48. After thorough preparation, the OC/T reviews the AAR agenda and gets ready to conduct the AAR. The OC/T then announces to unit leaders the AAR starting time and location at least an hour in advance. The time allows enough time for the OC/Ts to prepare and rehearse at the AAR site. Unit leaders use the time to account for personnel and equipment, perform actions required by unit SOPs require, and move to the AAR site.

Informal After Action Reviews

D-49. Often leaders have minimal time to prepare for AARs, so they identify and prioritize key observations as time permits. They then mentally review the training event from their personal observations and from subordinates' observations based on one of the three techniques discussed in paragraph D-46. The review and rehearsal allow the leader to mentally step through the AAR.

STEP 3: EXECUTE THE AFTER ACTION REVIEW

D-50. The AAR begins when the training exercise stops, AAR preparation is complete, and key players are at the designated AAR site. The leader or OC/T reviews the purpose and sequence of the AAR to ensure everyone understands why an AAR is conducted. It is now time to conduct the AAR. The purpose of the AAR is for participants to discover strengths and weaknesses, propose solutions, and adopt a COA to correct problems.

Provide an Introduction and Rules

D-51. First in the execution of an AAR is the introduction. In an introduction, the leader or OC/T requests the following:
- Everyone participates if they have an insight, observation, or question that will help the unit identify and correct deficiencies or sustain strengths. The AAR is a dynamic, candid, and professional discussion of training that focuses on unit performance measured against the task standards (as expressed in the T&EO).
- Participants avoid using the AAR as a critique. No one—regardless of rank, position, or strength of personality—has all the information or answers. AARs maximize training benefits by allowing Soldiers to learn from each other.
- The AAR focuses on identifying weaknesses to improve and strengths to sustain.

D-52. Soldier participation directly correlates to the atmosphere created during the introduction and command climate. The AAR leader makes a concerted effort to draw in Soldiers who seem reluctant to participate. The following techniques can help the leader or OC/T create an atmosphere conducive to maximum participation:
- Reinforce the fact that it is permissible to disagree respectfully.
- Focus on learning and encourage people to give honest opinions.
- Use open-ended and leading questions to guide the discussion of Soldier, leader, and unit performance.
- Enter the discussion only when necessary.

State the After Action Review Agenda

D-53. The leader or OC/T states the AAR agenda. The leader or OC/T reviews the commander's training objectives and restates the tasks being reviewed, including the conditions and standards for the tasks. Using tools—such as maps, operational graphics, terrain boards, sticks, and rocks—the commander or leader restates the mission, guidance, and concept of operations. The leader or OC/T may guide the discussion to ensure everyone understands the plan and the commander's guidance. Another technique is to have subordinate leaders restate the mission and discuss the commander's guidance and concept of operations.

D-54. In a formal AAR, the OPFOR commander explains the OPFOR plan and actions. The OPFOR commander uses the same training aids as the friendly force commander, so that all participants understand the correlation between the plans.

Summarize Events (What Actually Happened)

D-55. The leader or facilitator guides the review using a logical sequence of events to describe and discuss what happened. The facilitator—leader or OC/T—and participants determine to the extent possible what actually happened during the training event, phase, or operation. The leader gathers as many views or perspectives (such as from the OPFOR, squad leader, team leader, and rifleman) as possible. These varied perspectives help the facilitator to establish a common understanding. Leaders then understand the complexity of an event and work to solve complex, ill-defined problems. They discuss the unit's risk management integration and the Soldiers application of control measures to mitigate the risks. This is critical in helping Soldiers understand risk, act decisively, and accept prudent risk in the future.

D-56. The facilitator does not ask yes or no questions but encourages participation and guides discussion by using open-ended, leading questions. An open-ended question allows the person answering to reply based on what was significant to the Soldier. Open-ended questions are also much less likely to put Soldiers on the defensive; these questions are more effective in finding out what happened.

D-57. As the discussion expands and more Soldiers add their perspectives, a clearer picture of what really happened emerges. The leader or OC/T does not tell the Soldiers or leaders what was good or bad. The leader or OC/T ensures that participants reveal specific issues, both positive and negative. Skillful guidance of the discussion ensures the AAR does not gloss over mistakes or unit weaknesses.

Identify What Needs To Be Improved Or Sustained

D-58. The unit discusses both its successes and failures in the context of the training mission, objectives, and performance measures. Participants consider whether the resulting decisions and actions were ethical, effective, and efficient. To sustain success, the unit needs to know what it performs well. Also, participants concentrate on identifying what went wrong and not on the person responsible. If necessary, it is better to identify the duty position rather than the person. For example, they refer to "the platoon leader" rather than to "2LT Wilson."

Determine How the Task Should Be Done Differently

D-59. The facilitator—leader or OC/T—helps the unit determine a more effective method for the unit to perform the task in the future. The unit identifies conditions to modify to increase complexity. A more complex training environment challenges leaders and subordinates so they can better identify opportunities to take prudent risk within the commander's guidance. Additionally, the facilitator guides the discussion to determine a more effective method the unit can implement to train the tasks to achieve the commander's guidance.

Provide Closing Comments

D-60. During the summary, the facilitator reviews and summarizes key points identified during the discussion. The AAR ends on a constructive note and links conclusions to future training. The facilitator then leaves the immediate area to allow the unit or subordinate leaders and Soldiers time to discuss the training in private. Figure D-1 on page D-10 illustrates a notional AAR.

Appendix D

> The battalion commander has certified SFC Banks as an observer-controller for Company B's EXEVAL next month. In preparation for his duties, he gathered all the T&EOs and publications to reference. The T&EOs support the overall evaluation plan and specifically the collective tasks he is to evaluate.
>
> During the unit EXEVAL, SFC Banks observes 1st platoon, Company B executing the task, React to Direct Fire Contact, #07-3-D9501. Following the platoon's execution of the task, he conducts an informal AAR with the platoon and OPFOR personnel.
>
> SFC Banks facilitates the AAR by asking SSG Richmond of 1st platoon to describe what was supposed to happen. SSG Richmond describes the mission and scheme of maneuver the platoon was directed to execute from the company operation order.
>
> After SSG Richmond relayed what the platoon was supposed to do, SFC Banks asked PFC Smith to describe from his point of view what actually occurred. This generated some discussion in the platoon of what they believed went right and what went poorly. SFC Banks interjected at times, prompting platoon members to discuss how they could have executed the task to the published standard per the T&EO. Following this discussion, SFC Banks discussed his overall assessment of the platoon for this task. He also discussed how the platoon performed—with a go or a no go—for each performance step and measure as well as critical and leader steps. SFC Banks assessed the platoon as a P- based on his task evaluation and criteria met within the objective task evaluation criteria matrix as described in the T&EO.
>
> After 15 minutes, SFC Banks is satisfied that the platoon better understands how to execute the tasks to achieve the standard. He releases the platoon to retrain the task for another iteration.

Figure D-1. After action review scenario

STEP 4: ASSESS THE AFTER ACTION REVIEW

D-61. AARs are the link between task performance and execution to standard. They provide commanders a critical assessment tool to plan Soldier, leader, and unit training. Through the professional and candid discussion of events, Soldiers can compare their performance against the standard and identify specific ways to improve proficiency.

D-62. The benefits of AARs come from applying results in developing future training. Successful leaders use the information to assess unit performance and to plan future training. Leaders apply the information to correct deficiencies and sustain task proficiency.

Retrain

D-63. Units and Soldiers retrain tasks to meet the standard. A lack of resources may prevent retraining on some tasks during the same exercise. Without the necessary resources, leaders reschedule the mission or training. Leaders ensure that a lack of proficiency in supporting collective and individual tasks found during the AAR are scheduled and retrained. Effective leaders do not delay retraining. If the leader delays retraining, then Soldiers and the unit must understand that they did not perform the task to standard and that retraining will occur later.

Revise Standard Operating Procedures

D-64. AARs may reveal problems with unit SOPs. If so, unit leaders revise the SOPs and ensure units implement the changes during future training.

Appendix E
Lane Training

LANE TRAINING DEFINED

E-1. Leaders use situational training exercises (STXs) and lane training exercises (LTXs) to assess unit collective training. An STX is a mission-related, limited exercise. This short, scenario-driven exercise trains a group of related tasks or battle drills through practice. An STX usually contains multiple collective tasks linked to form a realistic scenario of a military operation, sometimes incorporating free play. STXs are used for training and evaluation, especially sustainment of task proficiency. STXs are developed by Army branch proponent schools reflected in the unit CATS or developed by a unit as required. See AR 350-28 for more on military exercises.

E-2. Leaders use lane training and LTXs to conduct training at the small-unit level. A lane is a standardized training exercise used to train on one or more collective tasks or the designated area or facility for the exercise. Lane training is a process—planning, execution, and assessment—for training company-size and smaller units on individual tasks, collective tasks, and battle drills that support a unit's METs. Although lane training is a technique for training company-size and smaller units (including platoons, sections, squads, crews, and teams), the emphasis is on the size unit, not the unit echelon. Commanders can use lane training to train small groups, elements, or staffs of any organization.

E-3. **A *lane training exercise* is a standardized and structured exercise or simulation used to train on one or more collective tasks that includes a designated area, terrain, or facility.** It usually focuses on one primary task. An LTX consists of the assembly area, rehearsal, lane execution, AAR, and retraining activities that culminate the lane training process. An LTX is an STX conducted using lane training principles and techniques. Trainers should consider the following when developing LTXs:

- An LTX is usually a mini-STX; however, it focuses on fewer collective tasks to enhance training efficiency.
- It has no free play.
- Its primary purpose is training, especially the development of task proficiency.
- LTXs are developed by units.
- A unit may train on several LTXs (several primary tasks) within a few days at one major training area.

E-4. An LTX is conducted in an LTX area. An LTX area is a training area selected and designed to train on one primary task. An LTX area is where the five LTX activities take place. The five LTX activities include assembly, rehearsal, lane execution, AAR, and retraining.

E-5. An LTX will include one or more lanes. A lane is a standardized and structured training exercise or simulation used to train on one or more collective tasks. A lane is designed to create the situation or conditions required for execution. When an LTX includes more than one lane, each lane can be used to train the same primary task. Ideally, units use different lanes for rehearsals, lane execution, and retraining on the same primary task.

E-6. Lane training is a systematic, performance-oriented training process. The rigor of the lane training process enables units to attain proficiency quickly and efficiently in tactical and technical tasks. It enables training to be effectively structured, administered, supported, and assessed by limiting the number of tasks, time, terrain, facilities, or other resources. Lane training provides a systematic and controlled approach to selected task proficiency.

Appendix E

LANE TRAINING USES

E-7. The purpose of lane training is to build or sustain proficiency in Soldier and leader individual tasks, collective tasks, and battle drills. Lane training enables leaders to—
- Conduct initial, developmental, sustainment, refresher, and enhancement training and assessment for tactical and technical tasks.
- Train similar units—simultaneously or sequentially—using mission-related scenarios.
- Test, standardize, and train TTP.
- Develop and refine unit SOPs that support unit METs.
- Efficiently control training objectives (including tasks, conditions, standards, and training proficiencies) during training.
- Support initial training and retraining.
- Vary training conditions to the training level of the unit (which may be at the initial, refresher, or sustainment level).
- Integrate (both vertically and horizontally) specific task training, battle drills, and exercises from different functional areas (including maneuver, maneuver support, and sustainment) into unit training programs.
- Achieve proficiency on multiechelon, multi-unit, combined, joint, multinational, or interagency procedures and on other difficult, infrequent, or teamwork-based tasks.
- Achieve maximum results when training Soldiers and units while efficiently leveraging limited resources (including land, facilities, personnel, and equipment).
- Prepare for both formal and informal assessments, internal evaluations, and EXEVALs.
- Conduct competitions.

E-8. In certain instances, lane training may be the most efficient and effective means to train small units to attain and sustain selected task proficiencies. Lane training techniques may be indicated as a training method—
- When training assessments indicate there may be changes or performance deficiencies in team, squad, section, platoon, or company collective tasks. Potential situations or indicators include changes in—
  - Doctrine.
  - Organization.
  - Materiel.
  - Personnel.
  - Training.
  - Leader development.
  - Task performance.
- When units need to prepare for assigned missions or specific operational environments.
- When leaders units need to prepare Soldiers and units for major training events, including annual training, gunnery exercises, combat training center rotations, and EXEVALs.
- When sustainment training is needed.
- When task proficiency is perishable or easily atrophied.
- When there is a need to evaluate performance on collective and supporting individual tasks further.
- When there is a need for integrated multiechelon or multifunctional training.
- When training requires significant planning, management, or resource support.
- When the use of other training techniques proves more expensive or impractical.
- When directed by higher headquarters.

LANE TRAINING CHARACTERISTICS

E-9. Lane training is a process for training company-size and smaller units on collective tasks that support a unit's capability or mission. The process consists of planning, execution, and assessment phases. In the planning phase, lane training emphasizes pre-exercise—
- Certification of trainers and leaders.
- Validation of training plans and materials.
- Rehearsals.

E-10. The execution phase (the LTX) focuses on specific collective tasks. Historically, lane training has usually been associated with tasks requiring movement over terrain (for example, conduct a movement to contact or conduct an attack); however, movement is not required. Lane training is appropriate for most small-unit maneuver, maneuver support, and sustainment collective tasks requiring teamwork and practice, whether conducted in fixed facilities or in a field environment.

E-11. Lane training is performance-oriented training. Since performance-oriented training requires training to the task performance standard, an inherent element is performance evaluation. This evaluation focuses on verification (or certification) that Soldiers, leaders, and units can perform tasks under specified conditions and standards. Effective lane training requires replication of missions and operational environments. Although lane training can be conducted in a live, virtual, or constructive training environment, it is normally conducted in a live environment (conducted in the field or duty site environment). However, the use of virtual or constructive environments to prepare for or to conduct lane training can dramatically enhance the effectiveness of lane training in live environments.

E-12. To ensure standardization, units develop LTXs to teach the doctrinally preferred way to perform specific missions or tasks. Initially, LTXs focus on a task or a few tasks at one time and exclude related tasks that may distract Soldiers from learning. However, once a unit is proficient in the tasks trained, more tasks may be included in more comprehensive LTXs to increase realism.

E-13. An LTX can consist of multiple lanes training the same task, but with different and varying conditions. LTXs are more flexible than drills, and units can tailor LTXs to meet a unit's METs or assigned mission requirements.

E-14. Lane training has characteristics that make it significantly different from other forms of training. Unit leaders consider these characteristics before planning and executing LTXs. These characteristics are listed in table E-1 on page E-4.

E-15. Leaders need an understanding of the tasks to be trained so they can develop a quality LTX. Leaders prepare themselves and their units. They coordinate training supplies and equipment well in advance of the LTX. Detailed and meticulous planning is critical in making an LTX that meets the training objectives.

E-16. Leaders conduct several activities prior to conducting an LTX. Trainers institute a pre-LTX training program to develop and verify the unit leaders' task proficiency. In this case, a pre-LTX training program means before the exercise or prior to arrival of the unit at the LTX area. Next, leaders institute a pre-LTX unit training and verification period after the leader training period. During this period, the unit's subordinate elements and personnel develop proficiency (through training and rehearsal) on prerequisite Soldier, leader, and collective tasks and battle drills.

E-17. After leaders and units develop proficiency on prerequisite tasks, they are ready to conduct LTX rehearsals. OC/Ts, OPFOR elements, leaders, and units all conduct rehearsals prior to the exercise. Leaders and units conduct rehearsals in the LTX area (in the assembly area or rehearsal area) just prior to lane execution. Rehearsals enable trainers to perform a pre-LTX validation, which is a tentative validation of training plans and materials prior to the exercise.

Appendix E

Table E-1. Characteristics of lane training

Characteristics	Description
Small-unit focus	A focus by units of platoon size or below (including staffs and small groups) on training a unit of company size or below.
Disciplined scenario	A disciplined scenario concentrating on mission-focused tasks and providing structured stimuli to prompt friendly force behavior.
Battle-focus	A focus on a limited number of collective tasks for each lane training exercise to improve effectiveness.
Validated tasks	Doctrinally and technically correct tasks and training objectives that have been validated against current doctrine and Army standards.
Controlled tasks and events	Highly controlled tasks, countertasks, and events that are structured to provide specific stimuli and elicit specific responses from the unit being trained.
Trained OC/Ts	OC/Ts trained and verified on specific OC/T and LTX tasks.
Trained OPFOR	Forces trained and verified on specific OPFOR countertasks required in the LTX in appropriate force ratios.
Support from outside the unit trained	Support (including OC/Ts, OPFOR, and resources) provided from sources other than the unit being trained.
LTX	A training exercise using lane training principles and techniques.
LTX lane training exercise OC/T observer-controller/trainer OPFOR opposing force	

E-18. Prior to conducting an LTX, trainers coordinate for post-LTX activities, including AARs, evaluations, retraining, and validation. For example, OC/Ts and unit leaders conduct AARs immediately following lane execution to provide feedback to units. AARs are facilitated by OC/Ts, are supported by the unit's leaders and OPFOR, and involve all unit participants. Post-LTX, senior unit leaders conduct a task performance evaluation. This evaluation determines whether units performed tasks to standard or not. The senior OC/T coordinates with the leader of the unit being trained. After an LTX, some units may require retraining. A retraining opportunity is an opportunity after the AAR to conduct retraining until a unit achieves standards. After retraining, the unit should have an opportunity to attempt the same tasks on a different lane, possibly with additional tasks, different conditions, or different leaders. Additionally, OC/Ts and unit leaders perform a validation of training and training materials after each iteration of the LTX.

E-19. The general flow of a lane follows a logical sequence of activities that includes rehearsals, task execution, AARs, evaluations, and the opportunity to retrain tasks not executed to standard. The lane can and should be repeated until the selected tasks are performed to the published standard. Figure E-1 shows an example of the lane training process, including the sequence of activities that occur as the lane is executed.

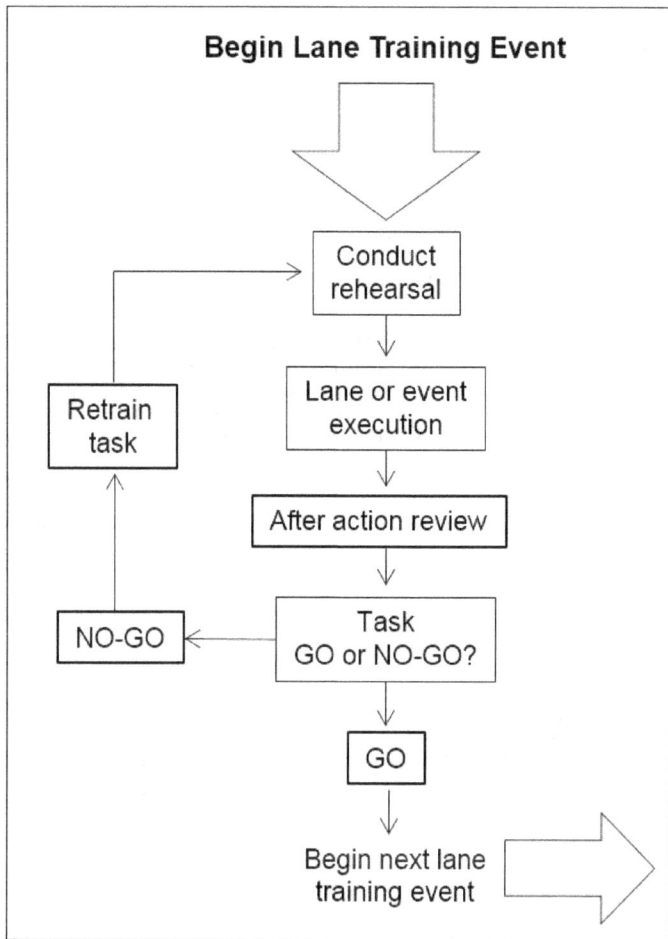

Figure E-1. General sequence of activities during a lane training event

COMPONENTS OF LANE TRAINING

E-20. As a focused and controlled training event, lane training includes components and personnel to ensure success. At a minimum, lane training includes the following components:
- The unit to be trained.
- Support structure conducting the training.
- OC/T teams.
- OPFOR teams, if appropriate.

E-21. A training exercise control cell may be created to manage lane training for one or more LTXs or units. (This cell is for training purposes only; it is not an operational cell.) The exercise control cell is supervised by an exercise director. It may be composed of operations, communications, administration, and logistics cells.

E-22. The unit two echelons higher than the unit on the lane usually manages lane training. For example, a brigade normally manages company lanes, a battalion normally manages platoon lanes, and a company normally manages squad and or section lanes.

E-23. Table E-2 on page E-6 lists key personnel involved in managing lane training. Other personnel involved in lane training (and generating management or coordination requirements) include—

Appendix E

- Exercise planners.
- Unit Soldiers.
- OPFOR Soldiers.
- Maneuver support or sustainment unit customers (for example, personnel from other units receiving services from a maneuver support or sustainment unit undergoing lane training).
- Role players.
- Higher headquarters' commanders, staffs, or representatives.
- Personnel from other units providing support.

Table E-2. Key personnel in managing lane training

Personnel	Description and Responsibilities
Exercise director	The individual responsible for managing all LTXs. This duty position is sometimes called chief controller or senior OC/T team chief.
Senior OC/T	The individual responsible for managing a specific LTX or LTX area. There is one senior OC/T for each LTX.
Other OC/Ts	Other personnel responsible for assisting senior OC/Ts or the exercise director. There may be an OC/T for each leader in a unit and each key event of each lane.
OPFOR leaders	Leaders of the element responsible for performing lane countertasks.
LTX resource managers	Personnel responsible for administration of logistic support for each LTX.
Unit leaders	Leaders responsible for the unit's training and for directing the unit during training.
Chain of command	Leaders responsible for supporting the planning, preparation, execution, and assessment of the unit's training.
LTX lane training exercise OC/T observer-controller/trainer OPFOR opposing force	

GENERAL PROCESS

E-24. Lane training is implemented using a systematic general process. This process includes planning, execution, and assessment phases. The activities described in table E-3 comprise the three lane training phases.

Table E-3. Lane training activities

Lane Training Phase	Activities Included
Planning (pre-LTX)	Actions involving unit assessment, training assessment, analysis, design, development, scheduling, resource acquisition, support coordination, pre-training, and preparation for training.
Execution (LTX)	Actions involving preparation, presentation, and performance of collective tasks to standard.
Assessment (post-LTX)	AARs and follow-up actions (such as update unit SOPs). Although frequently considered to be a post-exercise phase, assessment consists primarily of AARs conducted during or immediately after LTX lane execution.
AAR after action review LTX lane training exercise SOP standard operating procedures	

DETAILED PROCESS

E-25. Although lane training activities generally occur sequentially in the general process, lane training activities in the detailed process activities can occur simultaneously for different phases. For example, in figure E-2, "Perform AAR procedures" actually consists of the same procedures as the assessment phase's activity "Perform AAR preparation procedures" and "Conduct an AAR." Also, in the assessment phase, "Perform AAR planning procedures" takes place during the planning phase. Figure E-2 illustrates how the lane training process is composed of the three subordinate processes of planning, execution, and assessment.

Figure E-2. Detailed lane training process

LANE TRAINING EXERCISE CATEGORIES

E-26. LTXs (or lanes) may be classified into three categories. These are—
- Stand-alone.
- Integrated.
- Mission support.

STAND-ALONE

E-27. A stand-alone LTX is a single-function exercise requiring only one functional branch (for example, chemical) to accomplish a collective task. A stand-alone FTX is—
- Frequently executed at the lowest level (platoon, section, squad, or team) by units needing to develop proficiency.
- Able to provide OC/Ts the maximum flexibility and control over stopping the lane, resuming the lane, conducting AARs, and repeating the lane.
- Designed so several lanes may repeat identical tasks (sometimes with different conditions).
- More flexible than the integrated or mission support FTX because it has fewer constraints.

INTEGRATED

E-28. An integrated LTX is a multifunctional exercise requiring the integrated employment of two or more branches (for example, an infantry-armor company team) to accomplish a collective task. An integrated FTX is—
- Normally executed by units that exhibit high degrees of proficiency at the platoon or section level.
- Able to allow multiple units to interact, often interdependently, that are fully dedicated to training on the lane while participating under a master scenario.
- Difficult to restart as a single unit because that unit is a role player for another unit executing its task.
- More structured, complex, and time-phased than a stand-alone FTX, so OC/Ts have less flexibility and control.

Appendix E

MISSION SUPPORT

E-29. A mission support LTX is an exercise in which the unit undergoes lane training while performing a mission on behalf of, or associated with, other units. An example includes a petroleum, oils, and lubricants (POL) platoon performing a refueling mission. A mission support LTX—
- Is difficult for OC/Ts to stop and restart because the unit may be performing a real mission in support of other units.
- Limits the OC/T's control, requires more evaluation, is more complicated, limits controlled stimuli, and has less repeatability than a stand-alone or integrated FTX.

LANE TRAINING METHODOGY

E-30. Lane training is based on a crawl-walk-run methodology. This methodology has three phases: crawl, walk, and run. These phases are described in table E-4.

Table E-4. Crawl-walk-run characteristics in lane training

Phase	Description
Crawl (explain and demonstrate)	The leader describes the task step-by-step, indicating what each individual does.
Walk (practice)	The leader directs the unit to execute the task at a slow, step-by-step pace.
Run (perform)	The leader requires the unit to perform the task at full speed, as if in an operation, under realistic conditions.

E-31. Normally, the entire crawl-walk-run process occurs within a short time frame of only a few hours or days. This is determined by the tasks selected to train and the number of Soldiers to train. However, for lane training, the crawl-walk-run process can occur over several weeks, months, or years (especially for units within the Reserve Component). Lane training normally follows the crawl-walk-run methodology described in paragraphs E-31 through E-36.

CRAWL

E-32. During the crawl phase, each Soldier receives instructions from unit leaders on the common and specific individual tasks supporting the collective tasks that will be conducted during the LTX. Leaders review training objectives to demonstrate and discuss tasks, conditions, standards, and training proficiencies. This includes a review of supporting individual tasks for the collective tasks, battle drills, and T&EOs to train prior to and during the LTX. Leaders demonstrate a way to perform each task.

E-33. Junior leaders train their units on common and duty-specific individual tasks. After meeting the standards for all required individual tasks, junior leaders explain the units' collective tasks and drills. Individual and prerequisite collective training should be completed at a home station location prior to deploying for the training area to participate in the LTX.

WALK

E-34. During the walk phase, leaders conduct individual tasks and drills. Leaders train on each collective task until each unit meets the published standard. This phase is usually conducted without combat effects or the OPFOR. When possible, units complete supporting individual and collective training at a home station location so these tasks can be immediately performed at a run speed during the LTX to support the primary collective tasks to be trained. At the LTX area (in an assembly area or rehearsal area)—
- Unit leaders rehearse the primary collective tasks.
- Leaders and Soldiers rehearse supporting individual and collective tasks and drills.

Run

E-35. During the run phase, the unit actually performs the LTX. On a lane, the unit conducts training at combat speed under tactical conditions. Training multipliers such as TADSS, OPFOR, or live munitions may be used to enhance training. The LTX may integrate maneuver, maneuver support, and sustainment activities.

E-36. OC/Ts conduct (or facilitate) scheduled AARs at the end of the run phase. Although OC/Ts normally avoid stopping lane execution, OC/Ts may halt any phase of training to conduct an AAR at logical breaks in the training, whenever standards are not being met, or to address safety and environmental issues. If training standards are not achieved, the unit retrains until the standards are achieved.

LANE TRAINING EXERCISE ACTIVITIES AND SCENARIOS

E-37. Paragraphs E-38 through E-50 discuss lane activities and associated scenarios that depict how an LTX is developed and executed. If executed properly, the lane provides a realistic and demanding training exercise that achieves the training objectives required. It also provides an opportunity for the unit to retrain tasks not initially performed to the established standard. As necessary, a unit can perform multiple iterations of the lane (and its associated tasks) including opportunities to change task conditions and master the selected tasks so that the unit can perform them to the standard repeatedly.

LANE TRAINING EXERCISE ACTIVITIES

E-38. There are five basic activities that occur in the conduct of a LTX. These activities are executed sequentially and consist of assembly, rehearsal, execution, AAR, and retraining. These activities are described in figure E-3.

Assembly	Activities involving unit in-briefing, leader preparation, and troop leading procedures (including issuance of the unit's OPORD). These activities are normally conducted in an AA.
Rehearsal	Activities involving practices of unit task to be performed on the lane (or to execute the OPORD), normally at a crawl or walk speed. These practices may take place in rehearsal areas, in AAs, or on lanes.
Execution	Activities required to perform specific collective tasks on the lane (or to execute the OPORD), normally at a run speed. These activities may take place on a lane.
AAR	Activities required to provide— • A structured, interactive, group-oriented review and evaluation of the unit's task performance on the execution lane. • Suggestions on how to improve future performance These activities usually take place in an AAR area or on a lane.
Retraining	Activities required to enable the unit to perform lane tasks to the desired standards. These activities normally take place in a retraining area, rehearsal area, or on a lane.
AA assembly area	AAR after action review OPORD operation order

Figure E-3. Lane training execution process

E-39. Rehearsals, execution, and retraining activities may occur on different lanes within the LTX area. The execution of a lane follows a general pattern. A diagram of this pattern is depicted in figure E-4 on page E-10.

Appendix E

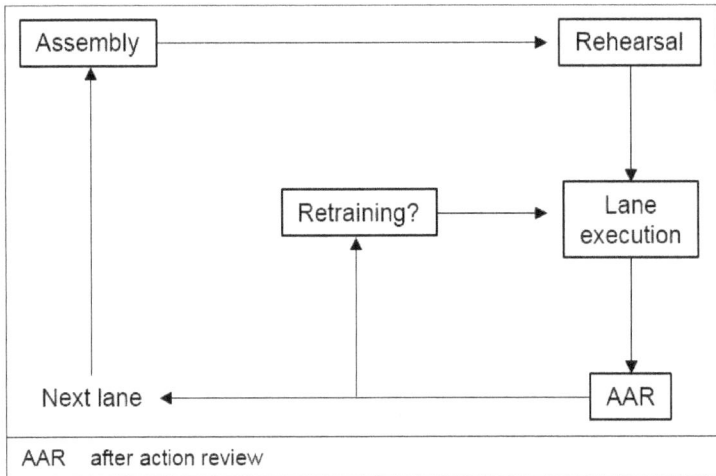

Figure E-4. Diagram of lane training

E-40. An LTX is used to train one collective task or a group of related tasks. The name of the LTX is the title of the primary collective task to be trained.

E-41. Exercise planners have flexibility in designing the structure of LTX lanes. The lane training structure can vary depending upon the tasks trained, the number of lanes and LTXs conducted, the number of units to be trained, and the size of the LTX area. Usually more than one LTX area is set up at a training area. This creates additional possibilities for LTX structures and improved efficiency, especially when several units are trained and necessary transportation is available.

E-42. A lane is usually illustrated using a graphic scenario or lane diagram. This diagram represents a series of events on the lane (often in the execution area).

E-43. The LTX events list includes supporting tasks or task steps associated with the collective task being trained. All unit events are conducted and assessed in the sequence they are normally performed during operations and in relationship to how they support the unit mission.

E-44. The event list may also indicate OPFOR events required for the lane. These events may include tasks or countertasks. OPFOR events are prefixed by a ">>." Key unit and OPFOR events performed on the lane are indicated in the graphic scenario or lane diagram.

E-45. AARs are planned to follow completion of lane execution but also may follow key supporting tasks or events occurring during lane execution. AAR events may also be indicated in a graphic scenario or lane diagram.

E-46. The following graphic control measures are frequently used for a lane involving unit movement:
- Assembly area.
- Start point.
- Line of departure.
- Phase lines.
- Boundaries (represented by lines with unit information).
- Objective.
- Release point.

Lane Training

LANE TRAINING EXERCISE SCENARIOS

E-47. Figures E-5 through E-8 on pages E-12 through E-14 depict examples of generic scenarios for LTX lanes. A lane has one primary collective task (or lane title) for a specific type of unit and one or more supporting collective tasks or task performance steps structured as events.

Note. An AAR is scheduled at the end of an LTX lane. Normally, an AAR is scheduled at the end of events for major collective tasks but not scheduled after events for task performance steps.

E-48. The LTX example lane in figure E-5 consists of three events for supporting collective tasks.

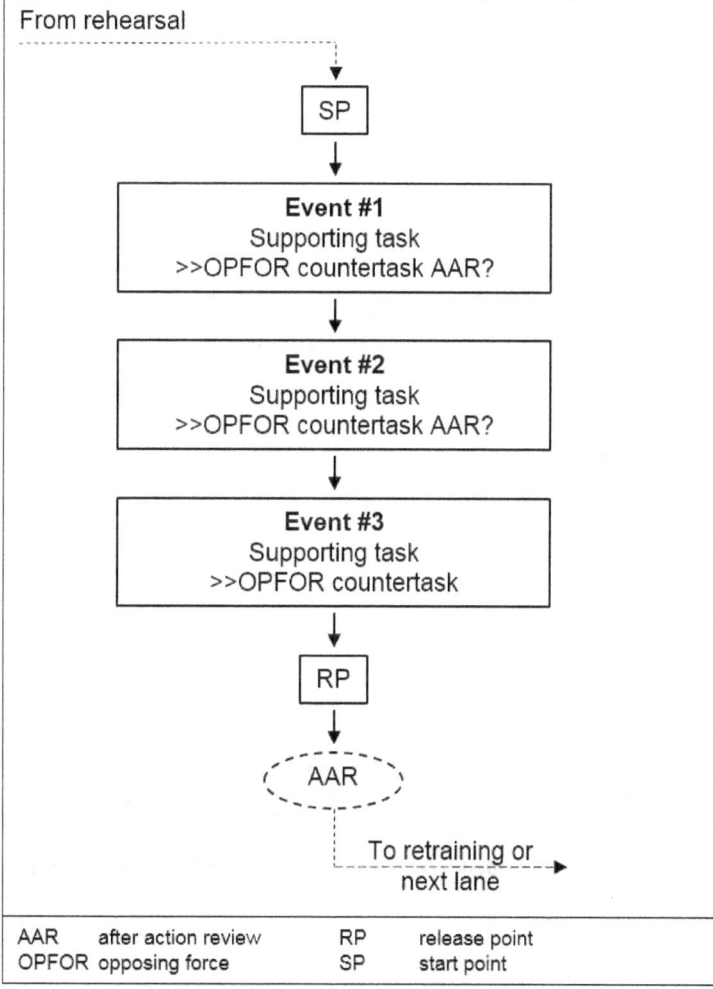

Figure E-5. Example generic lane scenario

Appendix E

E-49. The LTX example diagram in figure E-6 depicts an example of a scenario for one collective task with three task steps as events. The unit depicted is a platoon. The unit's task is to cross a radiologically contaminated area.

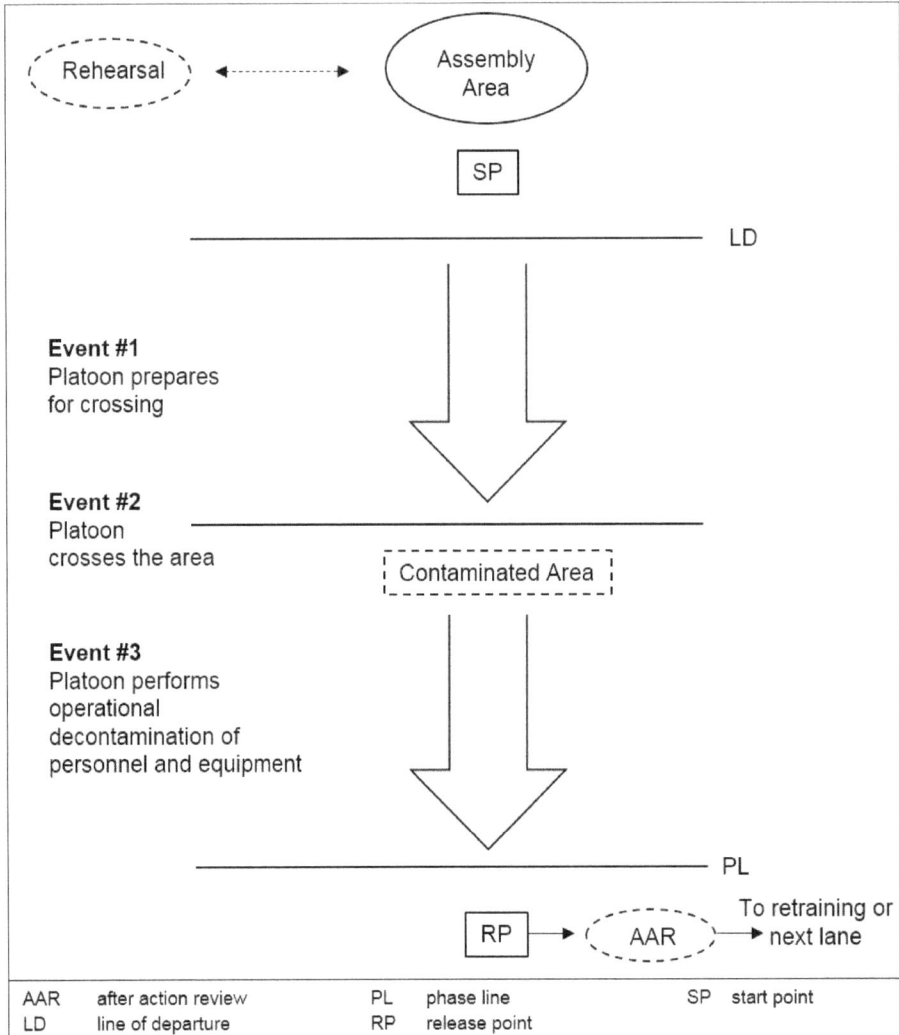

Figure E-6. Example scenario for one collective task with three task steps

E-50. Figure E-7 depicts an example of a scenario with several supporting or related collective tasks for a POL section. The scenario also has one OPFOR countertask. Normally, the unit should be proficient on each supporting or related collective task before the tasks are combined into a single lane. The exercise is for a POL platoon in a forward support company. The LTX task is to relocate a POL area.

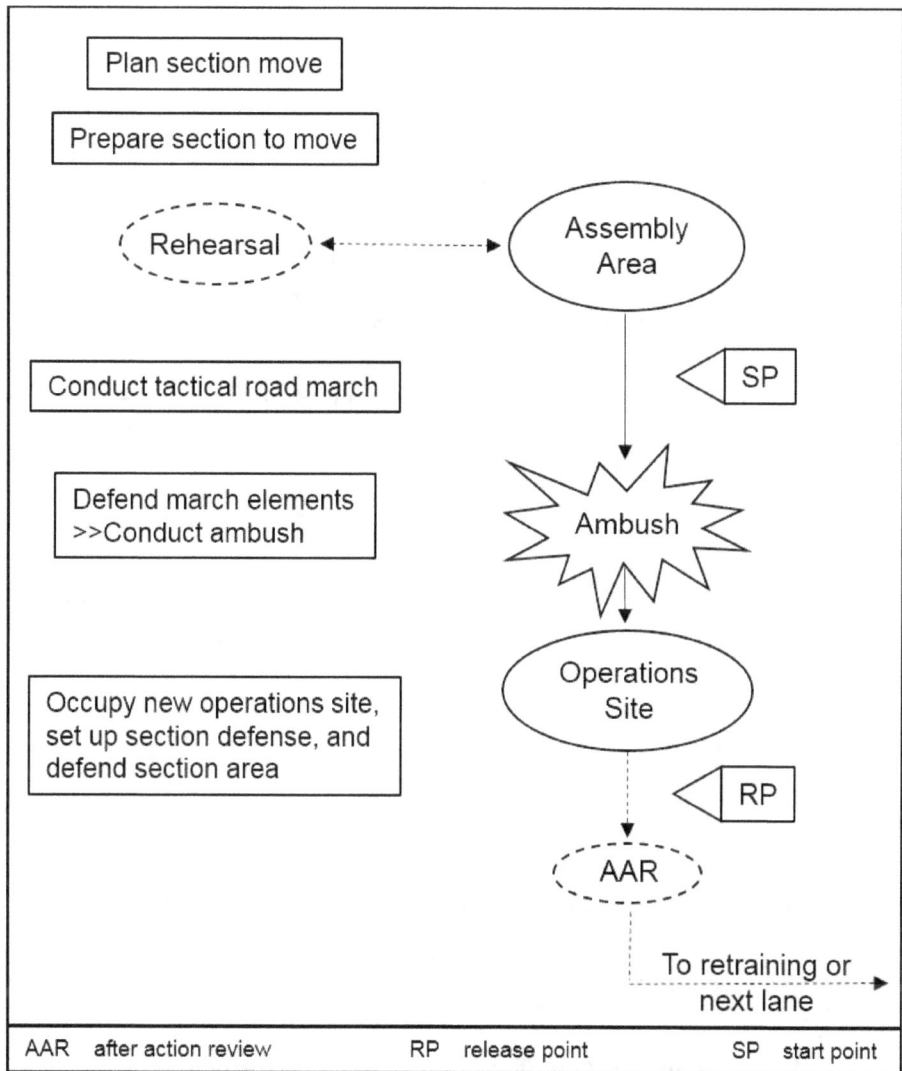

Figure E-7. Example scenario with several supporting or related collective tasks

Appendix E

E-51. Figure E-8 depicts an example of a scenario for a stationary unit (no movement is involved). Although the entire company is participating in the LTX, each element (including platoons or sections) trains and performs its own tasks in support of the company's higher level task. The exercise is designed for a unit ordnance maintenance company in general support. The LTX task is to conduct general support maintenance.

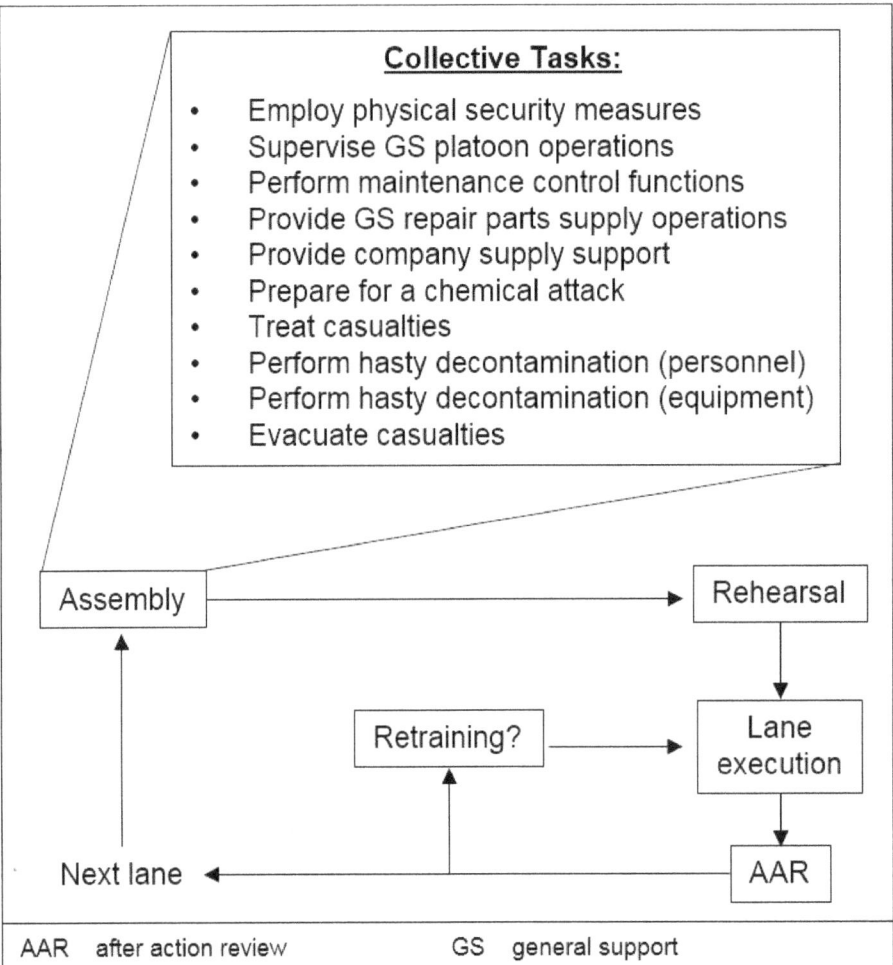

Figure E-8. Scenario for a stationary unit

SUPPORT REQUIREMENTS

E-52. Effective lane training requires support. FTX support requirements include (but are not limited to) the following items:
- Time.
- Personnel (lane planners, OC/Ts, OPFOR, customers, and role players).
- Doctrine and training publications and other training information.
- Training areas (maneuver areas, bivouac areas, ranges, and facilities).
- Materiel (vehicles, weapons, communications equipment, TADSS, tools, and special equipment).
- Supplies (ammunition, food, fuel, and POL).
- Funds.

Lane Training

- Operational tempo allocation.
- Other resources.

TIME

E-53. Sufficient time is required to conduct adequate planning, execution, and assessment. Variables affecting the time required include the following:
- Planning requirements.
- Number of METs, other collective tasks, and supporting tasks to be trained.
- Difficulty and complexity of tasks.
- Number of lanes to be conducted.
- Number of units to be trained.
- Size and echelon of the units trained.
- Task proficiency of units trained.
- Distances involved between—
    - Unit's garrison location and the training area.
    - Unit's bivouac areas and LTXs in training area.
    - Lane start points and release points.
- Safety and environmental issues.
- Available resources.
- Component of unit (Regular Army or Reserve Component). Reserve Component units have significantly fewer available work days per month than Regular Army units.
- Quality of lane training. Quality depends on effective leadership, planning, and resource support.

E-54. The lane training planning process is affected significantly by whether the unit is Regular Army or Reserve Component. Due to time constraints, planning for the Reserve Component must begin earlier than planning for the Regular Army.

E-55. The time required to conduct an LTX may range from a few hours to several days, primarily depending upon the layout of the LTX area, nature of LTX tasks, and number of tasks trained on a lane.

E-56. Although the time required to conduct an AAR can range from 30 minutes to 2 hours, the time required for planning and preparation is much longer. The time required to perform follow-up procedures depends upon the number and nature of issues identified during lane execution and subsequent AARs.

PERSONNEL

E-57. Lane training, especially for company or platoon-size lanes, can be manpower intensive for any size unit due to the large numbers of personnel involved in managing the planning, execution, and assessment of the lane training process. See paragraph E-23 for details on personnel.

INFORMATION

E-58. Training information is also an important resource. Sources of training information include CATSs, battle drill manuals, Soldier training publications, Army doctrine publications, Army doctrine reference publications, field manuals, Army techniques publications, training circulars, technical manuals, regulations, and SOPs. CATSs are a key source for information concerning tasks and resource requirements, although they do not address requirements for lane experts.

E-59. Several automated systems contain training information that can be used to support lane training. Among them are the components of the ATMS. This system provides access to unit and collective training information. Automated systems can also be used to develop training COAs, plans, T&EOs, resource statuses and allocations, UTP calendars, training schedules, briefings, and assessments.

Appendix E

SIMULATIONS AND SIMULATORS

E-60. The effectiveness of lane training can be enhanced by using simulations and simulators during lane training planning and execution. Trainers ensure that lane preparation and execution are supported by appropriate training multipliers such as TADSS. Simulators, simulations, and other TADSS are training multipliers. They—
- Enhance the realism of pre-LTX training.
- Increase proficiency on prerequisite and LTX tasks through practice and repetition.
- Enhance the realism of both force-on-force and force-on targeting LTX.
- Reduce safety and environmental hazards.

E-61. Trainers design and use simulations to conduct preliminary training (pre-LTX), rehearsals, lane execution, or retraining. Units can use simulations and simulators during lane training—
- Prior to the LTX by—
  - Having the exercise director and lane planners develop effective scenarios.
  - Enabling OC/Ts to refresh or enhance their proficiency on lane tasks and prerequisite tasks in the preparation for conducting the LTX.
  - Having the training unit or the OPFOR to develop, maintain, or enhance Soldier, leader, and unit proficiency on LTX tasks or prerequisite tasks.
- During the LTX to—
  - Rehearse tasks trained on the lane.
  - Conduct the lane within a simulation or simulator.
  - Conduct the lane with the use of weapons simulators to enhance realism.
  - Provide feedback during an AAR (including statistics and a replay of events).
  - Retrain the unit after an AAR.

Simulations and simulators can also be employed simultaneously with the LTX to provide training to staffs or other personnel or units not training on the lane.

E-62. Exercise planners and leaders should integrate simulations, simulators, and other TADSS into their lane training process. The use of TADSS can enhance the replication of an operational environment and increase training effectiveness. However, the use of TADSS normally requires long-range planning.

INTERNAL AND EXTERNAL SUPPORT

E-63. The unit on an LTX should not provide its own support. This action prevents full participation in the LTX by all the unit's members. The lane training process and LTXs are categorized based on the primary source of resource support as either internally supported or externally supported.

Internally Supported

E-64. Internally supported training is training for which resource support is provided from within the unit responsible for managing training. Internally supported lane training is normally used when—
- Only one unit is undergoing lane training. In this situation, support functions frequently can be accomplished adequately by the next higher unit.
- Several units are undergoing training on one or more LTXs. In this situation, the supporting headquarters (two echelons above the training unit) identifies and obtains resources from units within the command.

Externally Supported

E-65. Externally supported training is training for which resource support is provided from outside the unit responsible for managing training. Externally supported lane training is normally required when several units undergo training on one or more LTXs and resource support cannot be provided from within the command responsible for managing the training. In this situation, the supporting (or managing)

Lane Training

headquarters identifies desired resource requirements and obtains resources from outside the command. Efficient trainers use multiple lanes that require much more planning, scheduling, coordinating, and resourcing than single lanes require.

Resource Sources

E-66. Resource support for lane training may be available from a variety of sources, such as—
- Adjacent units.
- Higher headquarters.
- Installations.
- Centers of excellence or training proponents.
- Readiness groups, regional training teams, resident training detachments, and the Ground Forces Readiness Enhancement Program.
- Regular Army regional training brigades for OC/Ts.
- United States Army Reserve exercise divisions (for OC/Ts for example).
- Regional training sites.

Note. United States Army Reserve exercise divisions provide a turnkey lane training capability for United States Army Reserve and Army National Guard units by providing a complete support package of training materials and services to units planning to conduct lane training.

E-67. The sources listed in paragraph E-66 can assist units in developing mission-focused leader training and in verifying the doctrinal and training proficiency of leaders, OC/Ts, and OPFOR. Once verified, leaders train and verify their Soldiers on selected tasks. Regional training brigades, readiness groups, regional training teams, and resident training detachments can assist units in developing leader training and validating leader proficiency.

E-68. Long-range planning and coordination are essential to ensure adequate support for lane training. When external support is not available, leaders conduct internally supported lanes.

This page intentionally left blank.

Appendix F
Unit Training Plan

INTRODUCTION

F-1. Once the higher commander approves the COA at the TB, the plan is developed as the UTP. The commander—supported by the staff at battalion and higher—begins to organize the COA, the guidance given by the higher commander, and all additional clarifying information into a five-paragraph field order. When completed, the commander disseminates it to subordinate and higher units as appropriate and posts it to the DTMS.

STEP 7 – ORDERS PRODUCTION, DISSEMINATION, AND TRANSITION

F-2. Figure F-1 illustrates the seven steps of the MDMP. Figure F-2 (beginning on page F-2) illustrates a sample UTP OPORD for brigade, battalion, and company levels. See FM 6-0 for a complete discussion on preparing an OPORD.

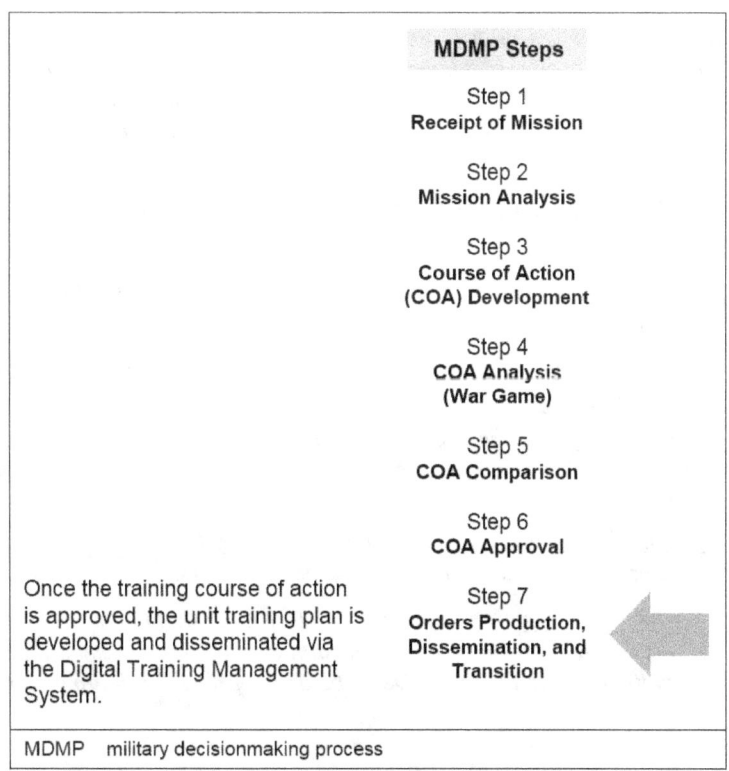

Figure F-1. Production and dissemination of the UTP

Appendix F

> [CLASSIFICATION]
>
> *Place the classification at the top and bottom of every page of the OPLAN or OPORD. Place the classification marking at the front of each paragraph and subparagraph in parentheses. Refer to AR 380-5 for classification and release marking instructions.*
>
>
>
> **Copy ## of ## copies**
> **Issuing headquarters**
> **Place of issue**
> **Date-time group of signature**
> **Message reference number**
>
>
>
> *The first line of the heading is the copy number assigned by the issuing headquarters. Maintain a log of specific copies issued to addressees. The second line is the official designation of the issuing headquarters (for example, 1st Infantry Division). The third line is the place of issue. It may be a code name, postal designation, or geographic location. The fourth line is the date or date-time group that the plan or order was signed or issued and becomes effective unless specified otherwise in the coordinating instructions. The fifth line is a headquarters internal control number assigned to all plans and orders in accordance with unit standard operating procedures (SOPs).*
>
> **OPERATION PLAN/ORDER [number] [(code name)] [(classification of title)]**
> Example: **OPORD 3411 (OPERATION DESERT DRAGON) (UNCLASSIFIED)**
>
> *Number plans and orders consecutively by calendar year. Include code name, if any.*
>
> **(U) References:** *List documents essential to understanding the operation plan (OPLAN) or operation order (OPORD). For example, higher headquarters training guidance, higher headquarters directives, OPORDs, ADP 7-0, ADRP 7-0, FM 7-0, Combined Arms Training Strategies (CATSs), Army Training Network (ATN), Digital Training Management System (DTMS), and decisive action standardized mission-essential task list (METL).*
>
> **(U) Time Zone Used Throughout the OPLAN/OPORD:** *State the time zone used in the training environment during execution. (Optional)*
>
> **(U) Task Organization:** *Describe the organization of forces available to the issuing headquarters and their command and support relationships. Refer to Annex A (Task Organization) if long or complicated.*
>
> **1. (U) <u>Situation</u>.** *Describe the conditions and circumstances of an operational environment for which the unit must train in the following subparagraphs:*
>
>   a. (U) <u>Training Environment.</u> *Use the operational variables to describe the environment at battalion and above and use the mission variables for company and below (a useful resource for the variables is ADRP 3-0, Operations).*
>
>   b. (U) <u>Friendly Forces</u>. *Briefly identify the missions of friendly forces and the objectives, goals, and missions of civilian organizations that impact the issuing headquarters.*
>
>   c. (U) <u>Training Risk, Challenges and Resources</u>. *List any significant training risks (such as insufficient time or resources) and challenges (such as difficulty obtaining resources or assets required to execute training) identified during planning. Describe any approved mitigating measures. This is not personnel safety risk.*
>
>
>
> [page number]
> [CLASSIFICATION]
>
>

Figure F-2. Operation plan or operation order format

[CLASSIFICATION]

OPLAN/OPORD [number] [(code name)] [issuing headquarters] [(classification of title)]

Place the classification and title of the OPLAN or OPORD and the issuing headquarters at the top of the second and any subsequent pages of the base plan or order.

    d. (U) <u>Attachments and Detachments</u>. List units attached or detached for training from the issuing headquarters. State when attachment or detachment is effective if different from the effective time of the OPORD. Do not repeat information already listed in Annex A (Task Organization).

    e. (U) <u>Assumptions</u>. List assumptions used for unit training plan (UTP) development, for example key challenges to training readiness, scarce or unique resources required to train, and estimated training time to achieve task proficiency.

2. (U) <u>Mission</u>. State the unit's mission—a short description of the who, what (task), when, where, and why (purpose) that clearly indicates the action to be taken and the reason for doing so. (Always include the mission-essential tasks [METs] and collective tasks in the mission statement, as they are the essential tasks to be trained as a result of mission analysis.)

3. (U) <u>Execution</u>. Describe how the commander trains the unit to proficiency in terms of commander's guidance, an overarching concept of operations, task assessment, specified tasks to subordinate units, and key coordinating instructions in the subparagraphs below.

    a. (U) <u>Commander's Training Guidance</u>. Provide commander's training guidance in a brief statement to include unit METs or collective tasks. The commander's training guidance is a clear and concise statement of the tasks' proficiency and leader traits and skills that the unit must achieve to successfully conduct operations in an anticipated operational environment. It succinctly describes what constitutes the success of the training plan and provides the purpose and conditions that define that desired end state.

    b. (U) <u>Concept of Operations</u>. The concept of operations is a statement that directs the manner in which subordinate units cooperate to obtaining MET or collective task proficiency and leader development. The concept establishes the sequence of actions and training events that the force will use to achieve the commander's training end state. It is normally expressed in terms of decisive, shaping, and sustaining operations. The UTP calendar helps portray the concept of operations and is located in Annex C (Collective Training Plan).

        (1) (U) <u>Decisive Operations (Collective Training)</u>. Describe the collective training plan that units will use to achieve MET or collective task proficiency. Refer to Annex C (Collective Training Plan) for the training focus for each training event on the calendar.

        (2) (U) <u>Shaping Operation #1 (Individual Training)</u>. Describe the individual training plan and how it supports the achievement of MET or collective task proficiency. Refer to Annex D (Individual Training Plan) for specific tasks.

        (3) (U) <u>Shaping Operation #2 (Leader Development)</u>. Describe the unit's leader development plan. Include leader certification, skills required to support the unit MET or collective task, officer professional development programs, and noncommissioned officer professional development programs. Refer to Annex E (Leader Development Plan) for specific tasks.

    c. (U) <u>Assessment</u>. Describe how the commander plans to assess training, MET or collective task proficiency, and leader development (may also require an annex or appendix).

    d. (U) <u>Tasks to Subordinate Units</u>. State the task assigned to each unit that reports directly to the headquarters issuing the order.

[page number]

[CLASSIFICATION]

Figure F-2. Operation plan or operation order format (continued)

Appendix F

[CLASSIFICATION]

OPLAN/OPORD [number] [(code name)]—[issuing headquarters] [(classification of title)]

e. (U) <u>Coordinating Instructions</u>. *List instruction and tasks applicable to two or more units not covered in the unit's training SOPs.*

(1) (U) <u>Timing</u>. *State the time or condition when the OPORD becomes effective and list the operational timeline.*

(2) (U) <u>Training Friendly Force Information Requirements</u>. *List the commander's plan to address key challenges to training.*

(3) (U) <u>Other Coordinating Instructions</u>. *List additional coordinating instructions and tasks that apply to two or more units.*

4. (U) <u>Sustainment</u>. *Describe the concept of sustainment, including priorities of sustainment by unit. Include installation requirements not included in SOPs. Include the projected dates of installation training resource conferences.*

5. (U) <u>Command and Signal</u>. *Include any changes from steady state (garrison) operations or state "no change."*

ACKNOWLEDGE: *Provide instructions for how the addressees acknowledge receipt of the OPLAN or OPORD. The word "acknowledge" may suffice. Refer to the message reference number if necessary. Acknowledgement of an OPLAN or OPORD means that it has been received and understood.*

[Commander's last name]
[Commander's rank]

The commander or authorized representative signs the original copy. If the representative signs the original, add the phrase "For the Commander." The signed copy is the historical copy and remains in the headquarters' files.

OFFICIAL:

[Authenticator's name]
[Authenticator's position]

Use only if the commander does not sign the original order. If the commander signs the original, no further authentication is required. If the commander does not sign, the signature of the preparing staff officer requires authentication and only the last name and rank of the commander appear in the signature block.

ANNEXES: *List annexes by letter and title. Army and joint OPLANs or OPORDs do not use Annexes I and O as attachments and in Army orders label these annexes "Not Used." Annexes T, X, and Y are available for use in Army OPLANs or OPORDs and are labeled as "Spare." When an attachment required by doctrine or an SOP is unnecessary, label it "Omitted."*

Annex A–Task Organization
Annex B– Training Environment
Annex C– Collective Training Plan
    Appendix 1 – METL with projected assessment for start of training and end of training
    Appendix 2 – Calendar
    Appendix 3 – Collective Training Event Objectives
Annex D– Individual Training Plan
Annex E– Leader Development Plan

DISTRIBUTION: A (example only)

[page number]
[CLASSIFICATION]

Figure F-2. Operation plan or operation order format (continued)

Appendix G
All Training Briefings

TYPES OF TRAINING BRIEFINGS

G-1. There are two types of TBs. These are the TB and the QTB (Regular Army) or YTB (Reserve Component). As described in chapter 3, at the TB the brigade and battalion commanders brief their UTP. These periodic QTBs or YTBs (discussed in chapter 3) provide the division commander updates on the status of UTP execution.

GENERAL FORMAT FOR THE TRAINING BRIEFING

G-2. The general format of a TB follows eleven basic slides:
- Brigade commander's training focus.
- Operational environment.
- Battalion training focus.
- Battalion's commander training guidance.
- Concept of operations: decisive operations.
- Concept of operations: shaping operations #1 (individual training).
- Concept of operations: shaping operations #2 (leader development).
- Assessment plans.
- Key resources required to train.
- Training risks.
- Training challenges.

G-3. To begin a TB, a brigade commander discusses the brigade training focus (see figure G-1) and the training environment to which the brigade will train (see figure G-2 on page G-2). All TB slides contain a title and bullet points. The figures in this appendix illustrate the details a user needs to add. Battalion commanders or command sergeants major follow the format of slides illustrated in figures G-3 through G-11 (beginning on page G-2) to complete the TB for their units. Commanders tailor the slides to meet their training requirements.

Brigade Commander's Training Focus

- State the brigade commander's training focus answering who, what, when, where, and why. The 'what' includes the METs the higher unit will focus training during the planning horizon.
- Include the training readiness rating (T-1 through T-4 in accordance with unit status reporting) the brigade will attain and sustain.

MET mission-essential task
T-   training week

Figure G-1. Sample slide for brigade training focus

Appendix G

Operational Environment

- Write a concise statement describing an operational environment the unit will train for (*train as you fight*).
- Break the statement down by operational variables—political, military, economic, social, information, infrastructure, physical environment, and time.

Figure G-2. Sample slide for training environment

Battalion Training Focus

- State the unit's training focus resulting from mission analysis and the backbrief to the higher commander.
- Answer who, what, when, where, and why. The 'what' includes the METs the unit will focus training on during the planning horizon to support the higher unit's training focus.

MET   mission-essential task

Figure G-3. Sample slide for battalion training focus

Battalion Commander's Training Guidance

- Write a concise (bulleted) statement of the commander's visualized end state for training.

- Include the current training proficiency assessments for each of the METs selected to train. Also include any additional training guidance given to subordinate units.

MET   mission-essential task

Figure G-4. Sample slide for training guidance

Concept of Operations: Decisive Operations

- Using the training strategy, state how the unit will train from the training start date to the end of the planning horizon.
- Refer to the long-range training calendar. Indicate the major training events and training objectives that the unit proposes to train (crawl-walk-run).
- Discuss dates of the EXEVAL and CTC rotations, planning, and execution status (as appropriate).
- Include the time management cycle.
- Discuss how the command will leverage the integrated training environment.

CTC   combat training center   EXEVAL   external evaluation

Figure G-5. First sample slide for concept of operations

All Training Briefings

Concept of Operations:
Shaping Operations #1 (individual training)

- Discuss individual training that supports the METs selected to train. The unit CSM is the primary briefer.
- CSM briefs the current and projected status of—
  - The unit's individual through section training.
  - Tasks that are nested with the unit's METs selected to train.

CSM   command sergeant major
MET   mission-essential task

Figure G-6. Second sample slide for concept of operations

Concept of Operations:
Shaping Operations #2 (leader development)

- Include the focus of leader development and the supporting training events during the planning horizon. Include subjects and details of the commander's leader development plans.
- Discuss how specific training events contribute to leader development.
- Discuss the leader assessment plan.

Figure G-7. Third sample slide for concept of operations

Assessment Plans

- Discuss how the unit plans to assess progressively and how it will develop training readiness as it executes the plan.
- Include—
  - How OC/Ts are trained and certified.
  - EXEVAL support requirements.
  - Resource support requirements for evaluations.

EXEVAL   external evaluation
OC/T   observer-controller/trainer

Figure G-8. Sample slide for assessment plans

Key Resources Required to Train

- State any major or unique resources required to meet training requirements.
- Include resources and facilities that are key to the unit achieving training readiness. Also include resources or facilities difficult to schedule or not readily available on the installation.

Figure G-9. Sample slide for key resources

Appendix G

> **Training Risk**
>
> State any training risk that the commander has identified that puts the plan at risk. This is **not a safety risk.** The risk exists because—
> - The key resources required to train are not available.
> - There is insufficient time to train to the readiness level required.

Figure G-10. Sample training risks

> **Training Challenges**
>
> State any additional challenges to the plan that will impact attaining training readiness.

Figure G-11. Sample training challenges

GENERAL FORMAT OF QUARTERLY OR YEARLY TRAINING BRIEFINGS

G-4. The QTB (for Regular Army) and the YTB (for Reserve Component) are periodic conferences on training between battalion commanders and division commanders. These TBs directly support the UTP. QTBs and YTBs are integral to the mid-range planning for training.

G-5. This discussion illustrates briefing slides for presenting QTBs and YTBs. The exact format and content will vary from command to command based on the commander's guidance and preference. Users can download slides for TBs slides from ATN. Staffs post the brigade and battalion UTP calendars in the meeting room for commanders to use as a reference throughout the briefing.

G-6. These TBs focus on reporting the overall progress of the UTP, identifying issues related to execution of the UTP, and ensuring the UTP as published is on track. The briefing gives battalion commanders a venue to discuss training previously conducted, training being conducted, and training planned for the future. These briefings can also be the venue for proposing and approving potential changes to the UTP as necessary. If changes are necessary, the base UTP OPORD requires a FRAGORD once the higher commander approves the modification.

G-7. The brigade commander begins a TB introducing the training focus and the training environment (see figures G-12 and G-13 [on page G-5]). Battalion commanders or command sergeants major follow the format of slides illustrated in figures G-14 through G-25 (beginning on page G-5) to complete the TB for their units. These figures provide sample slides to use as a guide to cover the minimum topics during a TB.

> **Brigade Commander Training Focus**
>
> - State the higher commander's training focus as stated in the unit training plan.
> - Include who, what, when, where, and why. The 'what' includes the METs the higher unit will train on during the planning horizon.
>
> MET   mission-essential task

Figure G-12. Sample slide for brigade training focus

All Training Briefings

Operational Environment
- Write a concise statement describing an operational environment the unit will train for (*train as you fight*).
- Break the statement down by operational variables—political, military, economic, social, information, infrastructure, physical environment, and time.

Figure G-13. Sample slide for training environment

Battalion Training Focus
- State the unit's training focus from the UTP.
- Answer who, what, when, where, and why. The 'what' includes the METs the unit will train on during the planning horizon to support the higher unit. If no mission is assigned, this should be the prioritized METL the unit will train.

MET   mission-essential task
METL mission-essential task list
UTP   unit training plan

Figure G-14. Sample slide for battalion training focus

Battalion MET Assessments
- List the unit METL (and METL for assigned missions if applicable). Include subordinate unit METs assessments.
- Indicate the current assessments of the METs selected to train. This helps frame the training strategy to improve and sustain proficiencies.

MET   mission-essential task
METL mission-essential task list

Figure G-15. Sample slide for battalion assessments

Last Quarter Training Highlights
- Review last quarter major multiechelon training events in accordance with the unit training plan. Review the associated training objectives and whether those objective were met or not met (and why).
- Discuss any training events planned but not conducted (and why).
- Discuss major training resources scheduled or ordered and not used (and why).
- Discuss plans to retrain and retry training objectives not met.

Figure G-16. Sample slide for last quarter training highlights

Appendix G

Current Quarter Training Highlights
- Review current quarter major multiechelon training events. Review the associated training objectives.
- Discuss any training events planned but not conducted (and why).
- Discuss major training resources scheduled or ordered and not used (and why).
- Discuss plans to retrain and retry training objectives not met.

Figure G-17. Sample slide for current quarter training highlights

---

Future Quarter Training Highlights
- Review plans for the future quarter (two quarters out) major multiechelon training events. Review the associated training objectives.
- Address other future training issues.

Figure G-18. Sample slide for future quarter training highlights

---

Training Resource Synchronization Conferences
- Discuss the unit's attendance at the last installation-level conference.
- Discuss the training resources (facilities and land) requested, not scheduled, and why.
- Discuss the unit's attendance at future installation training resource conferences (two quarters out).

Note: If possible, a representative of the installation DPTMS should attend the quarterly or yearly training briefing.

DPTMS   Directorate of Plans, Training, Mobilization and Security

Figure G-19. Sample slide for training resource synchronization conference

---

Soldier Training Assessment
- CSM and 1SG review individual Soldier training planned and conducted during the past, current, and future quarters.
- Discuss individual training planned, not conducted and why.
- Discuss the plan to retrain and retry individual tasks.
- Discuss the focus of opportunity (hip pocket) training tasks.

1SG   first sergeant
CSM   command sergeant major

Figure G-20. Sample slide for Soldier training assessment

Status of Schools

- Discuss the status of OES, WOES, NCOES, and troop schools' attendance for—
  - Current attendees.
  - Attendees projected two quarters out.
- Discuss personnel scheduled for training, but not attending and why.
- Discuss additional Soldier training needs of the unit.

NCOES   noncommissioned officer education system
OES   officer education system
WOES   warrant officer education system

Figure G-21. Sample slide for school statuses

Ammunition Status/Allocation

Show (by annual STRAC allocation/by DODIC and nomenclature):

Unit	Allocated	% Expended	Issues

DODIC   Department of Defense identification code
STRAC   standards in training commission

Figure G-22. Sample slide for ammunition status and allocation

Gunnery Scheduled

- Break out schedule in by-unit small arms, crew-served units, and by-gunnery units of gunnery and ranges scheduled and resourced two quarters out.
- Include basic rifle marksmanship and use of range simulations used in preparation for live-fire ranges and events.

Figure G-23. Sample slide for scheduled in gunnery

Appendix G

ITE Utilization

- Discuss unit utilization of ITE resources out to two quarters. Include constructive, virtual, and TADSS resources planned and coordinated.

- Discuss how these resources are planned and used in support of attaining training proficiency in METs selected to train.

Note: If possible, a representative of the installation DPTMS should attend the quarterly or yearly training briefing.

DPTMS Directorate of Plans, Training, Mobilization and Security
ITE integrated training environment
MET mission-essential task
TADSS training aids, devices, simulators, and simulations

Figure G-24. Sample for use of integrated training environment

Commander's Training Issues

- Discuss major training distracters last and current quarter.

- Discuss any unprogrammed taskings from higher headquarters that impacted approved, scheduled, and locked-in training.

- Discuss training issues the unit requires assistance to resolve.

Figure G-25. Sample slide for commander's training issues

Appendix H
T-Week Concept

PLANNING AND RESOURCING

H-1. The T-Week concept provides a detailed, backward-planning approach when planning training events. This concept also provides important considerations and specific activities for training event planning and coordination. Depending on the scope and complexity of the event, effective planners adjust activities that occur in each T-Week to fit resourcing and coordination requirements. When followed, planners ensure that they complete all actions to identify and coordinate leader and resource requirements prior to training. Each week previous to the execution of training requires planners to carefully coordinate all necessary training resources. These may include training areas, Class V requisitions, convoy clearances, and personnel certifications.

H-2. The degree of difficulty in planning training events varies. For example, preparations for conducting a class are significantly simpler than planning a FTX. More complex training events require more time to plan and coordinate.

H-3. Planners use the T-Week concept as a guide to assist in planning training activities that should occur in anticipation of each event. Each T-Week has an associated series of training activities that help guide planners and advise the commander of the actions the unit must accomplish to execute an effective training event.

H-4. The anchor point for the T-Week concept is the week training is executed. This is designated as T-Week. A minus sign (-) indicates the number of weeks prior to a particular training event execution. For example, T-5 is five weeks before the training event occurs. A plus sign (+) indicates the number of weeks following the event, for example, T+1 is one week after the training event. Units modify the T-Week concept to mirror their own local and command training requirements. See table H-1 on page H-2 as it breaks down hypothetical major T-Week activities.

H-5. The rest of this appendix breaks down major T-Week activities. Units can use this appendix as a guide for developing their own training activities and training events. Although this appendix contains extensive descriptions, they do not account for an individual unit or installation's particular resource requirements for planning and coordination. Additionally, each major training event falls into its own T-week construct as various points on the long-range, mid-range, and short-range planning horizons.

Appendix H

Table H-1. Illustrative T-Week concept

T-Week	Actions
UTP publication to T-13	Identify major training facilities
Week T-12	Conduct training event mission analysis
Week T-11	Refine training event requirements
Week T-10	Publish WARNORD and begin preexecution checks
Week T-9	Confirm resource requests
Week T-8	Execute reconnaissance and lock in resources
Week T-7	Publish the training event OPORD
Week T-6	Lock in training; publish training schedules
Week T-5	Complete plan and supporting products
Week T-4	Conduct certifications and complete prerequisite training
Week T-3	Conduct rehearsals
Week T-2	Finalize support and conduct OPFOR rehearsal
Week T-1	Draw equipment and supplies and execute subordinate rehearsals and checks
T-Week	Execute training
Week T+1	Recover, conduct final AARs, and assess training
AAR after action review OPFOR opposing force	OPORD operation order WARNORD warning order

Note. Reserve Component units should aggregate activities based on their monthly (rather than a weekly) schedule and published UTP.

UTP PUBLICATION TO T-13: IDENTIFY MAJOR TRAINING FACILITIES

H-6. Even before the UTP is published during the planning process, trainers begin to identify the major training resources and facilities that a training event will require. As soon as leaders identify the need for certain training resources and facilities, trainers actively begin to secure these for training. Successful planners and trainers require extensive knowledge of the facilities available on the installation. The installation Directorate of Plans, Training, Mobilization and Security is the primary source for the commander and trainers. This directorate documents and manages locally available training resources and the manner to schedule their use. These resources fall under the Army training support system. (See AR 350-2.)

TRAINING SUPPORT CENTER RESOURCES

H-7. An installation training support center is an organization that supplies training aids, devices, and facilities. Different installations offer different resources. A training support center may have the following resources available:
- Training land and training areas.
- Indirect firing points.
- Range facilities (to include multipurpose range complex, if available). Such facilities include range control facilities, processes, and may have certification requirements.
- Classroom facilities.
- LVC facilities.
- TADSS and TADSS warehouse.
- Medical Simulation Training Center.
- Flight simulators.
- Multiple Integrated Laser Engagement System (known as MILES) sets.

- Engagement Skills Training (known as EST) 2000.
- Improvised mock explosive training devices.
- Call for Fire Trainer (known as CFFT).

H-8. Early planning enables planners to schedule and lock in training facilities and resources for a unit. Depending on the installation, certain facilities are more heavily used than other facilities. Effective planners understand when and how to schedule such vital facilities. Once they schedule and reserve a facility for a unit, the commander ensures the unit occupies and uses the facility on the date and at the time scheduled. If planners or leaders cancel a training event, they do it as far in advance as possible so other units can schedule and use the facility.

INSTALLATION PLANNING AND FORECASTING TOOLS

H-9. Most installations publish a local supplement to provide training support requests for local procedures, tools, and timelines. Some supplements provide links to common forecasting tools, requesting tools, and unique training resources, such as—

- Total Ammunition Management Information System (known as TAMIS).
- Range Facility Management Support System (known as RFMSS).
- Integrated Training Area Management (known as ITAM).
- Mission training complexes.
- Training support centers.
- Medical evacuation (known as MEDEVAC) procedures and frequencies.

G-4s also publish procedures for all other classes of supply and services, food service, maintenance and transportation support, and nonstandard support items such as chemical latrines.

H-10. As the unit refines the plan, planners may need to cancel or modify training activities (planners do not cancel or modify activities when the unit is less than 6 weeks from that training). When planners identify that the unit will not need facilities and ranges early enough in the planning cycle, then other units can use the facilities. Installations usually conduct installation-level resource synchronization conferences to schedule and lock in major facilities (see paragraph 1-68 for a discussion on resource synchronization conferences). These conferences may be quarterly, semi-annual, or annual. They provide all units on the installation visibility of facility usage and availability for unit scheduling. Such facilities can include ranges, railhead training facilities, and simulation centers.

T-12: CONDUCT TRAINING EVENT MISSION ANALYSIS

H-11. In week T-12, planners conduct training event mission analysis. Gathering the information required to conduct training event planning is critical to developing successful events. Planners use historical information to begin mission analysis. Examples include AARs, inspection results, OPORDs, and troop lists. Historical information provides planners with the start point to shape future planning and for training assessment analysis.

H-12. Commanders refer to the approved UTP to re-confirm the METs and training objectives selected to train for each particular training event. Each training event requires a high degree of planning and coordination weeks in advance of execution. The resulting mission analysis ensures that planners account for the training event and the correct METs aligned in the UTP as they begin planning for the training event.

PREREQUISITE TRAINING

H-13. Prerequisite training is any training that a unit must complete or master before the planned training event. Prerequisite events can be any level event—such as classroom instruction, STXs, FTXs, and command post exercises—and are usually required at each progressive level of training difficulty. Commanders determine which events are prerequisites and ensure units perform the tasks to standard prior to beginning the next training event in the UTP. The CATS is the primary resource to view the proponent recommended prerequisite training. In the end, the commander decides whether to perform the CATS's recommended prerequisites, reduce or increase the CATS recommended frequencies, or choose a different prerequisite event based on the commander's experience.

Note. The Combined Report in CATS uses the term *training gates* to describe the recommended prerequisite events as well as the sequence (crawl-walk-run) for the events.

SERGEANT'S TIME TRAINING

H-14. As a subset of prerequisite training, commanders, sergeants major, first sergeants, and leaders at every level should always protect, support, incorporate, and maximize the importance of sergeant's time training (STT). STT is standards-based, performance-oriented, and mission-focused training. Commanders emphasize individual Soldier training in support of METs by allocating dedicated training time for NCOs using STT. STT recognizes the NCO's primary role in conducting individual, crew, and small-team training. If individual Soldiers and leaders cannot perform their basic tasks, the unit will never successfully accomplish or gain proficiency in its METs.

H-15. Units conduct this beneficial and effective training every week. Many installations reserve 3 or 4 hours each week for STT. The day or time of the week is not important. Units plan for, resource, rehearse, and execute STT with no external distracters.

H-16. STT builds cohesive teams. Based on their training assessment and platoon leader guidance, NCOs select specific individual, warrior, crew, and small-team tasks that support the unit's METs. Once these tasks are approved, NCOs plan for, prepare, rehearse, execute, and assess the training. Training the team to standard, not to time, is the bottom line; if additional time is needed or tasks must be retrained, the first line leaders must communicate these needs up the chain of command. Units can also use this time to train and educate Soldiers on the essential characteristics of the Army Profession.

H-17. STT develops junior leaders. Commanders demonstrate to junior leaders how to approve the selected tasks, provide the necessary resources, allocate time to prepare, and monitor the training. When subordinates demonstrate initiative, commanders exercise mission command to engage junior leaders. Command sergeants major or first sergeants supervise the training, and they coach, teach, and mentor junior NCOs.

T-11: REFINE TRAINING EVENT REQUIREMENTS

H-18. In week T-11, planners refine training event requirements. As the unit works through planning for the training event, planners require key pieces of information. An approved UTP contains initial training objectives for each training event, additional guidance, and MET or collective task proficiency requirements. Commanders and staffs review training objectives and refine them as necessary as well as identify additional tasks to train during the event. After refining objectives and tasks, commanders and staff refine the associated requirements for the objectives and tasks. These requirements can include facilities, resources, or materiel. Commanders and staffs refine these objectives and tasks as they execute the UTP and plan, prepare, execute, and assess each training event. Because every plan must be fluid and account for adjustments, commanders and staffs adjust the training objectives for each event during planning to reflect proficiencies mastered or required retraining after each event. See figure H-1 for a sample training objectives for a FTX.

---

17 – 21 February 2017
FTX Armor Company, Training Objectives

Task(s) Focus:
Conduct an Attack (07-2-9001)
Conduct Area Security (07-2-1324)
Breach an Obstacle (17-2-3070)

Conditions: In a complex, live environment, facing an enemy platoon in a prepared defense, occupying a village, conduct continuous operations, in both day and night and in various MOPP levels.

Standard: The company conducts operations in accordance with the SOP, the order, and higher guidance.

Training Proficiency: Achieve a T- proficiency rating in the collective tasks Conduct an Attack (07-2-9001), Conduct Area Security (07-2-1324), and Breach an Obstacle (17-2-3070).

| FTX | field training exercise | SOP | standard operating procedure |
| MOPP | mission-oriented protective posture | T- | trained |

Figure H-1. Sample training objectives

H-19. The UTP states a broad end state for each training event expressed as a training objective. Based on the commander's current assessment of unit training made during training meetings, training objectives may require refinement. This refinement ensures that the unit continues to progress at the training levels required to attain MET or collective task proficiency on time. An event end state clearly defines the task proficiency rating required at the end of the event. The end state focuses on the selected METs or collective tasks as well as on leader and individual Soldier training objectives.

H-20. After the training objectives for the event are refined, commanders and trainers refer to each task's T&EOs. This reference ensures the unit and OC/Ts can identify the standards for the tasks. OC/Ts also evaluate the training. A unit TDA—for units without proponent-published T&EOs for their tasks—may lack established standards. When no standard exists, the commander determines the conditions and standards, and the next higher commander approves the task. See appendix B for a discussion on T&EOs.

H-21. T&EOs are accessed via the "Task Search" on the ATN homepage. Users can also access T&EOs via the CATS Viewer and via DTMS on ATN, if the user has these privileges. T&EOs are also available on the CAR. Planners publish the applicable task T&EOs by task number and title in the OPORD and in separate packets to evaluating personnel. This ensures that commanders, planners, OC/Ts, and leaders at every level can reference and refer to published task standards prior to the commencement of the training event.

H-22. The UTP has an initial end state for the event expressed as a training objective. Based on the commander's assessment of training during training meetings leading up to the event, the training objective may also need to be refined or restated. This refinement ensures that the unit continues to progress at the training levels required to attain MET proficiency on time. The event end state should clearly define the performance proficiency level required at the end of the event. The end state focuses on METs as well as on leader and individual training objectives. Any refinement to the training objective includes refining requirements needed to complete the new objectives. For example, planners may need to schedule a range training event.

H-23. In refining training event training objectives, CATSs provide additional recommended training event details to consider. For example, commanders consider the integration of combat multipliers while conducting multiechelon training whenever possible. This integration optimizes the time available and ensures the unit trains as it will fight. The CATS also recommends the training audience to optimize the number of individual Soldiers trained during each event.

Appendix H

TRAINING EVENT PLANNING GUIDANCE

H-24. Commanders provide preexecution guidance to subordinate units early in the planning process. This ensures they meet the commander's guidance throughout the planning process. This guidance helps keep subordinate leaders and planners in synch with the commander's vision for the event. Preexecution guidance can include the following:
- Review AARs from previous events.
- Review training objectives for the event.
- Review applicable T&EOs for each MET trained.
- Review major resource requirements from the UTP.
- Train during normal duty hours unless requested otherwise.
- Identify and assess prerequisite training.
- Update during unit training meetings.

See also TC 7-101 for designing exercises. During T-11, planners review the preexecution guidance and refine the requirements as necessary.

TRAINER, EVALUATOR, OBSERVER-CONTROLLER/TRAINER, AND OPPOSING FORCE'S DUTIES

H-25. Based on the event training objectives, commanders determine the duties for trainers, evaluators, OC/Ts, and OPFORs. Successful planners clearly identify each part of the event to include the requirements and purpose. Planners also identify, qualify, and later refine supporting individuals (internal or external resource requirements) for an event. These personnel should be disinterested persons with regard to the outcome of the training event—typically personnel from outside the evaluated unit. In support of OC/T and OPFOR personnel duties, units often provide standardized evaluator packets based on their SOPs, so evaluators understand how the unit operates tactically.

T-10: PUBLISH WARNING ORDER AND BEGIN PREEXECUTION CHECKS

H-26. In week T-10, commanders publish the WARNORD and begin preexecution checks. Commanders conduct an initial countertask analysis. This analysis identifies requirements to train the tasks selected for the event, such as OPFOR actions required to stimulate the collective tasks. These tasks correlate directly to the training environment identified in the higher unit training WARNORD. Additional resources are available through the TRADOC Intelligence Support Activity (known as TRISA), Contemporary Operational Environment and Threat Integration Division (known as CTID) site, and the Training Brain Operations Center. AR 350-2 discusses the roles, responsibilities, and details on the training environment and OPFOR resources.

H-27. As part of the training event WARNORD, individual Soldier training objectives—the individual tasks trained by Soldiers during the event—are developed and published in the WARNORD. These training objectives should include individual-focused tasks and battle drills. These objectives directly correlate to the training environment identified in the training WARNORD. These are usually directed to be trained during the event, or included with all prerequisite training to be accomplished no later than T-4. Individual supporting tasks and battle drills are found in CATS listed under each of the collective tasks. The training gates are located in the CATS Combined Report and listed under the type of event (such as a FTX). Figure H-2 illustrates individual training objectives provided to a company by a platoon.

> *Individual Tasks*
>
> Individual training task focus (weeks T-9 to T-7) in preparation for the company FTX:
> - Move Under Direct Fire (071-COM-0502)
> - Direct Main Gun Engagements on M1-Series Tank (171-126-1322)
> - Direct Machine Gun Engagements on M1-Series Tank (171-126-1262)
> - Communicate in a Radio Net (113-571-1003)
> - Engage Targets with M16 / M4 Series Carbine (071-COM-0030)
>
> *Battle Drills*
>
> Battle drill focus training (weeks T-6 to T-4) in preparation for the company FTX:
> - React to an IED Attack While Mounted (05-3-D0017)
> - React to Direct Fire Contact (07-3-D9501)
> - React to Indirect Fire (07-3-D9504)
> - React to CBRN Attack (17-3-D8006)
> - Breach of a Mined Wired Obstacle (07-3-D9412)
>
> *Training Gates*
>
> Individual tasks and battle drills nested with training gates (from CATS) for an armor company FTX:
> - STX Attack
> - STX Defend
> - STX Breaching Operations
>
> | | | | |
> |---|---|---|---|
> | CATS | Combined Arms Training Strategy | IED | improvised explosive device |
> | CBRN | chemical, biological, radiological, and nuclear | STX | situational training exercise |
> | FTX | field training exercise | | |

Figure H-2. Example of individual training objectives

TRAINING ENVIRONMENT

H-28. As part of the training environment identified in the WARNORD, the staff analyzes potential operational environments to provide the requisite amount of realism to the training. A training environment that properly replicates a potential operational environment provides a higher degree of fidelity to the training scenarios developed in support of the event. Ultimately, it makes the training more challenging and realistic for the unit and at the Soldier level. When published in the WARNORD, information regarding the training environment helps subordinate units identify the necessary training resources to coordinate prior to the event.

H-29. Defining the training environment involves determining the tasks to be trained, the necessary OPFOR countertasks, and variables that provide the necessary physical, mental, and ethical stressors. The training environment provides a generalized representation of potential enemies and projected operational environment conditions that challenge unit task execution. For example, when this information is published in a WARNORD for a mission rehearsal exercise where an operational environment is known, trainers apply known information from the theater of operations to make training more realistic.

TRAINING SUPPORT

H-30. Training support includes selecting training environments, developing a base tactical scenario, and publishing a WARNORD. Once the tasks and the training environment are determined for an event, the training support enablers must be selected. Training support consists of TADSS; facilities (mission training complexes and ranges), and services (personnel running the ranges).

Select Training Environments

H-31. Collective training events take place in three types of training environments: LVC. Planners consider employing each environment independently (the easiest to plan and prepare) or a combination of two or

Appendix H

more environments to meet the objective. If using more than one training environment, then leaders use either a BTE or an ITE. Planners choose the environment based on the installation's openings in the fielding schedule and the environment that best enables the unit to accomplish its training objectives in the time allotted.

H-32. Just as a leader must understand an operational environment in combat, a leader must understand the training environment for a training event. Leaders and trainers take the initiative, quickly develop partnerships with the right people—personnel at the Directorate of Plans, Training, Mobilization and Security; range control, and the mission training complex—and familiarize themselves with training capabilities. Subsequently, they take subordinate leaders on a terrain walk of those facilities and capabilities.

Develop a Base Tactical Scenario

H-33. A primary driver to the training event is the development of a tactical scenario. The tactical scenario provides a realistic backdrop to training when it properly replicates an operational environment. Focused on the training objectives to achieve during the event, a tactical scenario simulates the situations that cause the unit and Soldiers to act and react to specific situations, whereby the training objectives (collective tasks) can be evaluated and assessed. After determining the OPFOR requirements, a determination of the initial requirements for scripting and role-playing as well as complete the MSEL. All the information gathered and developed during weeks T-11 and T-10 inform the commander of the personnel, logistics, and other resource requirements to support the performance of the training event.

Publish WARNORD

H-34. Once planners compile the information gathered and developed during weeks T-11 and T-10, the commander issues a WARNORD tasking subordinates and requiring coordination to support the event. The staff distributes the WARNORD at the end of mission analysis to facilitate parallel planning at the subordinate unit level. At a minimum, the WARNORD contains the training audience, training objectives, location, date, resources, and personnel support requirements and training environment guidance.

PREEXECUTION CHECKS

H-35. Preexecution checks are informal checks that units complete to coordinate prior to conducting training events; these are not precombat checks. The chain of command develops these checks to prepare participants systematically and to ensure that units resource and properly conduct training. As units develop training schedules, the checks become increasingly detailed. Preexecution checks provide the attention to detail needed to use resources efficiently.

H-36. Preexecution checks are an important component of preparation for training events. A unit goes through the checks intending to have a YES for every response. Checks with a NO response require the unit to make corrections. Sample questions for a preexecution checklist can include the following:
- Is the current level of collective or individual task proficiency rating a trained or fully trained?
- Have the lessons learned from the last time training been applied?
- Has the OPFOR been equipped and trained (if applicable)?
- Are combat multipliers integrated into planning and execution of training?
- Has a risk assessment been completed? Have safety considerations been completed?
- Are Soldiers trained on prerequisite tasks?
- Has the appropriate training support been requested?
- Has reconnaissance of the training site been conducted?
- Are ranges and maneuver books on hand?
- Are leaders certified to conduct range operations?
- Are leaders briefed on environmental considerations?
- Have convoy clearances been submitted and approved?

- Have TADSS been identified, requested, and approved?
- Can trainers properly operate all TADSS?
- Has Class I been requested?
- Has Class III been requested and picked up?
- Has Class V been requested per ammunition supply point requirements and picked up?
- Has transportation been requested?
- Are sufficient expendable supplies on hand?
- Is a rehearsal time programmed for trainers?
- Has a backbrief for the chain of command been coordinated?
- Are times scheduled for AARs at the end and throughout the exercise?

T-9: CONFIRM RESOURCE REQUESTS

H-37. In T-9, commanders confirm resource requests. When the UTP is published to T-13, the UTP identifies major resource requirements and the planners requisition and schedule all supporting resources with the local installation. In T-9, commanders and staff confirm resources requisitioned before T-13 to ensure their availability when and where needed during T-Week. The unit also continues to review and refine requirements for every class of supply to support both the administrative and tactical executions of the training event. Planners can access general resource requirements (Classes V and IX) and other information in the CATS. The commander modifies these general requirements based on the desired end state of training or the local training environment. Planners draw and confirm resource estimates from three main sources: CATS, tactical logistic planning tools, and request support.

H-38. Security classification of a training event and its associated measures can impact the administrative resource requirements. The higher the classification of an event, the more limiting the resources. For example, a training event with a higher classification may require more guards, protocols, and destruction capabilities.

COMBINED ARMS TRAINING STRATEGY

H-39. The CATS provides proponent-recommended resources necessary to conduct training. It provides units with a good starting point to begin determining their requirements. Successful planners review historic documentation from previous training events and gather experience from the commander and staff. Planners then refine and improve data gathered from the CATS and forecast their unit needs. The more resource-constrained the training environment, the more likely leaders will use virtual, constructive, or combined capabilities to support training.

H-40. After determining OPFOR requirements and the tactical scenario, commanders make a more informed estimate of the TADSS required to support the training event. The CATS contains general TADSS recommendations for each training event. The commander modifies the recommended TADSS based on the desired end state of training and the local training environment. Commanders and planners use the TADSS to refine or research their requirements. The CATS provides TADSS's descriptions, contacts for every installation, and a list of resources and supporting materials. Successful trainers check in with their local installation-level TADSS office first to determine locally available resources and to coordinate off-installation support when needed.

TACTICAL LOGISTIC PLANNING TOOLS

H-41. Commanders and planners use installation planning tools to confirm resource requests. Various planning tools such as the operational logistic planner are available for planning every class of supply. The operational logistic planner is the official U.S. Army tool for planning tactical logistic requirements, but others planners are readily available.

Appendix H

REQUEST SUPPORT

H-42. Almost every resource and class of supply has different systems, Web sites, procedures, and timelines for forecasting and requesting. Effective training requests require commanders and planners to verify that the installation or approval authority processes their requests promptly. Requests should be processed as soon as possible and in accordance with the required timelines set by higher.

T-8: EXECUTE RECONNAISSANCE AND LOCK IN RESOURCES

H-43. In week T-8, commanders execute reconnaissance and lock in resources. After determining the training environment and required training support resources, commanders conduct an initial reconnaissance of the training sites and facilities. A thorough and detailed reconnaissance ensures that the training environment provides the necessary conditions to facilitate the training of the collective tasks to the level of fidelity needed. This reconnaissance enables commanders to identify details to complete the plan, specifically the simulations architecture possibilities and limitations. This reconnaissance also helps commanders identify any previously overlooked resources and other issues including security issues, traffic control, and possible route concerns. A reconnaissance requires the following minimum personnel: leaders, evaluators, trainers, OC/Ts, and OPFOR.

TRAINING AREA RECONNAISSANCE QUESTIONS

H-44. A unit strives to have a YES or clarification for every response. Questions with a NO or vague response require the unit to make corrections. During the initial reconnaissance, commander and planners answer the following administrative questions:

- Are reconnaissance personnel familiar with the training event OPORD and commander's guidance?
- Are there safety-related environmental factors (flash flood area, electric hazards, or wildlife)?
- Does the terrain support administrative employment of equipment and personnel? How?
- Are sleep areas located in acceptable area?
- Is the maintenance area acceptable?
- Is the distance from garrison less than one mile?
- Is the amount of fuel required acceptable and sustainable? Confirm.
- Is heavy equipment transport an option?
- Are maps available?
- Is satellite imagery updated?
- Is the resupply point located in acceptable area? Confirm.
- Can roads and bridges support heavy vehicle crossing? Confirm.
- Is the road network in the area of operations sufficient to support the operation?
- Does the traffic flow inside the area of operations need to be marked?
- Is there an area sufficient for aerial medical evacuation?
- Are civilians cleared from the area? Confirm.
- Does logistic support exist on site? Does it include water, electric, and sewer?
- Does fixed site support exist on site? What type is it? Will it support the commander's objective?
- Is the access control point located in acceptable area?

H-45. During the initial reconnaissance, commander and planners answer the following tactical questions:

- Can the terrain support the commander's objectives?
- Is the area large enough to support the required unit-level maneuver?
- Does the terrain support tactical employment of equipment and personnel? How?
- Is the fuel point located at acceptable distance? Confirm.
- Is the ammunition distribution point located at acceptable distance? What is the blast area?
- Is the network available (for example cell phone, or satellite)?

- Are the command post and alternate command post located in acceptable areas?
- Is the amount of Class IV required acceptable and sustainable? Confirm.
- Is the prisoner exchange point acceptable and sustainable?
- Are enemy avenues of approach located? Identify locations.
- Are fields of fire identified? Identify areas.
- Is the safety danger zone identified? Identify area.
- Are the observations post located in acceptable locations? Identify locations.
- Are alternate and secondary positions in acceptable locations? Identify locations.
- Does terrain facilitate traffic management?

LOCK IN RESOURCES

H-46. Following initial reconnaissance, commanders and planners re-confirm that all resources are locked-in (request receipts verified and recorded in memo format) to ensure all equipment, facilities, and supplies are available for training. Effective commanders and planners check the local installation requirements for locking in resources. They often manage training resources via annual, quarterly, and weekly conferences or meetings. Common examples of such meetings include but are not limited to—

- A monthly training resource integration conference.
- A weekly range and training area scheduling conference.

T-7: PUBLISH THE TRAINING EVENT OPERATION ORDER

H-47. In week T-7, commanders publish the training event OPORD. After the commander has approved the plan, the OPORD is published on DTMS. Planners use the standard five-paragraph OPORD format with required modifications to the annexes to reflect training-specific requirements.

H-48. The base OPORD for the training event coordinates the actions necessary to manage the execution of the event. This does not include the plan and MSEL. The OPORD identifies the collective and individual tasks to be trained and the desired levels of task proficiency expected to be reached by the conclusion of training. The OPORD also addresses the actions to be taken to retrain the collective and individual tasks during the event if the desired end state is not achieved. See figure F-2 beginning on page F-2 for a sample OPORD. The staff can publish annexes later as a follow up.

H-49. Planners add the friendly force (training audience) and the OPFOR troop list to the published OPORD. The OPORD identifies trainers, evaluators, and OC/Ts. At seven weeks out, specific names may not yet be available; however, the OPORD identifies the grade and background necessary to fill the positions. These details help a subordinate or coordinating unit fill the tasking for support through higher headquarters. If planners know the names of individuals, this information is included in the OPORD.

H-50. The execution paragraph of the OPORD identifies the leader development plan. This plan addresses prerequisite training leading up to the event, the event itself, and the follow-on post event reviews. Effective training for leaders grows increasingly difficult and complex to train adaptable and agile leaders. Figure H-3 on page H-12 illustrates a leader development plan for a company-level training event.

Appendix H

---

17 – 21 February 2017
FTX Armor Company, Leader Development

METs or tasks to train:
    Conduct an Attack (07-2-9001)
    Conduct a Defense (07-2-9003)
    Conduct Area Security (07-2-1324)
    Breach an Obstacle (17-2-3070)

Leader Objective: Demonstrated ability to make sound tactical decisions enabling unit battlefield success.

Leader Training:
Crawl:
    Conduct professional development classes – Attack (T-8); Deliberate Breach (T-7); Defend (T-6); and Area Security (T-5)
    Review unit SOPs, collective task T&EO, and TTP (check on learning during rehearsal)
    Develop individual training objectives at all echelons (T-10)
    Conduct leader certification training as necessary (training area, driver training, and more)

Walk:
    Squad Rehearsal (T-3); Platoon Rehearsal (T-2); and Company Rehearsal (T-1)
    Conduct Pre-Execution Checks (T-10 – T-1)
    Conduct Pre-Combat Checks (T-Week)

Run:
    Conduct informal after action reviews at all echelons (T-Week)
    Conduct leader performance feedback at all echelons
    All leaders facilitate a positive learning environment (T-Week)

FTX	field training exercise	T&EO	training and evaluation outline
MET	mission-essential task	T-	training week
SOP	standard operating procedure	TTP	tactics, techniques, and procedures

---

Figure H-3. Sample leader development plan for an armor company

H-51. The logistic plan to support the training event is the last critical piece of the OPORD. This plan addresses the resources requested at T-9. The logistic plan also lays out the coordination requirements for attached support, such as medical, maintenance, chemical, engineer, and military police support. Figure H-4 depicts an example of a logistic support plan for a company-level training event.

> **17 – 21 February 2017**
> **FTX Armor Company, Logistic Support Plan**
>
> **Logistic Support Objective:** Provide continuous logistic support to the company, OPFOR and attachments during the FTX.
>
> **Class I:** Ration cycle M-M-A, Battalion logistics operations 1500 daily at designated resupply point. Estimated headcount – 96; OPFOR headcount – 32. Two days of supply on hand basic load.
>
> **Class III:** Resupply daily; estimated fuel consumption – 430 gal per day; OPFOR – 300 gal per day. Oil as required.
>
> **Class IV:** Located at the designated Class IV point; issue on order.
>
> **Class V:** L602 – 504; OPFOR 288
> K866 – 6; OPFOR 2
> A080– 4,080; OPFOR 2,040
> G950 – 8; OPFOR 4; OC/T 2
> L709– OC/T 30
> LG936 – OC 8
>
> Resupply from ammunition holding area to ammunition supply point on T-Day 1. Distribution on order.
>
> **Class VIII:** Combat lifesaver bags fully supplied (1 per vehicle); Medical attachment with basic load.
>
> **Class IX:** Prescriber load list items available on request.
>
> **Medical:** Medical team attached to the company; combat lifesavers trained – one per vehicle.
>
> **Maintenance:** Company maintenance and recovery team attached.
>
> FTX   field training exercise   OC/T   observer-controller/trainer   OPFOR   opposing force

Figure H-4. Sample logistic support plan for an armor company

H-52. After commanders identify and request TADSS requirements, commanders schedule the training necessary to ensure trainers and operators are trained and certified prior to the event.

T-6: LOCK IN TRAINING AND PUBLISH TRAINING SCHEDULES

H-53. At week T-6, commanders lock in training and publish training schedules. Failure to lock in training and adhere to published training schedules can ruin the unit's ability to execute effective training. The act of locking in training creates an atmosphere in which leaders and Soldiers at all levels build confidence in the unit's leaders to ensure training is predictable, protected, and supported by the chain of command. The message sent by such discipline is that training and leader development are unit priorities.

H-54. Training schedules are focused and published at the company level. Unit commanders issue training schedules as a written order and use them as the primary means to communicate the scheduled training to Soldiers. Training schedules cite the collective or individual tasks to be trained. Training schedules are usually organized by or coincide with training weeks and cover a full week or more. Units publish training schedules T-6 week from training. Training schedules are signed by the unit commander and approved by the next higher commander (see figure H-5 on page H-14). For example, a company training schedule is signed by the company commander and approved by the battalion commander. The commander ensures that training schedules are conspicuously posted in the company area and electronically provides them directly to unit personnel as necessary.

Appendix H

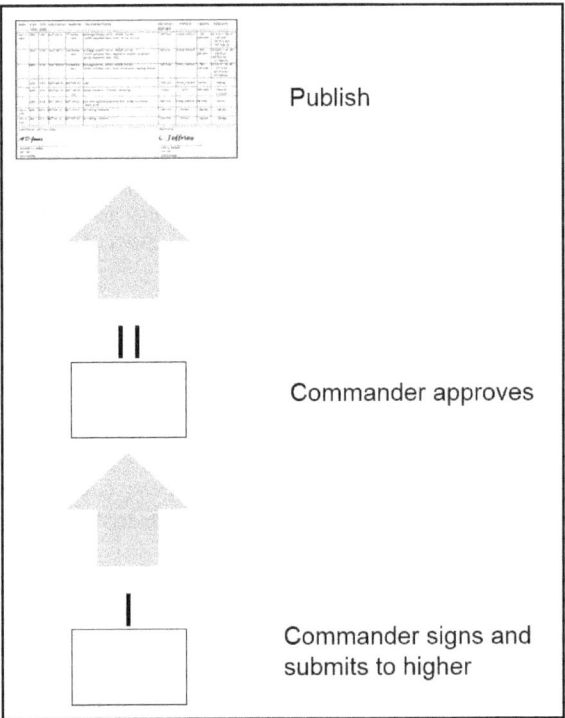

Figure H-5. Approval of company training schedules

CHANGES TO PUBLISHED TRAINING SCHEDULES

H-55. Changes to training are sometime unavoidable, but to the greatest extent, effective leaders keep changes to an absolute minimum. Higher commanders protect subordinate units from needless, unprogrammed taskings and other training distracters. One protection technique is to establish an approving authority for changes to company-level training schedules once published. For example, if a change occurs to a company training schedule, then the brigade commander must approve the change. This helps keep changes to an absolute minimum and makes training more predictable for Soldiers and trainers. See figure H-6.

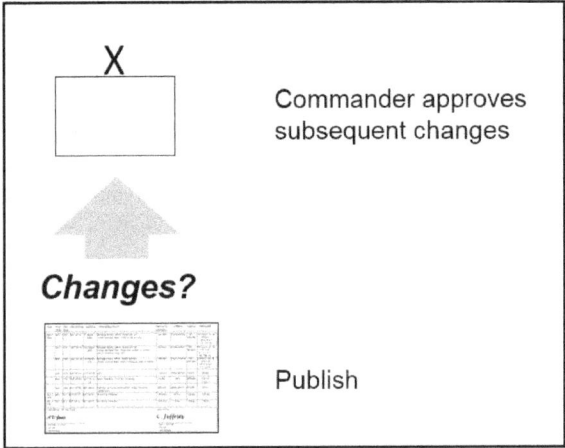

Figure H-6. Recommended approval process for changes

H-56. A training schedule specifies the tasks for a Soldier to train, the location to train, the time to train, the uniform to wear, and the equipment to bring. It also tells a Soldier any additional information, to include the references to read regarding the particular training task, event, or operation. A training schedule also identifies the instructors or trainers.

PUBLISHED TRAINING SCHEDULES IN DTMS

H-57. At T-6, the staff locks in and publishes the training schedules and calendars in DTMS upon approval in the unit training meeting. The company and battalion commanders approve and digitally sign the training schedule in DTMS. Once published, Soldiers can view their company's training schedules in their MyTraining Tab on ATN (see figure H-7). This access facilitates Soldier knowledge of UTPs and maximizes the Soldiers time to prepare in advance.

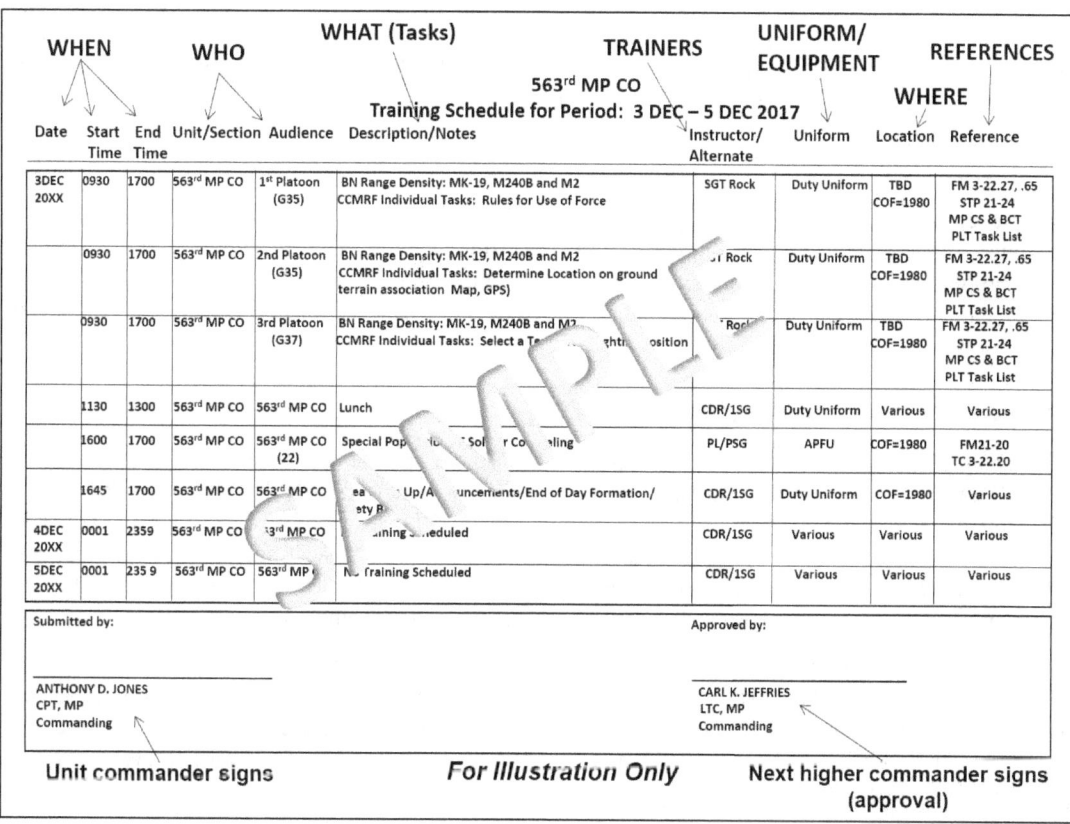

Figure H-7. Example company training schedule

DELIBERATE RISK ASSESSMENTS

H-58. The unit staff completes and submits a DD Form 2977 (*Deliberate Risk Assessment Worksheet*) to the higher commander for review and approval. More important than completing the form is the mental process used by the commander to identify and mitigate safety risks. Often, identifying the right leader positioned at the most dangerous place or time for the unit is the best mitigating control measure. See ATP 5-19 and the U.S. Army Combat Readiness Center's Risk Management courses for mitigating risk.

T-5: COMPLETE PLAN AND PROVIDE SUPPORTING PRODUCTS

H-59. At T-5, commanders complete the plan and provide supporting products. After publishing the OPORD, locking in the resources, and publishing the training schedule, the staff can begin to complete the rest of the plan.

Appendix H

COMPLETED PLAN

H-60. The plan covers both the friendly force and OPFOR. The plan drives the training to meet the training objectives. The T-5 plan identifies both the training audience and the OPFOR to ensure all training aids are synchronized and focused. If training involves multiple training support enablers, then identification of the audience and participants is important. Units will require assistance from a local mission training complex to ensure data are uploaded into the simulation.

COMPLETED MASTER SCENARIO EVENTS LIST

H-61. Units develop a MSEL at T-10 to develop the training scenario and set the conditions for the unit to display proficiency in the tasks evaluated during the training. The MSEL drives OPFOR actions that stimulate a friendly force reaction. A MSEL scenario is developed chronologically to stimulate friendly force actions from the beginning of the exercise to the end. The MSEL also provides the stimulus for evaluators to observe and evaluate the selected training objectives.

EXERCISE CONTROL PLAN

H-62. Developing an exercise control plan helps synchronize and manage the training event. For a small-unit training event, this can be a simple graphic with timelines and control measures. For a large-scale event, the plan may include a complex scenario, white cell personnel and equipment, OC/Ts, and rules of engagement. In addition to the scenario, a higher headquarters develops an OPORD to drive the training event.

OBSERVER-CONTROLLER/TRAINER PLAN

H-63. The OC/T plan addresses who (by name) the OC/Ts are and the assessment plan. It outlines how the OC/Ts (by name) are supported with supplies (and from whom) and details the OC/Ts' duties. The OC/T plan itemizes the OC/T packet contents. For example, the OC/T packet might contain unit SOPs, T&EOs, doctrine, pyrotechnics (Class V) on hand, and a Multiple Integrated Laser Engagement System (known as MILES) sets. OC/Ts read and make themselves familiar with both the friendly forces and OPFOR plans as well as attend key unit events (such as backbriefs, rehearsals, and precombat checks).

H-64. OC/Ts ensure all systems work properly prior to the training event to ensure accurate outcomes. OC/Ts familiarize themselves with the training support systems used for the event. Effective OC/Ts conduct work-arounds if live or simulated conditions cannot portray the realism necessary to achieve the training objectives. As with the leaders, OC/Ts ensure the unit conducts the training event safely. They address unsafe acts immediately.

EVALUATION PLAN

H-65. The evaluators may be internal or external to a unit. Evaluators must have a copy of the collective and individual tasks' T&EOs and be familiar with the scenario to ensure proper evaluation. Evaluators can be separate from the OC/Ts, allowing OC/Ts to be strictly trainers and facilitate AARs. OC/Ts can also be evaluators, depending on the commander's guidance and type of exercise. Upon completion, evaluators give evaluation packets to the commander for the commander's assessment.

T-4: CONDUCT CERTIFICATIONS AND COMPLETE PREREQUISITE TRAINING

H-66. At T-4, commanders conduct certifications and complete requisite training. Evaluators report to the commander. They must understand the collective tasks they are evaluating, the scenario, and the training environment. Commanders ensure the evaluators are prepared. The plan must have all link-up times and list items evaluators need to bring—T&EOs, references, and support if necessary. Evaluators also backbrief the commander prior to execution to ensure everyone is synchronized.

H-67. The OPFOR leaders backbrief the commander on their plan. The commander may adjust the OPFOR plan based on the training objectives. OPFOR capabilities should be sufficient to ensure flexibility during the event. The OPFOR must correctly portray the threat and be prepared to execute threat TTP. The commander or designated representative certifies that the OPFOR's portrayal is correct. The OPFOR must have countertasks identified so that they will prompt the unit to train and perform the collective and individual tasks to the Army standard (as stated in the T&EO).

TRAIN THE TRAINERS

H-68. Qualified OC/Ts have training to facilitate the appropriate type of AAR for the event (informal or formal). They must have full knowledge of the scenario, friendly forces, and OPFOR plans, training environment, and training objectives. They must understand all safety and medical evacuation procedures. The commander certifies the OC/Ts through backbriefs on the training and training requirements.

H-69. Qualified and competent trainers are critical in delivering quality, effective training to the unit. Trainers demonstrate task proficiency before teaching a task to others. Commanders and leaders ensure that trainers are prepared to conduct performance-oriented training to standard. They ensure adequate preparation time so the trainers—

- Understand the commander's guidance.
- Know the tasks, conditions, and standards to be performed.
- Have demonstrated the tasks to standard.
- Review references, such as ADP 7-0, ADRP 7-0, FM 7-0, ATN, T&EOs, CATS, CAR, Soldier's manuals, field manuals, and technical manuals as needed.
- Gather and prepare training support items as required.
- Conduct a reconnaissance of the training site prior to training.
- Prepare the training and materials needed.
- Integrate the risk assessment process.
- Schedule rehearsals for themselves and other trainers.
- Plan, prepare, and rehearse the conduct of AARs.

CERTIFICATION

H-70. Certification is a measure of individual, crew, or team technical proficiency. Unit commanders are responsible for creating and managing unit certification programs. Certification is not a normal part of day-to-day training. A higher headquarters decides to require certification after a deliberate process. Certification requirements for OC/Ts and individuals to supervise live-fire ranges and EXEVALs illustrate individual technical proficiencies that commanders may require to support training. Certification is more often applied to processes and procedures that support training and operations, like conduct of live fire ranges.

H-71. Commanders may require certification to confirm a unit's collective training proficiency to perform a specific type of mission or task. Certification of an infantry squad tasked to conduct a specific stability or support task is an example of unit collective certification. Higher headquarters on a by-exception basis normally directs this confirmation requirement.

Note. Individual Soldier certifications are recorded in DTMS in the "Soldier Manager" tab.

T-3: CONDUCT REHEARSALS

H-72. At T-3, commanders conduct rehearsals. Prior to conducting a rehearsal, staffs conduct the final reconnaissance of the training site. Staffs completed the initial reconnaissance at T-8 (five weeks previously). Since that time, changes may have occurred. Sometimes these changes alter the plan slightly, such as changing the location of the assembly area or the route to the training area. The staff publishes new timings or graphics in a FRAGORD.

H-73. A *rehearsal* is a session in which a staff or unit practices expected actions to improve performance during execution (ADRP 5-0). Units conduct rehearsals before training events and early enough to conduct multiple rehearsals, if necessary. Rehearsals provide an invaluable means of ensuring actions during training are synchronized and executed to standard. Rehearsals also provide a mechanism for leaders and Soldiers to visualize what is supposed to happen and to correct deficiencies during subsequent rehearsals, if necessary. Rehearsals allow leaders to—

- Identify weak points in the plan.
- Teach effective training techniques.
- Coach trainers until they feel comfortable.
- Ensure safety and environmental considerations are met and updated.
- Determine if subordinate leaders are tactically and technically proficient.
- Determine how the trainer will evaluate the Soldier's or unit's performance.
- Assess subordinate trainer competencies and provide feedback.
- Give subordinates confidence in their ability to train or operate.

H-74. FM 6-0 discusses rehearsals at length. Some leaders use the following checklist as a guide for conducting rehearsals:

- Rehearsal agenda.
- Conduct roll call.
- Participant orientation to terrain.
- Location of local civilians.
- Enemy situation brief.
- Friendly situation brief.
- Description of expected enemy actions.
- Discussion of friendly unit actions.
- Review of notes made by the recorder.

T-2: FINALIZE SUPPORT AND CONDUCT OPPOSING FORCE REHEARSAL

H-75. At T-2, commanders finalize support and conduct an OPFOR rehearsal. Staffs submit all administrative clearances and requests as necessary. These clearances and requests can include convoy clearances, wash rack requests, and range requests to include surface danger zone schematics.

SUPPORT FINALIZED

H-76. Commanders and planners complete a final review of all support requests for the event. They check and double check these to ensure that the support required and requested for the event in the T-weeks prior to T-2 will be present for T-Week. This includes a final check of all classes of supply, all ranges, training areas, TADSS, and all other required training support. This includes making personal contact between unit planners and facility and support managers. In many cases, training events fail because the unit did not make these crucial final support checks, which can result in training planned, but not conducted.

TADSS CERTIFICATION TRAINING

H-77. Units conduct TADSS certification training for trainers as scheduled during T-7.

OPFOR REHEARSAL

H-78. The OPFOR conducts a rehearsal to ensure its plan facilitates the friendly force achieving its training objectives. This rehearsal includes the administrative movement and preparation for the event as well as the

T-Week Concept

plan. The rehearsal enables subordinates to synchronize their plans with each other and enables leaders to address possible decision points. The evaluators and OC/Ts attend the OPFOR rehearsal to ensure they fully understand the execution of the event.

T-1: DRAW EQUIPMENT AND SUPPLIES AND EXECUTE SUBORDINATE REHEARSALS AND CHECKS

H-79. At T-1, if not previously done, the unit draws all required equipment and tests it to ensure it is operational, thereby providing time to work through problems before the event starts. Training support centers have exchange procedures for swapping unserviceable TADSS for serviceable items (if enough items are available). Units should plan sufficient time to exchange TADSS items, as necessary.

TRAINING SITE PREPARATION

H-80. Commanders conduct all final site preparation during T-1. If using a mission training complex to support training, commanders complete all preparations of the TADSS to be used.

UNIT REHEARSAL

H-81. Commanders conduct a unit rehearsal to ensure the plan is synchronized and enables the leaders to make decisions at the right time. The evaluators and OC/Ts attend the friendly force rehearsal to ensure they fully understand the execution of the event. The rehearsal can facilitate adjustments to the MSEL.

COMMUNICATIONS CONNECTIVITY TEST

H-82. Leaders conduct communications testing one week out from the event. This would include all unit communications devices, mission command systems, and TADSS connectivity, like the Multiple Integrated Laser Engagement System (known as MILES) equipment. Additionally, this includes any devices needed to support constructive or virtual training environments that drive the training event. Evaluator and OC/T communications checks are also conducted during this week.

T-WEEK: EXECUTE TRAINING

H-83. At T-Week, commanders execute training. This execution entails conducting precombat checks, drawing supplies, conducting training, conducting informal AARs, leading hip-pocket training, and retraining tasks not trained to standard.

PRECOMBAT CHECKS

H-84. T-Week begins with precombat checks. Units conduct these detailed final checks immediately before and during the execution of training and operations. Units include these checks in unit SOPs. Normally, units conduct them as part of TLP. These precombat checks can be as simple or as complex as the training or operation dictates. Units start precombat checks—such as applying camouflage, setting radio frequencies, and distributing ammunition—in garrison and complete them in the assembly area or in the training location. Commanders allocate sufficient time for subordinate leaders to execute precombat checks and inspections to standard. Precombat checks can include the following:

- Staff briefed the OPORD briefed, and leaders and Soldiers know the expectations.
- Unit completed safety checks and briefings.
- Unit has all required TADSS on hand and operational. For example, unit has Multiple Integrated Laser Engagement System (known as MILES) equipment and zeroed it.
- Unit completed before-operations preventative maintenance checks and services on vehicles, weapons, communications, and other equipment.
- Unit inspected equipment. For example, unit inspected compasses, maps, and binoculars.
- Unit inspected and camouflaged Soldiers and equipment. For example, unit inspected identification cards and driver's licenses as well as camouflaged weapons.

Appendix H

- Unit checked Soldier packing lists and enforced any discrepancies.
- Unit verified medical support present and prepared.
- Unit completed communications checks.
- Unit verified ammunition (Class V) drawn, accounted for, prepared, and issued.
- Unit checked and confirmed vehicle load plans as well as secured the cargo.
- Unit verified rations (Class I) drawn and issued.
- Unit briefed and dispatched quartering party.
- OPFOR personnel deployed and ready to execute their OPORD.

DRAW SUPPLIES

H-85. Successful units draw and inventory supplies at the beginning of the training week. The installation distributes classes of supply within the plan to ensure the event is properly resourced. Leaders report any shortage of requested supplies immediately.

CONDUCT TRAINING

H-86. The unit executes the plan developed and published earlier. While conducting training, the unit performs individual and collective tasks to the published standard as the plan evolves based on OPFOR action and reaction. Concurrently, the assessment plan is executed—OC/Ts observe and capture compliance with T&EO performance steps and measures—and staffs compile bottom-up feedback. As the plan develops, the unit tests its TTP; identifies new TTP; and develops or implements other TTP. The commander and all unit leaders are present and engaged and perform their tactical duties consistent with the plan.

INFORMAL AFTER ACTION REVIEWS

H-87. Evaluators and leaders conduct informal AARs at all levels (from crew to battalion). They can be done for a unit or an individual. They may be scheduled or as needed during the training. Evaluators and leaders can record observations, insights, and lessons for future use to identify trends and prevent reoccurrences of bad practices.

HIP-POCKET TRAINING

H-88. Hip-pocket training usually consists of individual tasks selected by the commander on which a unit can train when it experiences inactive periods during scheduled training. Hip-pocket training is another technique for managing sustainment training. The company commander selects tasks for this training so that the unit uses training time productively.

H-89. Hip-pocket training provides leaders confidence in their ability to train, which results in a more efficient use of Soldiers' time. While the tasks selected for this type of training are usually individual tasks requiring sustainment training, leaders can inject new training (if time), training levels, and circumstances allow. Ideally, leaders train selected tasks in 15 to 30 minutes. Initial individual training or collective task training ordinarily requires more time and resources. Effective leaders use their initiative to ensure their individuals are well trained and their time is not wasted.

RETRAIN

H-90. Leaders allocate sufficient time to retrain tasks during or after training events. Not all tasks will be performed to standard on the first or even second attempt. Commanders do not allow an organization to end training believing that a substandard performance was acceptable. Therefore, leaders allocate and schedule time and other resources for unit retraining of key collective and individual tasks in their training plans. Retraining allows participants to implement corrective action. Ideally, units complete retraining at the earliest opportunity, if not immediately after they attempt the task. In some cases, a restart of an event may be necessary before moving to the next training event.

T+1: RECOVER, CONDUCT FINAL AFTER ACTION REVIEW, AND ASSESS TRAINING

H-91. In T+1 week, commanders recover, conduct final AARs, and assess training. Recovery is part of every training event. Leaders plan for recovery to ensure all the resources and personnel are available to return to full operation. Evaluators and leaders conduct a final AAR of the training event. The final step in a training event is to assess the training, specifically the collective and individual task proficiencies demonstrated or attained.

Recovery

H-92. Recovery is critical to every training event. Leaders use recovery to ensure the resources and personnel return to standard. The recovery process is training. Once recovery is complete, it signifies the end of the training event. Captured AAR comments reflect the effectiveness of the recovery and modification to the SOP. Ideally, a unit performs the following sample recovery activities after a training event:

- Account for personnel health and welfare.
- Perform post-operations preventative maintenance checks and services.
- Ensure sensitive item accountability.
- Ensure accountability of organizational and individual equipment.
- Ensure that Class IV, Class V, TADSS, and other support items are maintained, accounted for, and turned in.
- Close out training areas and ranges.
- Conduct AARs.
- Allow time for the individual Soldiers to recover personal equipment and conduct personal hygiene.
- Conduct final inspections.

Recovery and Post Operations Checks

H-93. Post operations checks are those tasks a unit accomplishes at the conclusion of training. An effective unit SOP contains these checks. The checks vary depending on the type of training. For example, an FTX requires more extensive post operations checks than garrison-type training. Sample post operations checks include the following:

- Soldier accountability.
- Sensitive item accountability (such as weapons or communications security).
- Report closure of unit to higher headquarters.
- Ammunition and equipment turn-in (such as TADSS).
- Maintenance of vehicles, weapons, and communications including the following:
    - Equipment cleaned.
    - Thorough preventative maintenance checks and services after-operations checks.
    - Required services performed.
- Training assessments:
    - Leaders record results of training in leader books.
    - AARs completed.
    - After action report initiated, if appropriate.
- Soldier recovery.
- Chain of command inspections of Soldiers and equipment.

Appendix H

FINAL AFTER ACTION REVIEW

H-94. The final AAR takes place as soon as possible following the event. (Leaders conduct informal AARs as needed during the event.) This ensures that events are still fresh in the minds of all the participants, capturing the data as accurately as possible. OC/Ts, OPFORs personnel, and evaluators all provide their input to inform the commander's assessments. Using multiple recorders ensures a unit captures all lessons. Sound assessments of those lessons facilitate later success. A final AAR begins with the UTP. Leaders assess if event planning and preparation were sufficient and if the commander's training objectives were met. They also determine if administrative and tactical support were sufficient to conduct the training. OC/Ts, OPFORs, and evaluators record all the lessons learned and preserve them for retraining and future use.

MET ASSESSMENT

H-95. Commanders assess and evaluate training. The commander considers personal observations as well as observations, T&EOs, insights, and lessons from AARs and unit evaluations to inform both MET proficiency for the assigned mission and METL assessments for unit status reporting.

SOP REVIEW

H-96. Leaders conduct an SOP review after the event to implement recommended changes gleaned from the observations, insights, and lessons. Quickly implementing the right changes allows the unit to begin improving performance sooner.

Appendix I
Organizational Inspection Program for Training

PURPOSE

I-1. Unit training is a subset of the unit's overall Organizational Inspection Program (known as OIP). This appendix provides a training management inspector with the basic overarching program and then focuses on the specifics for training management. See AR 1-201 for details on inspections.

GUIDANCE FOR INSPECTORS

I-2. All inspections have a major purpose: to provide feedback to commanders so they can make decisions that will improve the Army. Inspections focus on measuring compliance against established standards to ensure that the Army as a whole can function effectively in its combat role. The five principles of Army inspections support the five basic elements of an inspection. Those five elements are—
- Measure performance against a standard.
- Determine the magnitude of the problem.
- Seek the root cause of the problem.
- Determine a solution.
- Assign responsibility to the appropriate individuals or agencies.

CHECKLIST STRUCTURE

I-3. Section I provides an inspector with a checklist for identifying training management processes in the unit. The presence of these processes imply that the unit has an understanding of the doctrine and contains the parts essential for planning, preparing, executing, and assessing unit training.

I-4. Section II focuses on evaluating the indicators of an effective training management program. It provides indicators of specific inspection items that allow for a more detailed assessment. The second section may require multiple observations of training planning, preparation, and execution to provide an accurate review of the unit's training program effectiveness.

SECTION I – BRIGADE, BATTALION, AND COMPANY INSPECTION CHECKLIST

I-5. This series of questions measures the unit's training. These questions enable an inspector to determine if the foundations of effective unit training exist. The series of questions is not an indicator of unit training effectiveness. The key to any training program is the commander's personal involvement. As the unit's primary trainer, the commander has direct involvement in the planning, preparation, execution, and assessment of training proficiencies and ensures compliance with the commander's vision and guidance for training. Ideally, a unit conducts annual formal inspections with semiannual internal informal inspections.

I-6. As a staff completes the checklist, it aims to answer each question in the affirmative (YES). If the staff cannot answer in the affirmative, it adds notes or comments to the checklist. Often those items require retraining.

Task

I-7. As staffs check each item in the checklist, they note if the unit sustains or improves the task and add a comment to elaborate.

Appendix I

Unit Training Plan

I-8. The UTP ensures units plan and prepare for training. Inspectors ask the following questions pertaining to the UTP:
- Is the higher headquarters UTP available and posted in DTMS?
- Is the inspected unit's UTP published? Is it posted to DTMS?
- Does the UTP contain the higher headquarters mission?
- Does the UTP contain the higher headquarters METL?
- Does the UTP contain the higher headquarters commander's training guidance?
- Does the UTP contain the unit mission?
- Does the UTP contain the commander's guidance?
- Does the UTP contain a concept of operations that includes—
  - A collective training plan?
  - An individual training plan in support of the collective training plan?
  - A leader development plan?
- Does the UTP contain a time management cycle?
- Does the UTP contain tasks to subordinate units?
- Does the UTP contain an assessment plan?
- Does the UTP contain the training environment?
- Does the UTP contain resources required?
- Does the UTP contain risks and mitigation for key tasks not trained?
- Does the UTP contain the UTP calendar?

Commanders' Dialogues

I-9. Commanders' dialogues ensure commanders communicate with each other. Inspectors ask the following questions pertaining to commanders' dialogue:
- Did commanders' conduct dialogues?
- Did the higher commander approve the unit's METs selected to train (key output of mission analysis)?
- Is the output of the mission analysis recorded?

Mission-Essential Task List

I-10. The METL ensures units have a list of tasks to attain. Inspectors ask the following questions pertaining to the METL:
- Is the unit METL available?
- Is the unit METL posted to the DTMS and to the CATS?
- For battalion and company, does the unit METL reflect the unit's as-designed capabilities as described by the TOE or TDA?
- Is the unit METL reportable on the unit status report?

Training Objectives

I-11. Training objectives are an essential part of the commander's training vision. Overall collective task objectives help sequence training events from simple to increasingly more complex tasks. The progressive nature of the training helps build upon previously mastered skills. Inspectors ask the following questions pertaining to training objectives:

Organizational Inspection Program for Training

- Are training objectives published for each major training event?
- Do the training objectives support training the unit METs for each event?
- Are objectives for the leader, collective leader, collective tasks, and individual tasks identified for each major training event?

Training Schedules

I-12. Training schedules are necessary to inform Soldiers and leaders and to focus support, project resource requirements, and allow companies optimum time to prepare for training events. Inspectors ask the following questions pertaining to training schedules:

- Are the company training schedules complete, approved, and signed by the battalion commander?
- Are company training schedules changed frequently?
- Are changes to the training schedules approved by the brigade commander?

Training Meetings

I-13. Training meetings ensure units complete training preparation, resource coordination, and provide opportunities for training plan corrections and modifications. Units use these meetings to keep the training plan on track and to prepare successfully for training events. Inspectors ask the following questions pertaining to training meetings:

- Are brigade, battalion, and company training meetings held?
- Do the right personnel attend?
- Is there a standard training meeting agenda?

Digital Training Management System

I-14. The DTMS ensures units engage in digital training. Inspectors ask the following questions pertaining to the DTMS:

- Does the unit use the DTMS?
- Is there a certified DTMS master trainer on hand? Is this individual appointed on orders by the commander (to include one alternate)?
- Is there a log of unit personnel with their privilege levels available and approved by the commander?
- Does each battalion have a DTMS operator?
- Is the DTMS used to manage company-level individual training records?
- Are incoming and outgoing personnel entered and removed from the DTMS as necessary?
- Has the unit published a DTMS SOP?

Assessment and Evaluation

I-15. Unit assessment plans help validate the current assessment of the unit METs and the UTP. Inspectors ask the following questions pertaining to assessment and evaluations:

- Does each major training event include an assessment plan?
- Are unit OC/Ts trained and certified by the unit commander?
- Does the unit conduct AARs during and at the conclusion of training events?
- Are AAR results available?
- Does the unit follow the AAR process as outlined in this publication (see appendix D)?
- Are AAR results provided to the commander and used for assessing MET task proficiencies?
- Are the latest training evaluations or inspection reports available?

Appendix I

- Does the unit use individual training records and T&EOs for collective, leader, and individual tasks?
- Are T&EOs used for bottom-up feedback that informs the commander's assessment of METs?

Training Briefing

I-16. The TB ensures higher commanders have visibility of UTPs. Inspectors ask the following questions pertaining to TBs:
- Are TBs conducted?
- Are the TBs tied to the higher commander's approval of the UTP?
- Are the TB's results recorded?
- Are installation staff, supporting unit, and gaining commanders present as appropriate?

Training Resource Management

I-17. Inspectors check resources concerning training ammunition. They ask the following questions:
- Are annual ammunition forecasts available?
- Does the unit have a plan to use annual forecasted ammunition?
- Is DA Form 581 (*Request for Issue and Turn-In of Ammunition*) on hand and does it support the applicable training event?
- Are projected shortfalls addressed during the commanders' dialogue and TB?
- Are Class V handlers certified by the commander?

I-18. Inspectors check resources concerning vehicle mileage. They ask the following questions:
- Is there a restriction on vehicle mileage?
- Does the UTP account for mileage caps?
- Does the unit use the CATS to help project unit mileage?

Live, Virtual, and Constructive

I-19. LVC training environments provide varied training environments for units. Inspectors ask the following questions pertaining to LVC training environments:
- Are the right LVC training environments assets considered and used to meet training objectives when necessary?
- Has the unit incorporated LVC assets into the training plan?

Training Aids, Devices, Simulators, and Simulations

I-20. TADSS ensures units train with varied items. Inspectors ask the following questions pertaining to TADSS:
- Does the unit incorporate the use of TADSS to support training events?
- Does the unit identify and adequately plan for TADSS that support collective and individual tasks?

Time Management

I-21. Time management ensures units manage their time. Inspectors ask the following questions pertaining to time management:
- Has the unit established or does it follow a higher headquarters or installation time management cycle (such as Green-Amber-Red cycle)?
- Has the unit established or does it follow a higher headquarters or installation external task 'lock-in' program that protects training time from unprogrammed requirements?

Leader Development

I-22. Leader development ensures units develop subordinate leaders. Inspectors ask the following questions pertaining to leader development:
- Has the commander established a unit leader development program?
- Is a leader certification program part of the leader development program?
- Are leader development training objectives and assessments integrated and identified in each major training event?

Rehearsals and Precombat Checks

I-23. Rehearsals and precombat checks ensure units practice training events. Inspectors ask the following questions pertaining to rehearsals and precombat checks:
- Does the unit schedule and execute rehearsals prior to each major training event?
- Do all applicable leaders and trainers attend the rehearsals?
- Does the unit conduct precombat checks and inspections prior to training execution?

Retraining

I-24. Retraining ensures units train to standard. Inspectors ask the following question: Does the unit schedule time to retrain tasks not meeting standards?

SECTION II – EVALUATION

I-25. The inspector interviews leaders throughout the unit to evaluate the effectiveness of training management execution. The inspector moves beyond simply measuring the presence of the required elements of the program (Section I) and begins to determine the magnitude of the problem, seeks the root cause of the problem, begins to determine a solution, and discovers where to recommend responsibility to the appropriate individuals or agencies.

I-26. By completing the earlier questions first, the inspector gains knowledge of any potential strengths and shortfalls in unit training. Inspectors ask the questions beginning in paragraph I-27 after completing the questions in Section I. By completing the earlier questions first, the inspector has knowledge of any strengths and shortfalls in the required elements of the training management program.

Commander and Leader Responsibilities

I-27. The inspector uses questions and considerations to determine if the commanders and subordinate leaders are meeting their responsibilities according to unit training. The questions are not all-inclusive but can help the inspector gain a basic understanding and lead to fuller conversation to determine the effectiveness of the program or root cause of any issues. For commanders at every echelon, the following questions apply:
- Do commanders use the principles of mission command to give subordinates latitude in determining how best to train their units to achieve commanders' visualized end state for training?
- Do commanders provide subordinates training objectives for each training event or suspense's for proficiency levels in their METs? Describe the processes.
- Do commanders provide subordinates the training time and resources they require? How? (Do they use the commanders' dialogue during development of the UTP? Do commanders allocate sufficient time for subordinates to train? When and how do commanders become involved in resourcing subordinate commanders and leaders?).

Appendix I

- Do commanders ensure subordinate leaders have the necessary skills and knowledge to manage unit training so that leaders and units can achieve desired levels of training readiness? How? Do commanders train subordinate leaders to use the unit training system? How?
- Do commanders ensure they were providing quality training to subordinates? Do commanders define quality training? How?

I-28. Paragraphs I-29 and I-30 apply to commanders and leaders at every echelon (select several at each echelon to determine if the programs in place are used throughout the command or if there are any systemic problems at certain levels).

I-29. How did commanders—

- Personally observe, participate in, and evaluate the quality and consistency of training at all echelons?
- Receive training feedback directly from subordinate leaders and Soldiers?
- Identify, resolve if possible, and bring to the chain of command's attention issues in training planning, leadership, management, support, resourcing, and other key functions?
- Check the adequacy of external training support and report inconsistencies to the chain of command?
- Maintain awareness of safety issues and make on-the-spot corrections?

I-30. The inspector uses some questions to gain an informed perspective of the commander and leader's understanding of their roles and responsibilities throughout the unit. Inspectors can add questions to explore any systemic problems or to develop recommendations to fix any issues found. Inspectors select several at each echelon to determine if the programs in place are used throughout the command or if there are any systemic problems at certain levels. The following questions apply to NCOs at every echelon:

- Do NCOs influence or plan training for individual Soldiers, crews, and small teams? How?
- Do NCOs make sure they conduct standards-based, performance-oriented training? How?
- Do NCOs use T&EOs?
- Do NCOs or the commander or platoon leader establish training objectives for the events NCOs controlled?
- Does an NCO identified individual, small-unit collective tasks and drills that support the unit METL? Identify individual.
- Does individual Soldier task training relate to the collective tasks the unit trains and do these relate to the unit's METL? How?
- Are NCOs involved in planning, preparing, and executing training, conducting AARs, and providing bottom-up feedback? How?
- Do NCOs maintain awareness of hazards and associated control measures during individual, crew, and small-team training? How?

Planning Training

I-31. When planning for training, instructors follow certain instructions. First, they review the OPORD or FRAGORD for the last several training events. Second, they compare the training objectives for the training events to the training objectives identified in the UTP. The inspector determines if the unit uses the operations process to develop its UTP, if the resulting plan nests with higher, and if adjusting the plan increases the difficulty as the unit masters or adjusts skills to overcome any training short falls.

I-32. When planning training, commanders and S-3s at each echelon answer the following questions:

- Do commanders and S-3s develop the UTP? What planning method do they use?
- Do commanders and S-3s use a different method to plan training events?
- Do commanders and S-3s conduct planning sessions? Who is involved in planning sessions?
- Do commanders and S-3s adjust the UTP or training events? How, when, and where did commanders and S-3s make these adjustments?
- Do commanders and S-3s manage the planning and preparation for training events? How?

I-33. The inspector drills down (by echelon) with questions. Inspectors use the questions to determine root causes, solutions, and where to recommend responsibility for fixes.

I-34. Brigade-level inspectors review the current UTP OPORD asking the following questions:
- Do the training objectives complement higher headquarters' training objectives for multiechelon events?
- Do the training objectives reflect mastery of previously identified training objectives?
- Do the event and UTP training objectives match?
- Is an evaluation plan articulated?
- Are prior evaluations available for planning?
- Does the higher unit's UTP calendar have unaccounted time available? How much?

I-35. Brigade-level inspectors ask the brigade executive officer, brigade command sergeant major, principal staff officers, staff NCOs, and drivers the following questions:
- Do executive officer, command sergeant major, principal staff officers, staff NCOs, and drivers provide input to the training plan?
- Are executive officer, command sergeant major, principal staff officers, staff NCOs, and drivers aware of the training objectives for the training events?
- Are the training objectives building upon previously mastered skill sets?
- Are executive officer, command sergeant major, principal staff officers, staff NCOs, and drivers using previous assessments for event planning?
- Is the staff section assessments maintained? Where?
- Are the procedures for processing and tracking training resource requests from the units acceptable? Confirm.

I-36. Battalion-level inspectors should review UTP OPORD and the UTP calendar. They review the OPORDs or FRAGORDs for the last two training events. They also review the unit SOPs for battalion-level training meetings and identify the date and time for the last four training meetings. Battalion-level inspectors ask the following questions:
- Are the training meetings scheduled at least weekly?
- Is there a set agenda for the training meetings?
- Does the agenda allow for timely identification and procurement of resources?
- Are the training meeting focused on training or are other issues addressed as well?
- Are the results recorded?

I-37. Battalion-level inspection asks the battalion executive officer, battalion command sergeant major, battalion staff officers, battalion staff NCOs, and battalion staff drivers these questions:
- Do battalion executive officer, battalion command sergeant major, battalion staff officers, battalion staff NCOs, and battalion staff drivers provide input to the training plan?
- Are battalion executive officer, battalion command sergeant major, battalion staff officers, battalion staff NCOs, and battalion staff drivers involved in the MDMP for developing the UTP?
- Are the training objectives building upon previously mastered skill sets?
- Are battalion executive officer, battalion command sergeant major, battalion staff officers, battalion staff NCOs, and battalion staff drivers using previous assessments for event planning?
- Do the training meetings focus on training?
- Do the training meetings allow for adequate planning?
- Do battalion executive officer, battalion command sergeant major, battalion staff officers, battalion staff NCOs, and battalion staff drivers provide planning input during the training meeting?
- Are procedures for processing and tracking training resource requests from the units acceptable?
- Is training time allocated to subordinates acceptable? How much time is allocated?

Appendix I

I-38. Company-level inspectors review the company UTP, the last two weekly training schedules, and OPORDs or FRAGORDs for the last two training events. These inspectors ask the following:
- Are the training meetings scheduled at least weekly?
- Is there a set agenda for the training meetings?
- Does the agenda allow for timely identification and procurement of resources?
- Are the training meetings focused on training or are other issues addressed?
- Are the results recorded?

I-39. Company-level inspectors ask the company commander, company executive officer, company first sergeant, platoon leader, platoon sergeant, section leader, and crew chief the following questions:
- Do company commander, company executive officer, company first sergeant, platoon leader, platoon sergeant, section leader, and crew chief provide input to the training event?
- Are company commander, company executive officer, company first sergeant, platoon leader, platoon sergeant, section leader, and crew chief involved in the TLP for developing the UTP?
- Are the training objectives building upon previously mastered skill sets?
- Are company commander, company executive officer, company first sergeant, platoon leader, platoon sergeant, section leader, and crew chief using previous assessments for event planning?
- Do the company training meetings focus on only on training?
- Do the company training meetings allow for adequate planning?
- Do company commander, company executive officer, company first sergeant, platoon leader, platoon sergeant, section leader, and crew chief provide planning input during the training meeting?
- Is training time provided adequate to plan training? How much time is allocated?

Preparing Training

I-40. Inspectors use this portion of the evaluation to determine the efficiency of the preparation activities of resourcing, rehearsing, and preexecution checks.

I-41. Inspectors ask commanders and S-3s at each echelon the following questions:
- Do commanders and S-3s have procedures for processing and tracking training resource requests? What are the procedures?
- Are there problematic resource requests? What are they?
- Are resources managed at echelon? What are they? How are they managed?
- Do commanders and S-3s begin preparation for training events? How?
- Do commanders and S-3s emphasize parts of preparation? What parts?
- Do commanders and S-3s plan your rehearsals? When
- How do you schedule rehearsals? When?
- Are commanders and S-3s' rehearsals evaluated? Who evaluates them?
- Do rehearsals help commanders and S-3s prepare for training? How?
- Do commanders and S-3s have procedures for conducting preexecution checks? What are they?
- Do commanders and S-3s plan for precombat checks? How?

I-42. Brigade and battalion-level inspectors ask the executive officer, command sergeant major, staff section officer, and staff section NCO the following questions:
- Do executive officer, command sergeant major, staff section officer, and staff section NCO assist units in training preparation? How?
- Do executive officer, command sergeant major, staff section officer, and staff section NCO give help to units in training preparation? How?

I-43. Battalion-level inspectors review the battalion training meeting agenda for specific training preparation topics. These inspectors ask the following questions:

- Are leader, trainer, and evaluator certification times discussed?
- Are rehearsal times discussed?
- Are preexecution times discussed?
- Do executive officer, command sergeant major, staff section officer, and staff section NCO track the progress of resource requests? How?

I-44. Company-level inspectors review the last four weekly training schedules. These inspectors ask the following questions:
- Are rehearsal times scheduled?
- Are preexecution inspection times scheduled?

I-45. Company-level inspectors ask the company commander, company executive officer, company first sergeant, platoon leader, platoon sergeant, section leader, and crew chief the following questions:
- Are preexecution checks standardized?
- Are trainers certified? Who certifies the trainers?
- Do company commander, company executive officer, company first sergeant, platoon leader, platoon sergeant, section leader, and crew chief from battalion and brigade receive preparation assistance? What preparation assistance is received?

Executing Training

I-46. Inspectors use this portion of the inspection to focus on training execution. Successful training execution results from good preparation and planning. Adaptive leaders help training execution through responsive assistance by maximizing training opportunities, creative conditions, and accurate assessments.

I-47. Brigade and battalion-level inspections for training execution focus on facilitating the training and providing resources. Brigade and battalion commanders ensure that they are simultaneously training their respective staffs and providing the necessary guidance for training execution.

I-48. Brigade and battalion-level inspectors ask the executive officer, command sergeant major, staff section officer, and staff section NCOs the following questions:
- Do executive officer, command sergeant major, staff section officer, and staff section NCOs have roles during subordinate unit training execution? What are they?
- Do executive officer, command sergeant major, staff section officer, and staff section NCOs evaluate their own ability to assist training execution?
- Do executive officer, command sergeant major, staff section officer, and staff section NCOs assist subordinate unit training execution? How?

I-49. Company-level inspectors ask the commander, executive officer, first sergeant, platoon leader, platoon sergeant, section leader, and crew chief the following questions:
- Do commander, executive officer, first sergeant, platoon leader, platoon sergeant, section leader, and crew chief make training challenging? How?
- Do commander, executive officer, first sergeant, platoon leader, platoon sergeant, section leader, and crew chief plan to capture and record training data during execution? How?
- Do commander, executive officer, first sergeant, platoon leader, platoon sergeant, section leader, and crew chief have a plan for retraining? During, after, or as separate events?
- Do commander, executive officer, first sergeant, platoon leader, platoon sergeant, section leader, and crew chief always achieve training objectives during allotted time for training events? If not, what do commander, executive officer, first sergeant, platoon leader, platoon sergeant, section leader, and crew chief do in response?
- Do commander, executive officer, first sergeant, platoon leader, platoon sergeant, section leader, and crew chief allot enough subordinate training time prior to collective and multiechelon events? How?

Appendix I

- Do commander, executive officer, first sergeant, platoon leader, platoon sergeant, section leader, and crew chief make sure adequate training areas are scheduled or used to train unit? How?
- Do commander, executive officer, first sergeant, platoon leader, platoon sergeant, section leader, and crew chief ensure that training is done to standard for the tasks to be trained? How?
- Are commander, executive officer, first sergeant, platoon leader, platoon sergeant, section leader, and crew chief able to get adequate resources routinely for unit training? What do they do when problems or shortfalls occur?
- Do commander, executive officer, first sergeant, platoon leader, platoon sergeant, section leader, and crew chief ensure leaders are present at the right place and time for training? How?
- Do commander, executive officer, first sergeant, platoon leader, platoon sergeant, section leader, and crew chief ensure the unit executes training safely? How?
- Do commander, executive officer, first sergeant, platoon leader, platoon sergeant, section leader, and crew chief make sure safety precautions do not limit training realism or reduce the impact? How?
- Do commander, executive officer, first sergeant, platoon leader, platoon sergeant, section leader, and crew chief train the OPFOR properly and ensure the OPFOR poses as an adequate challenging threat? How?
- Do commander, executive officer, first sergeant, platoon leader, platoon sergeant, section leader, and crew chief train, certify, and position OC/Ts to observe, control, and train the unit as necessary? How?
- Do commander, executive officer, first sergeant, platoon leader, platoon sergeant, section leader, and crew chief integrate Army mission command systems into exercises? How?

Assessing Training

I-50. Inspectors use this portion of the inspection to focus on the assessment of training. Assessment occurs throughout the training management process.

I-51. Brigade and battalion-level inspections focus on the assessment of their respective staff sections and assessment of their roles in subordinate unit training. Inspectors review recorded assessments to assess their thoroughness.

I-52. Brigade and battalion-level staff inspectors ask the executive officer, command sergeant major, staff section officer, and staff section NCOs the following questions:

- Do executive officer, command sergeant major, staff section officer, and staff section NCOs plan for assessment of staff sections, section leaders, and individuals? How and when?
- Do executive officer, command sergeant major, staff section officer, and staff section NCOs record assessments? How?
- Do executive officer, command sergeant major, staff section officer, and staff section NCOs use AARs to improve task proficiency and training quality?

I-53. Battalion-level inspectors ask the executive officer, command sergeant major, staff section leaders, and staff section NCOs the following questions:

- Do executive officer, command sergeant major, staff section leaders, and staff section NCOs train, certify, rehearse, and otherwise prepare the observers? How?
- Does the commander assess the unit METL and determine MET proficiency? How?
- Does the unit have procedures to ensure MET assessments are recorded in the DTMS?
- Do the training assessments address such areas as training support, force integration, logistics, and personnel availability? How?
- Are there procedures that link training proficiency to resources and does the UTP get adjusted based on training proficiency measures?

- Does the commander ensure observers are qualified and familiar with applicable T&EOs used to evaluate task execution? How does the commander review an observer's subjective assessment on the unit's ability to perform a task?
- When an AAR identifies a unit training strength to be sustained or a weakness to improve, does that information get routed back into the planning and trained in the continuum of the operations process for training? How?
- Do leaders use criteria to select appropriate times during a training event to conduct an AAR with the objective of improving future performance?
- Are immediate in-stride corrections allowed?
- Does the commander guide MET proficiency training? How?
- Are AARs used to improve task proficiency and training quality? How?
- Are AARs conducted as part of an open learning environment where facilitators, participants, and observers freely discuss successes and honest mistakes?
- Do executive officer, command sergeant major, staff section leaders, and staff section NCOs share lessons learned with other units?

This page intentionally left blank.

Glossary

The glossary lists acronyms and terms with Army or joint definitions. Where Army and joint definitions differ, (Army) precedes the definition. Terms for which ADRP 7-0 is the proponent are marked with an asterisk (*). The proponent publication for other terms is listed in parentheses after the definition.

SECTION I – ACRONYMS AND ABBREVIATIONS

1LT	first lieutenant
1SG	first sergeant
2LT	second lieutenant
AAR	after action review
ADP	Army doctrine publication
ADRP	Army doctrine reference publication
AR	Army regulation
ATMS	Army Training Management System
ATN	Army Training Network
ATP	Army techniques publication
BTE	blended training environment
CAR	Central Army Registry
CATS	Combined Arms Training Strategy
COA	course of action
CPT	captain
CTG	command training guidance
DA form	Department of the Army form
DA pam	Department of the Army pamphlet
DD form	Department of Defense form
DTMS	Digital Training Management System
EXEVAL	external evaluation
FM	field manual
FRAGORD	fragmentary order
FTX	field training exercise
G-4	assistant chief of staff for logistics
ITE	integrated training environment
JP	joint publication
LTX	lane training exercise
LVC	live, virtual, and constructive
MAJ	major
MDMP	military decisionmaking process
MET	mission-essential task

METL	mission-essential task list
MG	major general
MOPP	mission-oriented protective posture
MSEL	master scenario events list
NCO	noncommissioned officer
OC/T	observer-controller/trainer
OPFOR	opposing force
OPORD	operation order
P	practiced
P-	marginally practiced
PFC	private first class
POL	petroleum, oils, and lubricants
QTB	quarterly training briefing
S-1	battalion or brigade personnel staff officer
S-3	battalion or brigade operations staff officer
S-4	battalion or brigade logistics staff officer
SFC	sergeant first class
SGT	sergeant
SOP	standard operating procedure
SSG	staff sergeant
STT	sergeant's time training
STX	situational training exercise
T	fully trained
T-	trained
T&EO	training and evaluation outline
TADSS	training aids, devices, simulators, and simulations
TB	training briefing
TC	training circular
TDA	table of distribution and allowances
TLP	troop leading procedures
TOE	table of organization and equipment
TTP	tactics, techniques, and procedures
U	untrained
U.S.	United States
UTP	unit training plan
WARNORD	warning order
YTB	yearly training briefing

SECTION II – TERMS

*after action review

A guided analysis of an organization's performance, conducted at appropriate times during and at the conclusion of a training event or operation with the objective of improving future performance. It includes a facilitator, event participants, and other observers.

assessment

Determination of the progress toward accomplishing a task, creating a condition, or achieving an objective. (JP 3-0)

battle rhythm

A deliberate cycle of command, staff, and unit activities intended to synchronize current and future operations. (FM 6-0)

essential task

(Army) A specified or implied task that must be executed to accomplish the mission. (FM 6-0)

implied task

(Army) A that must be performed to accomplish a specified task or mission but is not stated in the higher headquarters' order. (FM 6-0)

*lane training exercise

A standardized and structured exercise or simulation used to train on one or more collective tasks that includes a designated area, terrain, or facility.

mission command

(Army) The exercise of authority and direction by the commander using mission orders to enable disciplined initiative within the commander's intent to empower agile and adaptive leaders in the conduct of unified land operations. (ADP 6-0)

*mission-essential task

A collective task on which an organization trains to be proficient in its designed capabilities or assigned mission.

*mission-essential task list

A tailored group of mission-essential tasks.

multiechelon training

A training technique that allows for the simultaneous training of more than one echelon on different or complementary tasks. (ADRP 7-0)

operational environment

A composite of the conditions, circumstances, and influences that affect the employment of capabilities and bear on the decisions of the commander. (JP 3-0)

planning horizon

A point in time commanders use to focus the organization's planning efforts to shape future events. (ADRP 5-0)

rehearsal

A session in which a staff or unit practices expected actions to improve performance during execution. (ADRP 5-0)

specified task

(Army) A specifically assigned to a unit by its higher headquarters. (FM 6-0)

*training and evaluation outline

A summary document that provides information on individual or collective task training objectives, resource requirements, and evaluation procedures.

Glossary

*training environment
: An environment comprised of conditions, supporting resources, and time that enables training tasks to proficiency.

*training objective
: A statement that describes the desired outcome of a training activity in the unit.

References

All URLs accessed on 14 June 2016.

REQUIRED PUBLICATIONS
These documents must be available to intended users of this publication.
JP 1-02. *Department of Defense Dictionary of Military and Associated Terms*. 08 November 2010.
ADRP 1-02. *Terms and Military Symbols*. 07 December 2015.

RELATED PUBLICATIONS
These documents contain relevant supplemental information.

JOINT PUBLICATIONS
Most joint doctrinal publications are available online: http://www.dtic.mil/doctrine/index.html.
JP 3-0. *Joint Operations*. 11 August 2011.

ARMY PUBLICATIONS
Most Army doctrinal publications are available online: http://www.apd.army.mil/.
ADP 6-0. *Mission Command*. 17 May 2012.
ADP 7-0. *Training Units and Developing Leaders*. 23 August 2012.
ADRP 3-0. *Unified Land Operations*. 16 May 2012.
ADRP 5-0. *The Operations Process*. 17 May 2012.
ADRP 6-0. *Mission Command*. 17 May 2012.
ADRP 7-0. *Training Units and Developing Leaders*. 23 August 2012.
AR 1-201. *Army Inspection Policy*. 25 February 2015.
AR 220-1. *Army Unit Status Reporting and Force Registration–Consolidated Policies*. 15 April 2010.
AR 350-1. *Army Training and Leader Development*. 19 August 2014.
AR 350-2. *Operational Environment and Opposing Force Program*. 19 May 2015.
AR 350-28. *Army Exercises*. 09 December 1997.
AR 380-5. *Department of the Army Information Security Program*. 29 September 2000.
ATP 3-90.1. *Armor and Mechanized Infantry Company Team*. 27 January 2016.
ATP 5-19. *Risk Management*. 14 April 2014.
DA Pam 220-1. *Defense Readiness Reporting System–Army Procedures*. 16 November 2011.
FM 3-21.10. *The Infantry Rifle Company*. 27 July 2006.
FM 6-0. *Commander and Staff Organization and Operations*. 05 May 2014.
FM 27-10. *The Law of Land Warfare*. 18 July 1956.
TC 7-101. *Exercise Design*. 26 November 2010.

WEB SITES
Army Training Network at https://atn.army.mil.
Center for Army Lessons Learned at http://usacac.army.mil/organizations/mccoe/call.
Central Army Registry at https://atiam.train.army.mil/catalog/dashboard.
Combined Arms Training Strategy at https://atn.army.mil/dsp_CATSviewer01.aspx.

References

Digital Training Management System at https://dtms.army.mil.

United States Army Combat Readiness Center Online Training at https://safety.army.mil/TRAININGCOURSES/OnlineTraining.aspx.

PRESCRIBED PUBLICATIONS

This section contains no entries.

REFERENCED FORMS

Unless otherwise indicated, DA forms are available on the Army Publishing Directorate Web site: http://www.apd.army.mil/. DD forms are available online: http://www.dtic.mil/whs/directives/forms/index.htm.

DA Form 581. *Request for Issue and Turn-In of Ammunition.*

DA Form 2028. *Recommended Changes to Publications and Blank Forms.*

DD Form 2977. *Deliberate Risk Assessment Worksheet.*

Index

Entries are by paragraph number.

8-step training model, 3-12–3-20

A

adaptability, A-15
after action review, 3-19, 3-58, A-11, D-1–D-64, H-94
    agenda, D-12–D-16, D-53–D-54
    assessment of, D-61–D-64
    benefits from, D-62
    characteristics, D-11
    climate, D-3, D-52
    closing, D-60
    contents, D-58
    defined, D-1
    evaluator, D-13, D-35–D-41
    events, D-14
    execute, D-50–D-60
    facilitator, D-8
    formal, D-7–D-8, D-44, D-49
    informal, D-9–D-10, D-39, D-43, D-48, H-87
    introduction, D-51–D-52
    lane training exercise, E-38, E-45
    locations, D-40
    opposing force and, D-54
    organization of, D-45–D-46
    participants, D-27, D-51
    plan for, D-13, D-19–D-31
    prepare for, D-32–D-49
    purpose, D-1–D-5, D-61
    rehearsal, D-47–D-49
    resources, D-28–D-30
    steps, D-17–D-64
    time, E-56
    training fundamentals, D-11
    types, D-6–D-10
    versus critique, D-3
approach
    backward planning, 2-56, H-1
    crawl-walk-run, 2-57–2-58, E-30
    top-down/bottom-up, 1-15–1-16, 1-33–1-35
Army Training Management System, 1-59–1-64, E-59
Army Training Network, 1-61, B-3, H-21
assembly, lane training exercise, E-38
assess
    checklist for training, I-50–I-53
    MET, 2-22–2-24
    training, 3-31–3-58

assessment, 3-52–3-57
    checklist, 1-15, I-50–I-53
    defined, 3-37
    input from, C-44
    make, 2-24
    mission-essential tasks, H-95
    platoon, C-28
    risk, H-58
    task, B-30
    training meeting and, C-28
    training plans, 1-14
assessment planning, 3-27
    requirements, 3-56

B

backbrief, 2-29
    mission analysis, 2-10, 2-27–2-32
    training briefing, 2-85
    unit training plan and, 2-32
backward planning, 2-56, H-1
    T-Week, 3-21
battle focus, 1-38–1-46, 2-1
    achieving in training, 2-38
battle rhythm
    activities and products, 1-49
    defined, 1-48
    establishing, 1-51–1-55
    training for, 1-48–1-70
battle task, 1-44
blended training environment, 2-63
    planning, 2-65
bottom-up approach, 1-15–1-16
breaks, in training events, D-25–D-26
briefing. See specific briefing types.
    yearly, 1-78

C

calendar
    command training guidance, 1-51–1-52
    coordination for, 1-69
capabilities, A-3
    mission, 2-21
    train to, 2-17–2-18
caution notice, B-34
Center for Army Lessons Learned, 1-67
Central Army Registry, 1-66
certification, H-66–H-71

trainers, H-77
challenges, A-8
    identifying, 2-70
    planning, 1-41
    training, 1-20
checks
    post operations, H-93
    precombat, H-84, I-23
    preexecution, 3-25, H-26–H-36
    preexecution coordination, C-37–C-40, H-35
    preexecution sample, H-36
course of action
    characteristics, 2-35
    decision briefing, 2-78
    decision matrix and, 2-75–2-76
    development, 2-33–2-69
    multiechelon training and, 2-45
    training events and, 2-49
    unit training plan and, 2-80
    unit training plan calendar and, 2-34
course of action analysis, 2-70–2-72
course of action approval, 2-79
course of action comparison, 2-73–2-77
coaching, D-4
    by leaders, D-9
collective tasks, 1-84, A-1
    assessment of, 3-38
    creation of, 2-20
collective training, A-9
    assessment of, E-1
Combined Arms Training Strategy, 1-62–1-63, H-39–H-40
    training events and, 2-66
    use of, 2-52, 2-58
command guidance, coordination and, C-35–C-36
command training guidance, 2-6–2-9
    format, 2-9
    guidance after, 1-53
    readiness and, 1-51
commanders. See also leaders.
    advisor to, C-10
    analysis by, 2-50
    approvals by, 2-85
    Army Training Management System and, 1-60
    assessment, B-41–B-46

Index

Entries are by paragraph number.

commanders (*continued*)
    assistance to, 2-74
    challenges for, 2-26
    communication by, 2-6–2-7
    communication from, 2-29
    considerations, 2-17, 2-23, 3-41
    decisions, 2-79
    dialogue, 1-71–1-73
    engagement by, 1-29
    external evaluation, 3-51
    guidance, 2-28, D-20
    meetings and, C-8
    responsibilities, 1-13, 1-15, 1-22, 1-33, 1-68, 1-86, 2-13, 2-84, 3-18, A-17, C-6, C-39, H-83, I-27–I-30
    role of, 1-27–1-35, D-5
    senior responsibilities, 1-70
    vision, 1-28
commanders' dialogue, I-9
communications, testing, H-82
company, unit training plan, 2-11
company training meetings, C-1–C-45
    purpose, C-1–C-6
complexity
    planning and, H-2
    training for, 1-1
conditions, changing, A-16
conferences, training, 1-68–1-70
considerations
    objective, 3-38–3-40
    subjective, 3-41
constructive
    training, B-23
    training environment, 2-60–2-61
coordination, 3-11
    lane training exercise, E-18
    resources, 1-77
    tasks, 1-40
    training, C-34–C-40
    training event, H-48
coordination measures, informal, 3-25
corrections, guidance and, D-4
crawl-walk-run, 2-57–2-58, E-30–E-36
critique, versus after action review, D-3
cue, B-33
culture, positive, 1-31

D

danger notice, B-34
decision briefing, 2-78
decision matrix, 2-75–2-76
decisive action training environment, 3-7
destruction notice, training and evaluation outline, B-12
Digital Training Management System, 1-64
    checklist, I-14
    training schedules, H-57
distracters, 2-84
    protections from, A-8
    training, 1-32
distribution restriction, training and evaluation outline, B-11

E

environment, B-58
    challenging, 1-1
equipment, B-55–B-57
    collecting, H-79–H-82
essential task, 2-3
    defined, 2-19
    MET and, 2-20
evaluation, 3-42–3-51
    checklist, I-16
    execution and, 3-30
    external, 3-49–3-51
    formal, 3-44, 3-47
    informal, 3-46
    internal, 3-48
    Organizational Inspection Program, I-25–I-53
    plan, H-65
evaluator
    after action review, D-13
    briefings by, C-40, H-66
    guidance from, D-41
    responsibilities, B-30, D-20, H-25
    selection of, D-21–D-22
    summary by, D-55
    training of, D-24
events
    critical, D-34
    summarized, D-55–D-57
execute
    training, 3-29–3-30
    training checklist, I-46–I-49
execution, lane training exercise, E-38
exercise control plan, H-62
external evaluation, 3-49–3-51, B-26
    requirements, 3-50

F

facilitator. *See* evaluator.
facilities, training, H-6–H-10
feedback
    evaluations, 3-45
    meeting and, C-2
    subordinates, 2-25
foreign disclosure, training and evaluation outline, B-13
formal evaluation, 3-47
framework
    planning, 1-45–1-46
    training, 2-4

G

graphic control measures, lane, E-46
Green-Red-Amber cycle, 2-40–2-43
guidance
    on tasks, 2-3
    review of, D-33
    support to, 2-28
    training, 1-16, 1-34

H

hip-pocket training, C-43, H-88–H-89

I

implied task, defined, 2-19
individual tasks, 1-84, A-1
informal evaluation, 3-46
information
    after action review, D-45
    automated, E-59
    lane training, E-58–E-59
information systems, stimulate, 2-64
initiative
    meetings and, C-9
    subordinate, 1-15
    training, A-15
inspection
    battalion checklist, I-5–I-24
    brigade checklist, I-5–I-24
    company checklist, I-5–I-24
    elements of, I-2
inspector
    guidance for, I-2
    responsibilities, I-25
instructors, responsibilities, I-31
integrated training environment, 2-64–2-68
    planning, 2-65
internal evaluation, 3-48
iteration, B-40

Index

Entries are by paragraph number.

L

lane training, E-1–E-68
    characteristics, E-9–E-19
    components of, E-20–E-23
    management of, E-22
    methodology, E-30–E-36
    personnel, E-23
    phases, E-24
    process, E-2, E-25
    support for, E-52–E-68
    techniques, E-8
    uses of, E-7–E-8

lane training exercise
    activities and scenarios, E-37–E-51
    categories, E-26–E-29
    coordination for, E-18
    defined, E-3
    focus of, E-10
    integrated, E-28
    location, E-4
    mission support, E-29
    order of activities, E-39
    scenarios, E-47–E-51
    stand alone, E-27
    trainers and, E-3

lanes, E-2, E-5, E-42
    graphic control measures, E-46
    multiple, E-13
    sequence in, E-19

leader development plan, operation order and, H-50

leaders
    assessment, 3-54, B-41–B-46
    considerations, C-31, H-32
    developing subordinates, H-17
    development checklist, I-22
    development, A-7
    Digital Training Management System and, 1-64
    input from, C-44
    lane training and, E-7
    meetings and, C-5
    observations by, 3-53
    opposing forces, H-67
    presence of, B-24
    rehearsals, H-72
    responsibilities, 2-67, 3-30, 3-31, 3-5, A-5, A-8, C-36, I-27–I-30
    roles of, 1-21–1-37
    subordinate, 1-22–1-23
    train, 1-22–1-23, 3-14, 3-24
    understanding, E-15

learning, adaptive, 1-67

library, training products, 1-66

live, training environment, 2-60

live fire, B-31

live training, B-21

location, lane training exercise, E-5

logistic planning, tools for, H-41

long-range planning horizon, 2-25

M

master scenario events list, H-61

measures. *See also* proficiency.
    coordination, 3-25
    performance, 1-6–1-11, B-27, B-38
    training, I-5

meeting, feedback during, C-2

meetings, training, 3-32–3-35

MET, 1-41–1-43
    assessment of, 2-22–2-24, H-95
    defined, 1-41
    determine, 2-16
    essential task and, 2-20
    identify, 2-22
    training events, 2-51
    training start and, 2-23
    updated assessments, C-32–C-33

methodology, crawl-walk-run, 2-57–2-58

METL
    checklist, I-10
    defined, 1-41
    non-standardized, 1-43, 2-30
    standardized, 1-42, 2-18

military decisionmaking process, training and, 2-33, F-2

mission
    assigned, 2-19–2-21
    capabilities, 2-21

mission analysis
    backbrief, 2-27–2-32
    training event, H-11–H-17
    unit training plan and, 2-12–2-32

mission command
    defined, 1-17
    philosophy, 1-26
    principles of, 1-19
    subordinates and, 1-17–1-20
    training, 1-15

mission-essential task. *See* MET.

mission-essential task list. *See* METL.

multiechelon training, 1-57–1-58
    defined, 1-57
    events, 2-44–2-48

N

noncommissioned officers, role of, 1-36

notes, B-36

O

objective task evaluation criteria matrix, 3-40
    caution notice, B-34
    commander assessment, B-41–B-46
    cue, B-33
    danger notice, B-34
    environment, B-58
    equipment, B-55–B-57
    iteration, B-40
    leader assessment, B-41–B-46
    live fire, B-31
    notes, B-36
    opposing force tasks, B-49
    performance measures, B-38
    performance steps, B-37
    prerequisite collective tasks, B-47–B-48
    remarks, B-35
    risk, B-32
    safety, B-59
    supporting collective tasks, B-50
    supporting drill tasks, B-52
    supporting individual tasks, B-51
    task performance and evaluation, B-39
    terms of references, B-18–B-30
    training aids, devices, simulators, and simulations, B-54
    training and evaluation outline, B-17
    warning notice, B-34

objectives, training, 2-54–2-55

observations
    collection of, D-42–D-44
    uses of, D-42

observer-controller/trainer. *See also* evaluator.
    plan, H-63–H-64

obstacles, training, 1-32

operation order, 3-16
    training event, H-47–H-52

operational domain, 1-24–1-26

operational environment
    defined, 2-15
    terms describing, B-19

operations
    preparations, 1-3
    versus training, D-12

Entries are by paragraph number.

operations process
    training applied, 2-4–2-5
    training framework and, 3-3

opposing force
    after action review, D-54
    lane training exercise and, E-44
    rehearsals, H-78
    tasks, B-49

orders, 2-81–2-82

Organizational Inspection Program, I-1–I-53
    checklist structure, I-3–I-53
    purpose, I-1

organizational training, 1-83

P

participants
    after action review, D-56
    perspectives of, D-57

performance measures, B-27, B-38
    critical, B-28
    leader, B-29
    rating, 1-6–1-11

performance steps, B-37

personnel, lane training, E-23, E-57

phase, training, E-30–E-36

plan
    premobilization, 1-84
    resources and, 1-56
    training checklist, I-31–I-39
    training events, 3-5–3-22
    training objectives and, 3-29

planners
    considerations, 2-36
    lane training exercise, E-41
    responsibilities, 3-28
    scheduling, H-8
    tasks, 3-6, 3-9–3-10

planning
    challenges, 1-41
    guidance, H-24
    logistic tools, H-41
    parallel, 1-54
    subordinate, 2-47
    timelines, 1-55
    tools for, H-9–H-10
    training, 1-34
    training guide, H-5
    T-Week concept, H-1–H-5

planning horizon, 1-71
    defined, 1-46
    framework, 1-45–1-46
    Reserve Component, 1-76

platoon assessment, training meeting and, C-28

post operations checks, H-93

postmobilization, Reserve Components, 1-81, 1-85–1-86

pre lane training exercise, E-16

precombat checks, H-84
    checklist, I-23

preexecution checks, 3-25, H-26–H-36
    coordination, C-37–C-40, H-35
    sample, H-36

premobilization
plans for, 1-84
    Reserve Component, 1-81–1-84

preparation, training, A-10

prepare
    training, 3-23–3-28
    training checklist, I-40–I-45

prerequisite collective tasks, B-47–B-48

prerequisite training, H-66–H-71

presence, commanders, 1-29

principles, training, 1-4

process, lane training, E-9

proficiency
    attaining, 3-4
    certification and, H-70–H-71
    measure, B-2
    ratings, 1-6–1-11
    shortfalls, C-29–C-31
    sustaining, 1-12–1-14
    task evaluation, 3-38
    tasks, A-1
    training, 1-5–1-20, 1-38

Q

quarterly training briefing, 3-36
    format, G-4–G-7

R

rating
    fully trained, 1-7
    marginally practiced, 1-10
    practiced, 1-9
    proficiency, 1-6–1-11
    trained, 1-8
    untrained, 1-11

readiness, 1-82
    assessment of, 2-22
    factors affecting, 1-12
    levels, 2-8
    sustaining, 1-12
    training, 1-3, 2-1–2-3
    training issues, 2-26
    visibility of, C-1

realistic training, A-1–A-18
    characteristics, A-4–A-18

reconnaissance, training areas, H-43–H-45

recovery, H-92–H-93

references, training and evaluation outline, B-14

rehearsal, 3-17, 3-26
    after action review, D-47–D-49
    checklist, I-23
    conducting, H-72–H-74
    defined, H-73
    lane training exercise, E-38
    opposing force, H-78
    subordinate, H-79–H-82

remarks, B-35

Reserve Component,
    considerations, 1-74–1-86
    planning horizons for, 1-76
    premobilization, 1-81–1-84
    resources, 1-77
    training briefings and, 2-86
    training meeting, C-21
    T-Week, 1-79–1-80

resource synchronization conference, 1-68–1-70, H-10

resources, 3-10
    confirmation, H-37–H-42
    coordination, 1-77
    lane training, E-66–E-68
    locking, H-46
    plans and, 1-56
    prioritizing, 1-70
    requests, H-37–H-42
    scheduling, 1-69
    selection of, D-28–D-30
    support, H-59–H-65
    training, 1-65–1-67, 2-71, D-10
    T-Week concept, H-1–H-5
    unit training, A-6

responsibilities, overlapping, 1-37

retrain, 3-20, D-63, H-90
    checklist, I-24
    lane training exercise, E-38
    requirement for, I-6

risk
    assessment, H-58
    safety, B-32

S

safety, B-59

schedule
    information for, 1-68
    meetings, C-1
    training, C-45, H-3
    T-Week concept, 3-22
    UTP and, C-42

scoring. *See* proficiency.

sergeant's time training, H-14–H-17

Index

Entries are by paragraph number.

simulations, E-60–E-62
situational training exercise, E-1
Soldiers. *See also* commanders, leaders, noncommissioned officers.
    perspectives of, D-14
specified task, defined, 2-19
staff
    responsibilities of, I-6
    tasks, 2-77
standard operating procedure,
    reviewing, H-96
    revising, D-64
standards
    achieving, 1-30
    collective task, B-1
    individual task, B-1
steps, performance, B-37
subordinates
    feedback from, 2-25, C-44
    leaders, H-17
    mission command, 1-17–1-20
    oversight of, A-17
    planning, 2-47
    rehearsals by, H-79–H-82
    responsibilities of, 1-18
    rewarding, 1-31
    time, 2-69
    training meetings, C-11–C14
supply, drawing, H-85
support
    external to lane training, E-65
    finalization of, H-75–H-76
    internal to lane training, E-64
    lane training, E-63–E-68
    requests for, H-42
    to training, 2-65, H-30–H-34
supporting collective tasks, B-50
supporting drill tasks, B-52
supporting individual tasks, B-51
sustainment, training proficiency, 1-12–1-14

T

tactical objective, 2-55
tactical scenario, base, H-33
task assessment, B-30
task condition, training and evaluation outline, B-15
task number, training and evaluation outline, B-6–B-9
task performance and evaluation, B-39
task standard, training and evaluation outline, B-16

task title, training and evaluation outline, B-10
tasks
    checklist, I-7
    conduct of, A-1, D-59
    coordination, 1-40
    evaluation of, 3-42
    grouped, 1-63
    identify, 2-19
    information on, 3-57
    lane training exercise, E-43
    measuring, 1-5
    performance steps, 3-39
    proficiency, 2-1, A-1, E-17
    retrain, D-63
    standardization, E-12
    training for, 1-30
team
    building, 1-23, H-16
    develop, 1-24–1-26
    training, 1-15, 1-33
teamwork, developing, 1-24
terms
    for operational environment, B-19
    objective task evaluation criteria matrix, B-18–B-30
    training environment, B-20–B-23
threats, 1-2
time
    lane training and, E-53–E-56
    managing, 1-32, 1-41, 2-69
    variables, E-53
time management, checklist, 1-21
time management cycle
    applying, 2-38–2-43
    enforcing, 2-39
top-down approach, 1-15–1-16
train to win, 1-1–1-3
trainers, 3-23. *See* evaluator.
    certification of, H-77
    considerations, E-3
    requirements of, H-69
    train the, H-68–H-69
training, 1-1–1-86
    actions during, 1-22
    assessing checklist for, I-50–I-53
    assessment of, 3-31–3-58
    challenges, 1-20, A-8
    company level, H-54
    conditions, 3-8
    conducting, H-86
    constructive, B-23
    coordination requirements, C-34–C-40
    culture, 1-31

    differences, 1-75
    distracters, 1-32
    executing checklist for, I-46–I-49
    execution of, 3-29–3-30, H-83–H-90
    facilities, H-6–H-10
    framework, 3-3
    future, C-41–C-42
    goals, A-1–A-3
    guidance, 1-16, 1-34, 2-12, 2-16
    guide to planning, H-5
    hip pocket, C-43, H-88–H-89
    intellectual, A-12–A-13
    lane, E-6
    live, B-21
    locking in, H-53
    performance oriented, A-14, E-11
    physical, A-12
    planning, 1-34
    planning checklist for, I-31–I-39
    preparation for, 1-3, 3-23–3-28
    preparing checklist for, I-40–I-45
    prerequisite, H-13, H-66–H-71
    principles of, 1-4
    proficiency, 1-5–1-20
    readiness, 2-1–2-3
    realistic, 2-60, A-1–A-18
    repetition, A-18
    requirement for, 3-2
    Reserve Component, 1-74–1-86
    resources, 1-65–1-67, D-10
    results of, A-3
    schedule for, C-45, H-3
    selectivity, 1-38
    shortfalls, C-29–C-31
    standards, B-1
    strategy characteristics, 1-62
    support, 2-65, H-30–H-34
    teamwork, 1-33
    unit, 1-24–1-26, E-14
    venues, 2-60–2-61, 3-9
    virtual, B-22
training aids, devices, simulators, and simulations, B-54
    checklist, I-20
training and evaluation outline, B-1–B-59
    access to, H-21
    defined, B-1
    destruction notice, B-12
    distribution restriction, B-11
    elements, B-4–B-5
    foreign disclosure, B-13
    objective task evaluation criteria matrix, B-17

Index

Entries are by paragraph number.

training and evaluation outline (*continued*)
  references, B-14
  repositories, B-3
  review of, D-23–D-24
  task condition, B-15
  task number, B-6–B-9
  task standard, B-16
  task title, B-10
training area, reconnaissance of, H-43–H-45
training briefings, 2-85–2-88, G-1–G-7
  checklist, I-17
  format, G-2–G-3
  quarterly, 3-36
  types, G-1
  yearly, 3-36
training domains, 2-2, A-7
training environment, 2-59, A-10, H-28–H-29
  checklist, 1-19
  comparisons of, 2-68
  creating, 3-6
  defined, 1-47
  selection of, H-31–H-32
  terms describing, B-20–B-23
  types, 2-60–2-68, H-31–H-32
  understanding, 2-67
training event, 2-5, 3-24, A-4
  CATS and, 2-66
  COA and, 2-49
  conducting, 3-1–3-58
  considerations for, 2-59
  coordination, H-48
  critical, D-34
  determining, 2-49–2-53
  develop, 2-82–2-83
  enhancing, A-2
  evaluating, 3-31, 3-43
  identify, 2-52, D-34
  lane training, E-20
  location, 3-15
  mission analysis of, H-11–H-17
  multiechelon, 3-4
  operation order, H-47–H-52
  plan for, 3-13, H-24
  posting, 2-44–2-48
  requirements, 2-53, H-18–H-25
  sequencing, 2-57

  standards achieved, B-2
  stop point in, D-25–D-26
  training meetings and, C-5
  UTP and, 3-1
training exercise control cell, E-21
training management
  identifying processes for, I-3
  program for, I-4
training meetings, 3-32–3-35
  agenda, C-22–C-31, C-41
  battalion and brigade, 3-33–3-34
  characteristics of, C-4
  checklist, I-13
  company, 3-35
  considerations for, C-20
  goals, C-3
  participants, C-8–C-17
  phases and agendas, C-23–C-25
  Reserve Component and, C-21
  review, C-27–C-31
  routine for, C-18–C-45
  time for, C-19–C-21
  time requirements, C-26
  training events and, C-5
training model, 3-12–3-20
training objective
  checklist, I-11
  defined, 2-54
  end state and, H-19
  evaluating, 3-31
  identify, 2-54–2-55
  plan and, 3-29
  review of, 3-5, D-33
training plan
  after action review in, D-7
  assessment of, 1-14
  completion of, H-60
training resource management, checklist, I-17–I-18
Training Resource Synchronization Conference, 1-68–1-70
training schedule
  changes to, H-55–H-56
  checklist, I-12
  publishing, H-53–H-58
training support center, resources from, H-7

T-Week concept, 1-79–1-80, 3-21–3-22, H-1–H-96
  planning, H-1–H-5
  resources, H-1–H-5
  training meeting and, C-22

U

unit
  assessments of, 3-55
  mission analysis, 2-30
  presence, B-25
  resources, A-6
  TDA, 2-30
  TOE, 2-18
unit training plan, 2-10–2-84, F-1–F-2
  analysis of, 2-10
  backbrief and, 2-32
  calendars, 1-69
  checklist, I-8
  COA and, 2-809
  developing, 2-1–2-88
  guidance after, 1-53
  mission analysis and, 2-12–2-32
  modify, C-2
  planning and, C-6
  publish, 2-80–2-84
  scheduling and, C-42
  training events and, 3-1, 3-4
unit training plan calendar, 2-37, 2-83
  COA and, 2-35
  scheduling, 2-69
  training events on, 2-44

V

virtual, training environment, 2-60–2-61
virtual training, B-22
vision, commanders, 1-28

W

warning notice, B-34
warning order, H-34
  publishing, H-26–H-27

Y

yearly training briefing, 1-78, 3-36
  format, G-4–G-7

FOR MORE TOP-FLIGHT MILITARY BOOKS

VISIT WWW.CARLILE.MEDIA OR SEARCH AMAZON FOR "CARLILE MILITARY LIBRARY"!

www.ingramcontent.com/pod-product-compliance
Lightning Source LLC
Chambersburg PA
CBHW082328220526
45470CB00008B/2438